BUS

Getting Rich

This book is about wealth mobility. It is about how some people get rich while others stay poor, and it is about the paths people take during their lives that determine how well-off they will be. The advantages of owning wealth and the elusive nature of true wealth have long made questions about who is rich and why broadly appealing. In recent years, dramatic economic changes, accompanied by rising wealth inequality, have created renewed interest in wealth and the wealthy. While basic facts about wealth inequality are no longer a mystery, we still know very little about who the wealthy are, how they got there, and what prevents other people from becoming rich. That is, we know very little about the process of wealth mobility. This book explores wealth by investigating some of the most basic questions about wealth mobility such as: how much mobility is there? Has the nature of mobility changed over time? How much does entrepreneurship matter? How much does inheritance matter? What other factors encourage or prevent wealth mobility and how do these change over the course of a person's life?

Lisa A. Keister is Professor of Sociology and Associate Dean in the College of Social and Behavioral Sciences at the Ohio State University. She is recipient of the National Science Foundation's Faculty Early Career Development award and author of *Wealth in America* (Cambridge 2000) and *Chinese Business Groups* (2000).

GETTING RICH

AMERICA'S NEW RICH AND HOW THEY GOT THAT WAY

LISA A. KEISTER
Ohio State University

CAMBRIDGE
UNIVERSITY PRESS

CAMBRIDGE UNIVERSITY PRESS
Cambridge, New York, Melbourne, Madrid, Cape Town, Singapore, São Paulo

Cambridge University Press
40 West 20th Street, New York, NY 10011-4211, USA

www.cambridge.org
Information on this title: www.cambridge.org/9780521829700

First published 2005

Printed in the United States of America

A catalog record for this publication is available from the British Library.

Library of Congress Cataloging in Publication Data

Keister, Lisa A., 1968–
Getting rich : America's new rich and how they got that way / Lisa A. Keister.
p.   cm.
Includes bibliographical references and index.
ISBN 0-521-82970-4 (hb : alk. paper) – ISBN 0-521-53667-7 (pb : alk. paper)
1. Wealth–United States.   2. Income distribution–United States.
3. Millionaires–United States.   I. Title.
HC110.W4K44   2005
339.2′2′0973–dc22   2005000241

ISBN-13   978-0-521-82970-0 hardback
ISBN-10   0-521-82970-4 hardback

ISBN-13   978-0-521-53667-7 paperback
ISBN-10   0-521-53667-7 paperback

To JWM

To JWM

Contents

PREFACE

I am extremely grateful for the assistance of a very large number of people and organizations. Grants from the National Institutes of Health program on Intergenerational Family Resource Allocation (funded by the National Institutes of Child Health and Human Development and the National Institute on Aging) and the National Science Foundation (Social, Behavorial and Economic Research, SES-0239995) supported this work. Emily Click, Beth Crosa, Joshua Dubrow, Donald McGrath, and Alexis Yamokoski all provided research assistance at various stages of the project. Tina Drenovas of the Department of Sociology provided clerical assistance, and the Initiative in Population Research, the Center for Human Resource Research (CHRR), and the Mershon Center at Ohio State University gave me space to work on the research. I drew on joint work with Phillip Kim and Howard Aldrich in Chapter Seven and previously published papers in Chapters Five and Six. In addition, I previously published related work in several places, including the following: "Sharing the Wealth: Siblings and Adult Wealth Ownership," Demography, 2003, 40:521–42; "Race, Family Structure, and Wealth: The Effect of Childhood Family on Adult Asset Accumulation," Sociological Perspectives, 2004, 47:161–87; and "Religion and Wealth: The Role of Religious Affiliation and Participation in Early Adult Asset Accumulation," Social Forces, 2003, 82:173–205.

PART ONE

I'D RATHER BE RICH

This book is about wealth mobility. It is about how some people get rich while others stay poor. In particular, it is about the paths people take during their lives and how these paths influence how well-off they become. In the 1964 movie *I'd Rather Be Rich*, people were typical in their willingness to go to great lengths to get rich. In the movie, the goal was to inherit from a dying grandfather, but people have all manner of ways of trying to hit it big. There is a general sense that being rich is better than not being rich, but wealth – and the processes that lead to wealth ownership – may be even more important than most people realize.

Wealth is the things people own, including their homes, savings, investments, real estate, businesses, and vehicles. It is usually measured as net worth, the sum of assets less the sum of debts. Owning wealth has many advantages, from the obvious financial freedom it provides to the even more enduring social and political privileges and power accessible to the wealthy. These advantages and the elusive nature of true wealth make questions about who is rich and why broadly appealing. Dramatic economic changes in recent years, accompanied by rising wealth inequality, have created renewed interest in wealth. These changes have also generated speculation about new patterns in the ways people become wealthy. The visibility of Internet millionaires created speculation that there may be an increasing number of entrepreneurs among the wealthy, and the subsequent devaluation of technology stocks and the bankruptcy of scores of dot-com companies raised questions about the role the sectoral shifts play in wealth ownership. Through all this, an increasingly skewed wealth distribution has raised questions, at least in some corners, about why there continue to be people who accumulate little even during periods of unprecedented economic growth.

While basic facts about wealth ownership and inequality are no mystery, we still know very little about who is wealthy and why. That is, we still know very little about wealth accumulation and wealth mobility. Wealth accumulation is the way people acquire assets and debts during their lives. Wealth mobility refers to changes in relative positions within the distribution of wealth. That is, if all people were sorted according to how much wealth they have, mobility refers to how a person's position in this list changes over time. Clearly, wealth accumulation is central to these changes. Those who accumulate assets quickly are going to move upward more rapidly. Of course, wealth mobility is also related to wealth distribution. Given that wealth ownership is highly concentrated and that it has become more concentrated during the time I will be considering here, moving into the upper positions in the distribution is difficult.

Researchers have shown that there is considerable concentration of wealth ownership and have estimated trends in the growth of wealth owned by households. There are also estimates of the role that macroeconomic and demographic trends played in shaping recent changes in wealth ownership. Yet the processes by which people accumulate wealth, the way their wealth ownership changes over their lives, and the way their positions in the distribution change over time have received little attention. This book explores wealth by investigating some of the most basic questions about wealth mobility, such as: How much mobility is there? Has the nature of mobility changed over time? Who is rich? Are most wealthy people entrepreneurs, did they inherit their wealth, or did they become wealthy in some other way? And what behaviors and processes in middle- and working class families propel some people out of these classes while others remain poor throughout their lives?

The starting point for this book is the notion that understanding wealth and the processes that create wealth are not only interesting but also of critical importance to understanding the way people sort themselves socially and economically. That is, understanding wealth ownership is central to understanding inequality. The approach used here directs attention primarily toward the paths people take during their lives in order to understand how these paths shape the distribution of wealth. From this perspective, life paths include the starting point as well as many of the key points of change people encounter during their lives. Being born into a wealthy family, of course, makes it easier to be wealthy as an adult. But decisions about education, work, marriage, children, and saving also matter, and these interact with each other in complex ways to create trajectories. The paths people take are also a product of circumstances and influences that individuals do not directly control but that impede or enhance these trajectories. To understand why people occupy certain positions in a distribution, it is necessary to understand how these processes interact. The objective of this book is to explore the life paths that underlie wealth mobility in order to better understand both the wealthy and those who never become wealthy.

WEALTH AND WELL-BEING: ARE THE RICH REALLY BETTER OFF?

There is growing evidence that having wealth, at least some wealth, is critically important to well-being. *Wealth* is the value of the property that people own. It is *net worth* or total assets less total debts. For most families, this includes tangible assets such as the family home and vehicles. Other families also own vacation homes, other real estate, and business assets. In addition, assets include financial wealth such as checking and savings accounts, stocks, bonds, mutual funds, Certificates of Deposit, and other financial assets. Debts or liabilities include mortgages on the family home, other mortgages, consumer debt, student loans, car loans, home equity loans, and other debt to institutional lenders or informal lenders such as family members. *Financial wealth* is the value of liquid assets, such as stocks and bonds, but does not include housing wealth or the value of business assets or investment in real estate. Wealth is different from income. *Income* is a flow of money over time, such as wages and salaries from work, government transfer payments, or interest and dividends earned on investments. Unlike income, wealth is not used directly to buy necessities such as food and clothing; rather, wealth is the total amount of property owned at a point in time.

Studies of inequality and the distribution of financial well-being tend to focus on income and how income changes over time. However, wealth may be an even more important indicator of well-being because it provides both direct financial benefits and other advantages. The family home, for example, provides shelter and other current services to the owner. At the same time, home ownership can be one of the most beneficial investments a family can make. Wealth also provides a financial cushion that can alleviate the impact of an emergency. For those without savings, a medical emergency, the unemployment of a primary income earner, or a family breakup can be devastating. Wealth can be used to directly generate more wealth if it is invested and allowed to accumulate. It can also be used to indirectly generate more wealth if it is used as collateral for loans for further investments, such as in the purchase of a home or business. Wealth can be used to purchase luxuries, and it can be used to buy physical protection and a safe and pleasant living environment. In the extreme, wealth can also buy leisure when its owner is able to decide whether to work or not. When family savings provide sufficient current income, income earned from wages and salaries is unnecessary.

Wealth ownership may also generate political and social influence. In a representative democracy, the distribution of political influence is often related to the distribution of wealth, and wealth carries with it social connections that can be used in important ways. Wealth expands educational and occupational opportunities for the current owner, and because wealth can be passed from one generation to the next, it often expands educational and occupational advantages intergenerationally. Of course, the truly rich may attract media attention, solicitations for donations, and other unwanted recognition. Wealth also invites security threats, may be socially isolating, and can dampen motivation. Yet the benefits of wealth ownership generally outweigh the disadvantages, and most agree that the rich are generally better off as a result of their asset ownership.

THE ALLURE OF WEALTH: WHY DOES WEALTH FASCINATE US?

The rich have perhaps always been fascinating, and dramatic changes in economic conditions in recent years created even more interest in wealth and the wealthy. Social registers and other written accounts of the lives of the wealthy captivated attention in earlier eras much like magazines and television shows that offer a glimpse into the lives of the rich do today. During the 1990s, changing economic conditions drew even more attention to wealth accumulation. Spectacular stock market booms, sustained economic growth, low inflation, low unemployment, and decreased fear of historic international rivals combined to create economic conditions that matched or surpassed numerous historic records. A subsequent economic slowdown reminded investors that good economic times must eventually become more normal. Before the downturn, however, there were important changes in the amount of wealth owned by households, changes in who owned it, and changes in how it was distributed. The magnitude of these changes generated new interest in who gets rich and how.

EXPANDING INTEREST IN WEALTH

The total wealth owned by American households began to grow in the 1960s, and it continued to expand through the 1990s. Total household assets increased more than four times during that period, from about $8 trillion in 1960 to more than $33 trillion in 1994 (all estimates are in year 2000 dollars unless otherwise noted). By the end of 1999, total household assets were valued at more than $50 trillion, decreasing to just more than $45 trillion at the end of the first quarter of 2001. Figure 1.1 illustrates the extent of growth of assets and liabilities held by households during the late 1990s and shows that changes in net worth reflected changes in assets more than they reflected changes in liabilities. During the 1980s and 1990s, fluctuating real estate prices increased the importance of housing assets in the portfolios of American households. There were bigger shifts, however, in the role of financial assets in the portfolio, particularly stock assets.

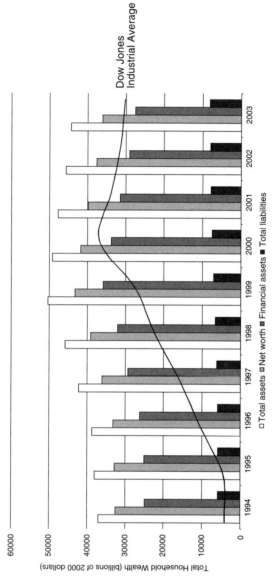

Figure 1.1. Trends in household wealth: Wealth owned by all U.S. households, 1994–2003. *Note:* Wealth values are from the Federal Reserve Board's *Balance Sheets of the U.S. Economy* converted to 2000 dollars using the Consumer Price Index (Federal Reserve System 2001). Dow Jones Industrial Average ranges from $3,700 in 1994 to a high of $11,400 in 2000 (scale not indicated on graph). Values for this figure are included in the Appendix.

Indeed, changing stock market values had a relatively large effect on household wealth throughout the 1990s and beyond 2000. During the 1970s and early 1980s, the stock market was relatively stable, and middle-class families were relatively unlikely to own stocks. This changed in the late 1980s and 1990s, when stock market booms, combined with increased availability of stock mutual funds, made stock ownership both more common and more lucrative for families. The trend line imposed over Figure 1.1 indicates the Dow Jones Industrial Average during the period included in the graph. During the later years included there, many households watched their portfolios expand enormously. Decreasing stock values between 2000 and 2003, however, also accounted for much of the decline in household assets at the end of the period pictured in the figure. As the economy slowed, many of the same households were forced to watch the value of their portfolios diminish almost overnight. More recently, increases in stock values are once again increasing household wealth, a testament to the importance of aggregate trends in outcomes at the household level.

Figure 1.2 focuses on changes in the composition of household wealth ownership that occurred between 1994 and 2003. The figure illustrates the percentage of total household assets that was accounted for by real estate, corporate equities, and mutual fund shares during that period. Between 1994 and 1999, the relative importance of housing wealth declined while the importance of corporate equities and mutual funds increased. These trends reflected inflated stock prices and a growing propensity for households to own corporate equities and (to a lesser degree) mutual funds, rather than changes in the propensity of households to own homes. Corporate equities and mutual funds became an increasingly significant portion of American household portfolios during the 1990s. At the same time, saving and investing increased during the mid-1990s because favorable economic conditions made investing more appealing, because baby boomers had begun to increase their saving for retirement around that time, and because changes to financial instruments created new opportunities for families to save. The introduction of Individual Retirement Accounts, for example, allowed some Americans

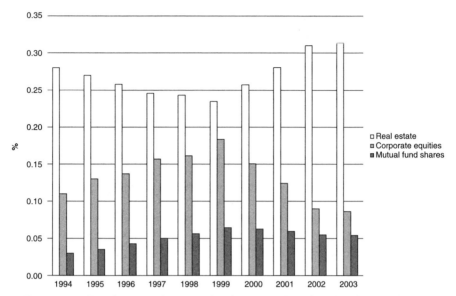

Figure 1.2. The relative importance of real estate and stock in family portfolios. *Note:* Estimates are from the Federal Reserve Board's *Balance Sheets of the U.S. Economy* (Federal Reserve System 2001). Corporate equities are at market value. Mutual fund values are based on the market values of equities held and the book value of other assets held by mutual funds. Real estate includes vacant land and vacant homes for sale. Estimates for 1994–2002 are for end of the year; values for 2003 are for the first quarter.

to save for retirement, tax-free, in ways in which they were not able to in the past. Similarly, while mutual funds have been around for decades, they also became easier to use during the 1990s, and more people accordingly began to save at least a small amount in mutual funds. Technological and other changes, such as the ability to invest easily on the Internet, also changed the way people save. In particular, during the 1990s, it became relatively common to buy stocks, bonds, mutual funds, Certificates of Deposit, and other financial assets online.

Beginning in 2000, the relative importance of real estate in total household wealth increased while the importance of stock ownership declined. This trend reflected declining stock values, evident in Figure 1.1. However, it also reflected increasing home ownership rates and the ability of families to pay off mortgages resulting

Table 1.1. *Household Wealth*

	1989	1992	1995	1998	2001
Net worth					
Mean	239,110	247,340	228,75	283,230	325,180
Median	60,700	51,300	50,220	63,600	65,690
% WITH ZERO OR NEGATIVE	18	18	19	18	17
Financial wealth					
Mean	190,800	188,300	175,540	222,400	254,900
Median	14,200	12,300	11,100	18,650	19,800
% WITH ZERO OR NEGATIVE	27	28	29	26	25

Note: Estimates from the Surveys of Consumer Finances. All monetary values are in 2000 dollars.

from declining mortgage interest rates. In the late 1990s and early 2000s, the proportion of families owning their primary residence increased by 1.5 percent to nearly 68 percent, and mortgage interest rates reached historic lows (Aizcorbe, Kennickell, and Moore 2001). As a result, more families owned homes, and home equity increased, contributing to a relative increase in the importance of real estate in the household portfolio.

Consistent with these patterns, wealth ownership at the level of families fluctuated quite a bit, with those at the upper ends of the wealth distribution enjoying most of the gains. In the early 1960s, mean net worth was about $116,000 (in 2000 dollars), but it has been consistently greater than $170,000 since the early 1980s. Similarly, financial wealth increased from about $92,000 to more than $134,000 between the 1960s and the late 1990s. Table 1.1 summarizes trends in wealth ownership between 1989 and 2001. Changing stock and housing values caused mean net worth to fluctuate somewhat dramatically over that time, particularly at the upper levels of the distribution. Median net worth (the central value in the distribution) varied less in response to stock market changes and is perhaps a better indicator of the true average household wealth. What is perhaps most noticeable from these estimates is that while net worth fluctuated, the percentage of the population that owned no wealth remained high throughout this period. In each year included in the table, at least 17 percent of households had no net worth, and at least

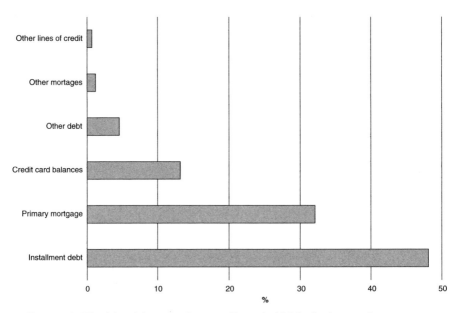

Figure 1.3. The debt of the poor: Sources of household debt for those with negative net worth (% of total debt). *Source:* Survey of Consumer Finances. Net worth was estimated in 2001 dollars.

25 percent of households had no financial wealth. In other words, approximately one-fifth of the population owned no wealth at all.

In order to have negative net worth, of course, it is necessary to have debts. In addition to making decisions about saving and investing, families also affect their net worth by acquiring debt. Including total liabilities in Figure 1.2 is not particularly instructive, because the value of total debt is minimal compared to the value of total assets and trends in aggregate debt do not vary as dramatically as changes in assets. However, the composition of total household debt for those with negative net worth sheds light on the reasons so many families have no wealth. Figure 1.3 shows the debt sources of poor families for 2001. As this figure demonstrates, the largest percentage of debt is installment debt. In 2001, nearly 50 percent of the total liabilities of families with zero net worth was installment debt, and an additional 13 percent was credit card balances. Installment debt refers to loans with fixed payments and a fixed term, including student loans,

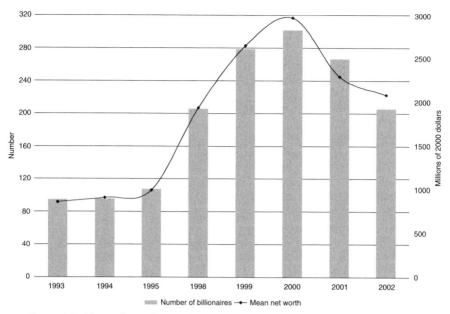

Figure 1.4. How rich is rich? Number of billionaires and mean wealth of Forbes 400. *Source: Forbes* magazine. Number of those in Forbes 400 with net worth greater than $1 billion (in 2000 dollars). Mean net worth in 2000 dollars for all Forbes 400.

automobile loans, and loans to buy furniture, appliances, and other durable goods.

When wealthy households are examined in isolation, increasing asset values are much more evident than estimates of all households. Indeed, there are more millionaires and billionaires in America than there were in the past. Figure 1.4 shows the increase in the number of families whose wealth is greater than $1 billion and the mean wealth of the Forbes 400. This increase is net of inflation – the estimates are derived from wealth estimates in constant (1995) dollars – suggesting that the increase in millionaires has been considerable. There is also evidence from the Forbes 400 that the wealthiest Americans have gotten even wealthier in recent years. Consistent with the fact that the largest gains in wealth ownership have been enjoyed by those who are already rich, the mean net worth of the Forbes 400 has increased dramatically in recent decades. In the early 1980s, the mean net worth of this group of the wealthiest Americans was

$408 million (in 2000 dollars). The mean increased slowly in the early 1990s, as Figure 1.4 indicates, and it rose dramatically between 1995 and 2000. In 2000, the mean net worth of the Forbes 400 exceeded $3.4 billion. Moreover, the number of Americans with more than $10 billion in assets has increased noticeably in recent years. In 2000, approximately 75 percent of the members of the Forbes 400 were billionaires (in 2000 dollars), whereas fewer than 10 percent were billionaires through 1986. In 1996, only three of those in the Forbes 400 had net worth greater than $10 billion (current year dollars), while in 2000, 23 of the Forbes 400 had amassed more than $10 billion in net worth.

The wealthy are also amassing billion-dollar fortunes faster than they used to, in part because of highly valued (perhaps overvalued) Internet companies that create enormous paper fortunes when they go public. Jay Walker, the founder and CEO of the Internet auction service Priceline.com, is an interesting example. His company was worth less than $100 million in mid-1998, but after the company went public Walker's wealth soared to more than $1 billion, and he became the fourteenth richest person in the world (Dolan 1999). Of course, not all of the very rich got that way through inflated valuations of their company's stock. Martin S. Fridson, author of *How to Be a Billionaire*, insists that frugality still plays a role in the making of fortunes. His anthology of superrich icons does point to a number of cost-cutting personal behaviors of the wealthy, including John D. Rockefeller's insistence on using old golf balls in situations in which he was likely to lose the ball. Yet this anthology of the rich ultimately underscores popular images of the changing nature of the upper class.

The Reality of Wealth Inequality

Wealth has also attracted attention because its distribution is extremely unequal. Many Americans have enjoyed remarkable and increasing prosperity, but for others, reports of sensational economic conditions in recent years bore little resemblance to their own experiences. Those in the middle and lower segments of the wealth

Table 1.2. *Wealth Inequality Before 1900*

Percentage Held by the Top 1%	
Baltimore (1860)	39
Boston (1848)	37
New York (1845)	40
New Orleans (1860)	43
Philadelphia (1860)	50
St. Louis (1860)	38

Source: Williamson and Lindert 1980.

distribution have continued to own little or no wealth, and many have watched their economic standing deteriorate. Basic facts about wealth inequality throughout American history have become fairly well understood. The facts are somewhat vague before 1900, but even for early historical periods, it is possible to piece together information that shows extreme inequality. Williamson and Lindert (1980), for example, show that the percentage of total wealth held by the top 1 percent of households was at least 37 percent in six major U.S. cities prior to 1900. Table 1.2 reproduces the estimates of the percentage of total wealth held by the top 1 percent of households in these cities. As the table indicates, inequality was most extreme in Philadelphia, but there was considerable inequality in each of the six metropolitan areas.

Evidence from historical records also suggests that levels of wealth inequality varied drastically during the first part of the twentieth century, but wealth inequality was consistently extreme. Lampman (1962) is usually credited as being among the first to identify wealth inequality as a source of social problems. He used estate tax data to document trends in wealth ownership and inequality in the decades between 1920 and 1960. His findings indicated that between 1922 and 1953, the top 1 percent of wealth holders owned an average of 30 percent of total household sector wealth. While inequalities varied with macroeconomic trends during the decades Lampman studied, he provided convincing evidence that inequality was consistently extreme throughout that period. Table 1.3 summarizes the trends in the percentage of total wealth owned by the top 1 and 5 percent

Table 1.3. *Wealth Inequality in the First
Half of the 20th Century*

	Percentage Held by the	
	Top 1%	Top 0.5%
1922	31.6	29.8
1929	36.3	32.4
1933	28.3	25.2
1939	30.6	28.0
1945	23.3	20.9
1949	20.8	19.3
1953	24.3	22.7
1954	24.0	22.5
1956	26.0	25.0

Source: Lampman 1962, pp. 202, 204.

of households between 1922 and 1956. Across these decades, the richest families consistently owned more than 20 percent of total wealth and as much as 32 percent of the total.

Other historical estimates have produced similar evidence of inequality during the early twentieth century. Wolff and Marley (1989) used various data sources to study wealth inequality over the entire 1920–1990 period. For the early part of the century, their results were consistent with Lampman's findings. They demonstrated that those in the top 1 percent of the wealth distribution owned an average of 30 percent of total net worth between 1922 and the early 1950s. The share of wealth owned by the top 1 percent increased from about 29 percent to about 32 percent between 1922 and the 1929 stock market crash. During the 1930s and 1940s, the concentration of wealth declined, so that the top 1 percent owned less than 30 percent by the late 1940s. During the 1950s, economic prosperity brought with it increased wealth inequality, and by the late 1950s, estimates suggest that the top 1 percent of households owned nearly 35 percent of total wealth.

Wealth data, and the corresponding estimates of wealth distribution, began to improve in the 1960s. In 1962, the Federal Reserve Board's Survey of Financial Characteristics of Consumers (SFCC) became the first comprehensive survey of wealth holdings in the

Table 1.4. *Wealth Inequality in the Second Half of the 20th Century*

	Gini Coefficient	Top 1%	Next 4%	Next 5%	Next 10%	Top 20%	2nd 20%	3rd 20%	Bottom 40%
Net worth									
1962	0.80	33.5	21.2	12.5	14.0	81.2	13.5	5.0	0.3
1983	0.80	33.8	22.3	12.1	13.1	81.3	12.6	5.2	0.9
1989	0.85	37.4	21.6	11.6	13.0	83.6	12.3	4.8	−0.7
1992	0.85	37.2	22.9	11.8	12.0	83.9	11.4	4.5	0.2
1995	0.85	38.5	21.8	11.5	12.1	83.9	11.4	4.5	0.2
1998	0.85	38.1	21.3	11.5	12.5	83.4	11.9	45	0.2
Financial wealth									
1962	0.88	40.3	23.8	12.8	12.7	89.6	9.6	2.1	−1.4
1983	0.90	42.9	25.1	12.3	11.0	91.3	7.9	1.7	−0.9
1989	0.93	46.9	23.9	11.6	10.9	93.4	7.4	1.7	−2.4
1992	0.92	45.6	25.0	11.5	10.2	92.3	7.3	1.5	−1.1
1995	0.94	47.2	24.6	11.2	10.1	93.0	6.9	1.4	−1.3
1998	0.94	47.3	21.0	11.4	11.2	90.9	8.3	1.9	−1.1

Note: Estimates from the Survey of Consumer Finances. Cells indicate the percentage of net worth or financial wealth held by households in each segment of the distribution.

United States. Table 1.4 contains estimates of wealth distribution from the SFCC and SCF panels for the 1962–2001 period. These estimates demonstrate that a very small portion of households have consistently owned the vast majority of household wealth. In 1962, the top 1 percent of wealth owners owned 33.5 percent of total net worth, and the top quintile owned more than 80 percent of total net worth. Wealth remained unequally distributed but relatively constant between 1962 and the mid-1970s because of an extended stock market slump and the growth of welfare programs such as Aid to Families of Dependent Children (AFDC) and Social Security (Smith 1987). Using estate tax data, Smith found evidence that after 1973 wealth inequality began to drop once again. Others using similar methods have found that between 1972 and 1976, the share of total wealth owned by the top 1 percent of wealth owners declined from 29 to about 19 percent of total wealth (Smith 1987; Wolff 1992).

Wealth inequality began to rise considerably after 1979, a trend that continued throughout the 1980s. By 1983, wealth inequality had returned to, and indeed surpassed on some measures, the 1962 levels. In fact, the share of wealth owned by the top 1 percent of wealth holders was 33.8 percent in 1983 and 37.4 percent by 1989. Real mean wealth grew at 3.4 percent annually during this six-year period, a rate that was nearly double the rate of wealth growth between 1962 and 1983. Others have found similar trends (Danziger, Gottschalk, and Smolensky 1989; Wolff 1993). Wolff (1993) found that mean family wealth increased 23 percent in real terms, but that median wealth grew by only 8 percent over that period. His research also suggested that the share of the top 0.5 percent of wealth owners rose by 5 percent during this period, from 26.2 percent of total household sector wealth in 1983 to 31.4 percent in 1989. The wealth of the next 0.5 percent remained relatively constant at about 7.5 percent of total household wealth, but the share of the next 9 percent decreased from 34.4 percent in 1983 to 33.4 percent in 1989.

Most striking is evidence of the decline in the wealth of the poorest 80 percent of households. The wealth of this group decreased by more than 2 percentage points between 1983 and 1989, leaving their share at just more than 16 percent at the start of the 1990s. Moreover, the top 20 percent of the distribution accumulated nearly all growth in real wealth between 1983 and 1989, and their share of total wealth grew to nearly 84 percent. Past research has also suggested that in the 1980s, wealth inequality in the United States became severe relative to that found in European nations. Studies of wealth in the 1920s suggested that wealth was much more equally distributed in the United States than in Western European nations. Yet research suggests that by the late 1980s, household sector wealth was considerably more concentrated in the United States than in Western Europe (Wolff 1995).

While mean and median household net worth declined during the 1990s, the distribution of wealth continued to worsen. The wealth of the top 1 percent of wealth holders increased from 37 percent of total wealth in 1989 to nearly 39 percent in 1995. However, between 1989 and 1998, the proportion of net worth owned by the top 1 percent of wealth owners rose from 30 percent to more than 34 percent. At the same time, the proportion of net worth owned by those in the bottom 90 percent declined from 33 percent to just over 30 percent (Wolff 1998). The average Forbes 400 member's wealth grew by 177 percent between 1990 and 2000. Between 1989 and 1998, the net worth of the median U.S. household declined by 8.6 percent. In 2000, the Forbes 400 owned as much wealth as the bottom half of the U.S. population combined. The Gini coefficient, an indicator of the degree of inequality comparable to the Gini coefficient used to measure income inequality, increased from 0.85 in 1989 and 1992 to 0.87 in 1995. The Gini coefficient ranges from 0 to 1, with 0 indicating perfect equality and 1 indicating perfect inequality. Conceptually, if a single household were to own all wealth, the Gini coefficient would equal unity (Weicher 1995, 1997). The Gini coefficient for financial wealth, that is, when real assets such as the family home and other real estate are excluded, reached 0.94 in the late 1990s (Keister 2000c).

Yet another way to think about wealth inequality is to consider spread, or the difference between the wealthiest and the poorest households. Because there is a great deal of inequality in wealth ownership, the spread is naturally quite large. What is perhaps most striking, though, is the degree to which the spread in wealth inequality exceeds the spread in income inequality. Table 1.5 compares the variance (or spread) in household income to the variance in net asset ownership in three years to demonstrate the changing nature of wealth inequality and the relative size of income inequality. The estimates in this table are from the National Longitudinal Survey of Youth, 1979 Cohort (a detailed explanation of these data is given in the last section of this chapter). As the table indicates, the variance in household ownership of net assets was extremely large in each year included in the table, but particularly in 1990 when other estimates indicate that wealth inequality was at historically high levels. The spread in income inequality was also quite large, but as the ratio between the two measures indicates, inequality in wealth ownership surpasses inequality in income by tremendous margins. In 1990, for

Table 1.5. *Ratio of Variance of Natural Log of Wealth to Variance of Natural Log of Income*

	1985	1990	1998
Variance in income	1.56	2.01	3.38
Variance in net assets	45.18	215.80	113.21
RATIO	0.034	0.009	0.030

Note: Ratio is calculated using the NLS-Y79. Income is total household income; net assets is the sum of assets less the sum of debts; both wealth and income are in 2000 dollars (adjusted using the CPI). The sample size varies between income and net assets because missing values are different for the two variables.

instance, variance in net asset ownership was more than 100 times greater than variance in income.[1]

Racial inequality in wealth ownership is among the most extreme and persistent forms of stratification in general and wealth stratification in particular (Conley 1999; Keister 2000b; Oliver and Shapiro 1995). Blacks and Hispanics, in particular, own considerably less wealth than whites. In 1992, while median income for blacks was about 60 percent of median income for whites, median net worth for blacks was only 8 percent of median net worth for whites. In that same year, 25 percent of white families had zero or negative assets, but more than 60 percent of black families had no wealth (Oliver and Shapiro 1995). Longitudinal estimates suggest that between 1960 and 1995, whites were twice as likely as minorities to have more wealth than income and nearly three times as likely to experience wealth mobility (Keister 2000c). Minorities are also underrepresented among the very wealthy. In 1995, 95 percent of those in the top 1 percent of wealth holders were white, while only 1 percent were black (Keister 2000c; Wolff 1998). The wealth position of nonblack minorities has attracted less attention, but there is evidence that the wealth accumulation of whites also exceeds that of Hispanics and Asians (Campbell and Kaufman 2000; Wolff 1998).

---

[1]   There are other surveys such as the Survey of Consumer Finances (SCF) that provide more precise measures of inequality, but the estimates here are comparable to similar estimates from the SCF.

Wealth Mobility: The Missing Link

While basic facts about the distribution of wealth have become taken for granted, understanding of the processes that account for wealth inequality is still limited. Efforts to explain wealth inequality have typically focused on the role of aggregate influences such as market fluctuations and demographic trends. There is evidence that because the wealthy are more likely to own stocks, wealth inequality worsens when the stock market booms (Keister 2000c; Smith 1987; Wolff 1995, 1998). Similarly, when real estate values increase, those who own houses and other land improve their position. Because those who are already well-off are more likely to own appreciable land, wealth inequality tends to worsen. With rising land values, however, the middle class has historically benefited more than it does with stock booms because home ownership has been more common among middle-class families. Recent changes in portfolio behavior (i.e., the combination of assets families own) thus have important implications for wealth ownership and inequality. This type of pattern was evident in recent years when the effect of stock market booms on wealth inequality was lower than it might have been because more middle-class families owned stocks (Keister 2000c).

There is a limited amount of research exploring how wealth varies by age and race. Keynesian economics, the predominant form of economics during the 1930s and 1940s, emphasized the role that individual saving played in the larger economy and proposed that current income was the primary determinant of saving (Modigliani and Brumberg 1954). Modigliani and Brumberg's Life-Cycle Hypothesis (1954), a reaction to the simplicity of the Keynesian approach, held that wealth increases until retirement, after which it declines. Empirical support of this hypothesis has been limited and inconsistent (Keister and Moller 2000; Osberg 1984) because the timing of death is uncertain and because people want to leave an inheritance to their offspring (Davies and Shorrocks 1999; Hurd 1990). Modigliani's own research shows that inter vivos transfers between living parents and their heirs and bequests made after the giver's death account for only 20 percent of the net worth of U.S. families

(Modigliani 1988a, 1988b). Most researchers agree, however, that inheritance accounts for at least 50 percent and perhaps as much as 80 percent of the net worth of U.S. families (Gale and Scholz 1994; Kotlikoff and Summers 1981).

Wealth ownership also varies in important ways across racial groups. Status attainment theorists have argued that educational differences are central to explaining racial differences in wealth (Campbell and Henretta 1980; Henretta 1979, 1984; Henretta and Campbell 1978). Others have argued more generally that structural barriers and discrimination create these differences (Baer 1992; Blau and Graham 1990; Oliver and Shapiro 1995; Parcel 1982). Social scientists generally agree that redlining in housing, dampened educational and occupational opportunities for minorities, and other structural constraints contribute to inequality (Horton 1992; Jackman and Jackman 1980; Oliver and Shapiro 1989; Williams 1975). Others have shown that differences in portfolio behavior (i.e., decisions about how to allocate savings) vary systematically by race and may contribute in important ways to racial differences in well-being (Galenson 1972; Keister 2000b; Terrel 1971). The reasons that portfolio behavior varies racially, however, are less clear, although the dominant explanation suggests that differences in willingness to postpone consumption are important (Brimmer 1988; Lawrence 1991). Of course, social influences on current consumption (i.e., decisions about whether to save or buy a new car) are likely quite strong, but current data restrict empirical examination of such influences (Keister 2000c).

There is reason to believe that family structure also plays an important role in creating and maintaining differences in wealth ownership, although evidence here is still limited. Some researchers have argued that a relatively small percentage of the increase in poverty in the 1970s through the 1990s was accounted for by changes in family structure (Gottschalk and Danziger 1984). Two separate studies contended that the "feminization of poverty" between 1960 and the mid-1980s was a result of changes in relative poverty rates for various household compositions rather than changes in family structure, particularly for blacks (Bane 1986; Danziger, Haveman, and Plotnick

1986). Yet evidence continues to mount that suggests some role for change in family structure. Few wealth researchers address issues of family structure, but both survey and simulated estimates suggest that gender and family structure affect both cross-sectional wealth ownership and longitudinal patterns of wealth mobility (Keister 2000a). These estimates suggest that at any given point in time, family structure is highly correlated with wealth ownership, net income, education, and race. In particular, there is evidence that marriage and widowhood increase wealth ownership, while family size and family dissolution through divorce or separation have the opposite effect (Kennickell and Starr-McCluer 1994; Kennickell, Starr-McCluer, and Sunden 1997). Researchers have also shown that family structure continues to affect poverty when it is defined in income terms (see McLanahan and Kelly 1999 for a review of the literature on the feminization of poverty).

Other elements of family background and characteristics of the adult family are also likely to shape adult wealth. For example, there is reason to suspect that wealth varies in significant ways with religious affiliation and participation during both childhood and adulthood. Religion can be among the most significant defining traits of a family, but previous research on wealth ownership has not moved beyond relatively casual references to these influences in understanding wealth accumulation and inequality. Religion is likely to affect asset accumulation *indirectly* because it shapes many of the processes that determine family wealth. A rich tradition of research demonstrates clear religious differences in childrearing, marital stability, divorce, and fertility (Alwin 1986; Ellison, Bartkowsi, and Segal 1996; Lehrer 1996; Sherkat and Ellison 1999) and other outcomes such as earnings, education, and female employment rates (Darnell and Sherkat 1997; Lehrer 1999; Wuthnow and Scott 1997). Religion is also likely to affect wealth ownership *directly* for a number of reasons. Religion shapes values and priorities, and wealth may be one of the values identified as worth pursuing. Religious beliefs transmitted through parents and during religious ceremonies also contribute to the set of competencies from which action is constructed, and these competencies may increase or impede wealth accumulation. In addition, religion provides social contacts that may improve opportunities to accumulate assets by providing information or assistance. Research on wealth occasionally references the potential importance of religion, but these studies focus almost exclusively on the role of income, investment behavior, and inheritance, without systematically exploring the relative importance of religion (Keister and Moller 2000; Menchik and Jiankoplos 1998; Spilerman 2000).

Researchers have made considerable strides explaining mobility both within and between generations, but this literature has focused on income, educational, and occupational mobility. Decades ago, sociologists began to study the intergenerational transmission of status (Bendix and Lipset 1966; Blau and Duncan 1967; Lipset and Bendix 1959), and the study of mobility remains active today in research on the United States and other countries (Biblarz and Raftery 1993; Warren and Hauser 1997; Western and Wright 1994; Wong 1992). Using longitudinal data, sociologists usually approach the subject of mobility by comparing parental standing (e.g., occupational prestige, income) with the standing of adult offspring. Status is usually measured categorically using transmission matrices that indicate the probability that an individual in class i in time t is in class j in time $t + 1$. Economists have also studied the intergenerational transmission of well-being, usually approaching the subject as the intergenerational persistence of status. In this literature, the typical approach is similar to that used in sociology, but the focus tends to be on continuous measures of status, and the methodological approach usually involves cross-generational correlations rather than transmission matrices. Estimates of the extent of intergenerational persistence range dramatically, but there is growing consensus that persistence is quite pronounced (Bowles and Gintis 2001; Mulligan 1997).

What is missing is a comprehensive exploration of the processes that lead to wealth accumulation and, thus, mobility. To fill this gap, we first need to explore how much wealth mobility there is. This is the task of Chapter Two. While the common wisdom remains that it is possible to get ahead financially in America, social scientists have yet to agree on how much mobility there actually is. When it comes to wealth mobility, researchers have barely begun to explore even the basic facts. Researchers have studied the wealthy in a number of ways in the past, often using estimates from public rosters such as social registers, other sources such as the Forbes 400 that publicize lists of wealthy individuals (Klepper and Gunther 1996; McAllister 1890; Watkins 1907), or in-depth studies of wealthy families (Chandler and Salsbury 1971; Colby 1984; Hurt 1981; Korporaal 1987). Often these studies ask compelling questions about the processes that generate wealth ownership and mobility, and these have arguably contributed to the understanding of the details of how particular fortunes are made. The drawback of this approach, however, is that it pays no attention to how typical or rare the stories might be.

My approach is to use representative samples but to focus on the variation and patterns that underlie aggregated estimates of inequality. My aim is to take advantage of variation while maintaining a focus on representativeness. In Chapter Two, I describe previous research that debates the extent of mobility. I conclude that past studies focused very little attention on wealth mobility, and I provide additional estimates to fill this gap. I argue that there is less mobility than we would expect by chance, but there is still considerable movement among segments of the wealth distribution. I draw on survey data that has tracked the same individuals for more than 20 years to explore these patterns empirically, and I show that there is considerable mobility, both within and between generations. This is not to say that there are not enormous impediments to wealth mobility. There certainly are. Yet there is enough movement to warrant investigation into why some are mobile while others spend their entire lives at about the same level of well-being.

In order to understand wealth accumulation, it is helpful to understand who the rich are. In Chapter Three, I argue that there is a new group of wealthy families in the United States, an educated rich that is more mobile than the wealthy of previous generations. I start by identifying the richest families in the United States and investigating the sources of their wealth. I then investigate how wealthy the very richest families are. In a first effort to understand what factors account for their fortunes, I look at the way the wealthy invest, and finally, I begin to explore the educational attainment patterns of these families.

The processes that create or impede wealth accumulation and upward wealth mobility are subtle and complicated. The estimates I provide in Chapters Two and Three underscore this fact, and in Chapter Four, I propose a general conceptual model of the processes that lead to wealth accumulation and mobility. Underlying my exploration is the notion that even with similar starting points, no two people make the same set of choices regarding education, work, marriage, children, and a host of other behaviors and processes that interact to create wealth. My objective is to identify the behaviors and decisions that contribute to wealth accumulation and mobility. The conceptual model that I propose in Chapter Four not only highlights the importance of education in the wealth accumulation process but also incorporates important elements of family background, inheritance, work experience, financial literacy, and adult family.

I then begin to examine the conceptual model empirically. In Chapter Five, I explore the role that family background plays in adult wealth ownership. I focus on the relative importance of inheritance and adult behaviors. I incorporate racial differences into the model, and I also explore the role that childhood family structure and siblings play in adult wealth. In Chapter Six, I continue to explore the importance of family background by investigating the role of religion, family culture, and other contributing factors that are somewhat more difficult to quantify. In Chapter Seven, I identify and study how individual differences, in both childhood and adulthood, shape wealth. I include discussions and analyses of the role of such factors as occupational and work behavior in creating adult wealth accumulation and mobility. Finally, in Chapter Eight, I explore the role that adult family issues play in the process. My objective is to present a relatively comprehensive conceptual and empirical exploration of the factors that interrelate to produce wealth accumulation. Naturally, it is not possible to address every contributing factor, but I highlight the most critical factors and provide a sense of how these factors work together to shape wealth ownership.

Getting the Facts Straight: Empirical Issues in Studying Wealth Mobility

Answering questions about wealth mobility creates several challenges that are typical of wealth studies and mobility studies. Most people are not willing to reveal details about their assets, and those who control most of the wealth often do not know details about their portfolios, even if they are willing to talk about them. Moreover, studying intergenerational processes requires information on at least two generations, and studying processes over the course of individual lives requires comprehensive data over long periods of time. Questions about wealth mobility have received little attention in the past because data on wealth ownership over time have been scarce. But this is changing. The collection of large-scale longitudinal data sets on the social and economic behavior of individuals and households began in the 1960s, and several of these data sets follow families through the present. As a result, researchers now have large amounts of information about the same individuals, covering more than 30 years in some cases. One of these data sets, the National Longitudinal Survey, contains extremely rich information about a large sample of respondents, including information about their wealth holdings. Surveys such as these make it possible to examine patterns in wealth mobility and wealth accumulation for large samples of people and to begin to answer some basic questions about who is rich, who is not, and why. In addition, increasing interest in wealth ownership has prompted efforts specifically focused on the collection of information about the wealth holdings of families. Most notably, the Survey of Consumer Finances collects detailed information on wealth ownership and savings behaviors and related information for a cross section of households every three years. I draw on these and other data sources to examine patterns of wealth mobility.

NATIONAL LONGITUDINAL SURVEYS

I primarily use data from the National Longitudinal Survey of Youth 1979 (NLS-Y79) cohort. The NLS-Y is a longitudinal survey that began with a sample of nearly 13,000 young adults (aged 14–22 years) in 1979. The same respondents completed interviews annually through 1994 and every other year after that through 2000. That is, the survey was administered 19 times between 1979 and 2000. The NLS-Y includes detailed information about the respondents, and, because it is longitudinal, the data set is well suited for assessing the impact of traits of the family of origin on later-life outcomes (McLanahan and Sandefur 1994; Sandefur and Wells 1999; Wu 1996). The data are also considered highly reliable because the response rate has continued to exceed 10,000 through the most recent survey.

The NLS-Y wealth data is one of the few data sets that contains detailed, longitudinal wealth data for a large sample. A comprehensive series of questions about wealth was added to the NLS-Y in 1985, when the respondents were all at least 20 years old. The NLS-Y wealth modules first ask respondents if they own an extensive series of assets and debts. For those who are owners, the survey then asks for the current market value. Because the survey has been conducted frequently and has maintained high participation rates, it contains extensive information on the dynamics of wealth ownership (Zagorsky 1999). In the remainder of this book, I use wealth data from the NLS-Y from 1985 to 2000 to model wealth accumulation and mobility. I also draw on the 1979 survey and other years between 1979 and 1985 to explore the impact of family background and related traits on adult wealth position.

I chose to use the 1979 cohort because information on their wealth holdings is more detailed and current. Respondents in the 1979 cohort reported their wealth in 1985, 1986, 1987, 1988, 1989, 1990, 1992, 1993, 1994, 1996, 1998, and 2000. In addition, the NLS-Y is ongoing, which will allow for future follow-up to this research. The 19-year time period over which the NLS followed this sample allows for observation of wealth dynamics over a relatively long period. In this sample, information about family background and life events is extensive and allows for considerable probing about the factors that contributed to the wealth ownership and mobility trends that appear in the data. In contrast, the NLS of mature men includes less detailed information about wealth, covers 15 years, and ends in 1981. The Longitudinal Retirement History Survey includes information between 1969 and 1979, and the Panel Study of Income Dynamics includes only the five-year period from 1984 to 1989. The longest panel in the Survey of Consumer Finances is 1983–1989.

OTHER DATA SOURCES

I supplement my analyses of the NLS-Y79 data with estimates from several other data sources. I include estimates of trends in aggregate household wealth from the *Balance Sheets of the U.S. Economy* and the Dow Jones Industrial Average. I provide estimates of patterns in the wealth of the richest Americans from *Forbes*. I also include estimates of wealth distribution and mobility from other household surveys, including the National Longitudinal Survey of Mature Men, the Survey of the Financial Characteristics of Consumers, and Surveys of Consumer Finances. The Appendix includes more detailed descriptions of each data source.

CHAPTER TWO

TRENDS IN WEALTH MOBILITY

To understand the processes that lead to wealth accumulation and mobility, it is first useful to ask how much wealth mobility there is. The task of this chapter is to draw on both previous research and updated data to investigate this ambitious question. In a single chapter, it would be impossible to completely array all previous efforts to explore who the wealthy are and where they came from. To do this *and* to add new estimates of wealth mobility is probably much too large a goal. Yet, before attempting to explain wealth mobility in subsequent chapters, it is critical to first understand whether there is enough mobility to explain. Thus the aim of this chapter is twofold. First, I draw on research that has used a variety of different methods to study wealth mobility in the past, and I synthesize the information contained in this research to draw a complete picture of what we know about wealth accumulation and mobility. No one else, to date, has combined information found in in-depth studies of wealthy families, studies of social registers, and survey-based research in a coherent way. Second, I provide additional estimates of wealth mobility using multiple methods to explore patterns in the same data sets. The result is a more complete and robust portrait of the state of wealth mobility than was available previously.

A great deal of past research on the wealthy has relied on public rosters such as social registers and other lists of the wealthy such as the Forbes 400 (Klepper and Gunther 1996; McAllister 1890; Watkins 1907) or in-depth studies of wealthy families (Chandler and Salsbury 1971; Colby 1984; Hurt 1981; Korporaal 1987) to understand how many rich people were born rich and how many were upwardly mobile. Often these studies ask compelling questions about the processes that generate wealth ownership and mobility, and they have arguably contributed to understanding how particular fortunes are made. The drawback of these approaches, however, is that their methods tend not to be systematic and their samples are definitely not representative. These studies provide little information about how typical or atypical these patterns are, and they do not address how much variation there is across the population in the occurrence of the patterns they identify. As a result, it is difficult to determine from these studies how likely it is that a person will become rich. There is some research that uses representative data, but efforts of this sort are quite limited. My task in this chapter is to begin to unravel these issues by exploring what we know from previous research on the wealthy and then to provide more systematic estimates of how much wealth mobility Americans experience.

In Chapter One, I demonstrated that there is considerable concentration in wealth ownership in the United States. Given this inequality and the relatively unrestricted manner in which wealth is transferred among generations in the United States, I anticipate that there is less wealth mobility than we would expect by chance. That is, if wealth were assigned randomly at birth, we would expect much more wealth mobility than I anticipate finding. However, I also anticipate that there is, indeed, considerable wealth mobility in the United States. This expectation is consistent with the small number of studies of wealth mobility that researchers have conducted in the past, primarily using simulation models that have demonstrated considerable consistency both between and within generations in wealth ownership (Davies and Kuhn 1988; Keister 2000c; Menchik and Jianakoplos 1997, 1998). Yet, I also anticipate that a considerable number of Americans do get rich over their lives. Indeed, changes in the composition of the wealthiest segments of the population in recent decades suggest that education, in particular, is one path through which wealth mobility is possible. The difference between intergenerational mobility (between generations) and intragenerational mobility (within generations) is an important one, and I differentiate these two types of mobility in my discussion that follows. I anticipate that there are differences in the amount of mobility found between and within generations and that the processes that lead to mobility vary inter- and intragenerationally. In this chapter, I concentrate on describing trends in mobility. I begin explaining these trends in the next chapter.

Perspectives on Mobility

Sociologists have made enormous strides in understanding social mobility, broadly defined. Yet sociologists have largely restricted their research to occupational and, to a lesser extent, income mobility. Early work focused almost exclusively on occupational mobility, exploring the extent to which occupational prestige persists across generations (Bendix and Lipset 1966; Blau and Duncan 1967a; Featherman and Hauser 1978). Studies of broad job categories, such as manual and nonmanual, were common early in the history of this research. Later work ranked jobs by their perceived prestige and demonstrated that there is a remarkable amount of consensus in the United States and in other countries in the ranking of occupations (Zimmerman 1992). Sociologists have shown that persistence in occupational prestige and income is pronounced across two generations (Lipset and Bendix 1959; Sewell and Hauser 1975; Zimmerman 1992). There is also evidence that intergenerational persistence is evident across three generations (Warren and Hauser 1997). A complete review of this research is beyond the scope of this book, but findings from mobility studies imply that there is likely to be a great deal of intergenerational persistence in wealth ownership. Moreover, because wealth is passed directly from one generation to the next, this literature implies that persistence in wealth ownership likely exceeds persistence in either occupational prestige or income.

Sociological research on elites, those who are at the top of social and political power structures, also offers clues into the state of wealth mobility. C. Wright Mills' *The Power Elite* (1956) is among the earliest sociological works that identified elites as an important focus of inquiry and the elite study as a useful analytic strategy. Mills proposed that there exists a cadre of people whose positions enable them to operate outside the ordinary environments in which the majority of people spend their lives. The elite is a group of people who can and do make decisions that have wide-reaching consequences. Mills (1956) saw the elite as those who both had "the most of what there is to have" and who are powerful, or "able to realize their will even when others resist it." Power and wealth are almost always shared according to Mills, and power is centered in three highly interlocked arenas: corporations, the military, and politics. People are installed in power, and power and wealth are perpetuated intergenerationally through education and the transfer of wealth. Keller (1963) referred to powerful elites as strategic elites, those who are at the top of certain pyramids of power and whose decisions and behaviors have important consequences for many members of a society. Both of these works, and a number of related arguments that emerged around the same time in sociology and the other social sciences, shared the important theme that power and wealth are concentrated in a few, relatively small, closed circles (Dahl 1961). Clearly, the implication of this is that wealth is not accessible to all and that if there is any mobility, it is limited.

Empirical research on elites provides support for theoretical arguments that mobility in the United States is likely to be restricted. Studies of politics and government demonstrate that there is no real concentration of power in an upper class elite; rather, various groups of leaders who draw on a variety of resources dominate political decision making (Dahl 1961; Polsby 1963; Wolfinger 1974). The majority of work on elites, however, concurs that there is a core of upper class individuals and families who dominate socially, economically, and politically (Domhoff 2002; Dye 1995; Elliott 1959). In fact, reanalysis of New Haven, the city that formed the core of earlier research leading to the populist conclusion, shows that a relatively small cadre of business elites controlled the city while Dahl was doing his research (Domhoff 1978). Subsequent research focused largely on business elites and explored the degree to which a small cadre of influentials controlled banking and business (Useem 1979, 1980, 1984). There is a great deal of evidence that banks and those who control banks, in particular, have tremendous power

(Mintz and Schwartz 1985; Mizruchi 1994; Mizruchi and Stearns 1994). Mintz and Schwartz's (1985) model of financial hegemony, for example, suggests that banks and other financial institutions have power because they shape the environment in which nonfinancial organizations function and because they reserve the right to intervene in corporate affairs even if they seldom do.

These studies do not explore wealth mobility directly, nor do they ask about the processes that lead elites to be in the positions they are in. Yet this research contains a number of important insights for understanding wealth mobility. First, elite studies underscore the importance of studying the wealthy and movement into the wealthy class. The power that is associated with wealth can be tremendous, and the normative significance of our interpretation of wealth inequality is likely to be different if the same people or families have power across generations.

Second, elite research suggests that, in fact, there is likely less wealth mobility than we would expect by chance (Domhoff 2002). Evidence that the same families populate the elite for multiple generations supports the impression that most casual observers would have of wealth ownership in the United States. That is, not only is wealth ownership concentrated, but the inhabitants of the extreme positions in the wealth distribution do not change much over time. Third, elite research suggests that there is likely to be a severe underrepresentation of women and minorities among the upwardly mobile (Vianello and Moore 2000; Zweigenhaft and Domhoff 1982). This is consistent with our understanding that racial inequality in wealth ownership is among the most persistent and severe forms of inequality in the United States. Yet we have little understanding of racial differences in wealth mobility.

Finally, however, elite research does suggest that wealth mobility *is possible* and, indeed, that it is likely that there is noticeable movement among segments of the wealth distribution. Researchers do not agree completely on who the elite are, even in a single place at a single time. Moreover, evidence that there are many changes in the structure of elites, both locally and nationally, suggests that there is some movement into and out of elite ranks (Vianello and

Moore 2000). Unfortunately, because previous elite research has not explored this movement systematically, there is little direct evidence of how much mobility there is and what accounts for the mobility that does occur.

Although economists began studying mobility after sociologists, they have done most of the theoretical and empirical research specifically addressing *wealth* mobility. Economists studying mobility fall into two camps. The first group begin by defining a stochastic process such as a first-order Markov process that underlies the distribution of income or wealth (Champernowne 1973; Shorrocks 1976). The second group uses deterministic models such as human capital models in the case of income mobility (Schiller 1977) and life-cycle models in the study of wealth mobility (Jianakoplos and Menchik 1997; Steckel and Krishman 1992). The life-cycle model proposes that households accumulate wealth during their working years and spend during retirement, generating a hump-shaped accumulation pattern (Modigliani and Brumberg 1954). This process varies across households because of differences in earnings, rates of return on assets, initial endowments, and bequest intentions. As Jianakoplos and Menchik (1997) point out, wealth mobility occurs when the age–wealth relationship leads to a change in a person's position in the overall distribution of wealth.

This research points to four factors that likely shape wealth accumulation and thus mobility. First, intergenerational transfers increase accumulation and mobility. Second, higher savings resulting from higher income, or a high propensity to save, increase accumulation and mobility. Third, fortunate people who earn higher rates of return accumulate more; likewise, entrepreneurs tend to accumulate more wealth. On the reverse side, discrimination and practices such as redlining in housing markets are likely to reduce accumulation and the chances for mobility. Finally, life-cycle differences in age shape accumulation and mobility patterns. For example, members of this generation on average delayed childbearing longer than their parents did (Keister and Deeb-Sossa 2000). As a result, baby boomers tend to be older than their parents were when facing large expenses, such as those for their children's college educations. Life-cycle differences such as these clearly have important implications for patterns of mobility that extend beyond individuals.

Public Rosters and Mobility

There is also important information to be learned from estimates of who are wealthy and how much they own that are found in social registers and public rosters such as the Forbes 400. The notion of creating and disseminating a roster of wealthy families dates to Ward McAllister's registry of upper class families in New York Society in 1892. Samuel Ward McAllister, born to wealthy parents in 1827 in Savannah, Georgia, married a millionaire's daughter and became the arbiter of New York and Newport, Rhode Island, Societies. His memoir, *Society as I Have Found it* (1890), served as a companion to the roster by bringing to life many of the people on the registry. At the head of McAllister's list of the wealthy was Caroline Astor, wife of William Astor, one of the wealthiest people in America at that time. Mr. Astor, whose family accumulated their wealth during the fur trade in Colonial times, was not interested in socializing or his position in Society. In contrast, Mrs. Astor was obsessed with the defining and regulating of Society and, with Ward McAllister's guidance, became the head of the New York social scene. Together Mrs. Astor and Mr. McAllister defined who was "In" and who was not. Their list of the top 400 actually only included about 300 names and only a small number of the wealthiest people at that time. Legend has it that the name of the list was derived from the number of people who could fit into Mrs. Astor's ballroom, and New York Society subsequently became known as "The Four Hundred."

McAllister's list and his narratives about wealthy families are important for a number of reasons. Naturally, they are important because they defined the circle of wealthy people at that time. McAllister also provided a vivid description of New York Society during the Gilded Age (1878–89) and a description of the inner workings of wealthy circles at the time. McAllister's book reads like a how-to manual for entering and properly interacting with the wealthy. He included descriptions of the important characters, stories about their interactions and faux pas, and instructions for such activities as introducing a young woman into Society, throwing a large party, and interacting with royalty. What is perhaps most instructive about McAllister's narration, however, is that he elucidated the process by which those in Society actively attempted to prevent new entrants. By documenting the deliberate efforts taken by those who were "In" to build barriers around their ranks, McAllister removed any questions about whether the barriers to entering Society were conscious or intentional.

Since McAllister's efforts to create a list of the most notable New Yorkers, a large number of rosters that identify and describe the wealthy have been compiled. Around the turn of the century, the *New York Tribune* (1892) and the *World Almanac* (1902) published lists of millionaires. More recently, Ferdinand Lundberg published lists of wealth families in his *America's 60 Families* (Lundberg 1939 [1937]) and *The Rich and the Super-Rich* (Lundberg 1968). C. Wright Mills also describes a number of efforts to document Metropolitan 400s in several American cities (1959). One of the most provocative uses of such lists is actually a relatively early publication by G. P. Watkins called *The Growth of Large Fortunes* (Watkins 1907). Watkins attempted to identify the activities that facilitate wealth accumulation. He argued that wealth accumulation depended more heavily on the type of capital invested and the area of the economy in which an entrepreneur worked than on personal attributes or connections. He classified the wealthy into various occupational sectors such as rentiers, financiers, agriculturalists, manufacturers, and miners. Watkins proposed, for instance, that the importance of agriculture was declining because it did not employ large-scale production methods and could not incorporate the corporate form of organization.

More recent efforts to catalog the wealthy include the Forbes 400 and the Wealthy 100. Starting in 1982, *Forbes* magazine began to compile an annual list of the 400 wealthiest Americans. The Forbes 400 is derived from public records and includes estimates of the size of the members' estates. In contrast to some earlier rosters of the wealthy, the Forbes 400 makes little attempt to screen members or pass judgment on who should be included and who should not. Moreover, although it likely omits some wealthy people, *Forbes* has developed a reputation for being both relatively comprehensive and fairly accurate in its estimates of wealth holdings and as a result has been used widely by scholars to describe trends in wealth ownership and the origins of great wealth (Broom and Shay 2000; Canterbery and Nosari 1985).

A related, and particularly broad, roster is *The Wealthy 100*, a unique effort to identify the 100 wealthiest Americans ever (Klepper and Gunther 1996). Whenever possible, the compilers of this list estimated wealth at the time of death and included only individuals who died after the founding of the United States in 1776. They used multiple estimates of wealth as often as possible, but they omitted people who lost their fortunes after making them. The list, and the book built around the list are intriguing because they include the names of the wealthiest individuals, estimates of their estates relative to GNP at the time of their deaths, and descriptions of the origins of their fortunes. Although the authors of this list make no effort to draw causal relations between behaviors, historical circumstances, and the origins of the estates they discuss, patterns undeniably emerge from stories they tell. The list needs to be taken lightly because of the large number of assumptions made to compile it, but it does provide a bit of insight into the changes in the wealthy class over time.

A much less systematic, but in some ways equally intriguing effort to identify notable people is the Marquis' *Who's Who*. The comprehensive *Who's Who* includes nearly 1 million people in all arenas, and so it is not a listing of the very top of the wealth distribution. What is useful about this roster, however, is that it includes rather detailed and often quite accurate biographies of those included on the list. Used in conjunction with other lists, the *Who's Who* is an effective way to determine who is rich and why. Equally provocative are international equivalents of these rosters that allow comparisons of trajectories in the lives of the U.S. wealthy with the wealthy from other countries. Forbes compiles international equivalents of its American list including the Forbes Richest People in the World and the Forbes affiliate in Germany (*Forbes von Burda*). Similarly, *Business Review Weekly*,

Table 2.1. *The 100 Wealthiest Americans Ever: The Sources of their Wealth*

Primary Source of Wealth	Percent of People in Top 100
Transportation, long distance (railroads, shipping)	18
Banking/finance	14
Natural resources (fur, land, lumber, mining)	12
Retail	10
Industry, heavy (automobiles, steel)	9
Oil	8
Agriculture/food(beverages (beer, cereals, tobacco)	7
Industry, light (chemicals, medical, textiles)	7
Publishing/communications	5
Technology (computers)	4
Transportation, local	4
Inheritance	2

Source: Author's calculations from Klepper and Gunther 1996. Appendix A includes the full list of the richest Americans, with the source of their wealth.

Australian Business, the *London Sunday Times*, *Money* magazine in Great Britain, and the *Financial Post* in Canada all compile modern lists of wealthy individuals around the world.

Although rosters do not provide the most systematic information about the wealthy, it is possible to derive clues from these lists that can enlighten more systematic efforts to understand wealth accumulation and mobility. The sectors in which wealth is made and how these change over time, for example, suggest a great deal about why some people are rich and others are not. Table 2.1 summarizes the "Wealthiest 100" by source of wealth (the full list is included in the Appendix). Table 2.2 summarizes the Forbes 400 between 1982 and 2002 by source of wealth. In the list of the wealthiest Americans of all time, the most common form of wealth is long-distance transportation such as railroads and shipping. Eighteen percent of people in the list of 100 built their wealth in transportation, followed by 14 percent in banking and 12 percent in natural resources. In contrast, in the Forbes 400 between 1982 and 2002, publishing/communications and real estate (both at 13 percent) are tied as the most common forms of wealth, with banking and finance and technology-related industries (12 percent) accounting for equally large groups in the lists. These

Table 2.2. *The Forbes 400, 1982–2002: The Source of their Wealth*

Primary Source of Wealth	Percent of People in Forbes 400
Publishing/communications	13
Real estate	13
Banking/finance	12
Technology (computers)	12
Natural resources	11
Industry, light	10
Other services	9
Retail	8
Industry, heavy	6
Transportation	3

Source: Author's calculations from *Forbes* magazine, yearly edition, listing the wealthiest Americans.

lists underscore some trends that are well known. For instance, they show that the importance of high-tech industry has clearly grown in recent years. They also suggest some patterns that may be less apparent, such as the continued importance of heavy industry. Scholars still take these lists quite seriously, and there are current efforts to deduce patterns in the sectoral origins of wealth (Broom and Shay 2000).

Kennickel (2003) also shows that there has been a great deal of change in the membership of the Forbes in recent years. He shows that of the 400 people in the Forbes list in 2001, 230 were not listed in 1989. He points out that this is a relatively long period, but notes that if there were little mobility, such movement would be less pronounced. Kennickel also looks at changes between 1998 and 2001, obviously a much shorter period. He shows that nearly 25 percent of people in the list in 1998 were replaced by 2001. It is possible that this change reflects mortality and changes due to the inheritance of great fortunes. Yet Kennickel's evidence suggests that this is the reason for the disappearance of only 20 percent of those who disappeared from the list between 1989 and 2001. Kennickel's evidence suggests that the greatest amount of persistence in the Forbes lists occurred in the top 100, where 45 of those who were list in 1989 were still on the list of top 100 in 2001. In contrast, of those in the lowest 100 of the listed in 1989, only 29 were still somewhere on the list in 2001. While these comparisons do not provide conclusive evidence for a shift in the way wealthy people earn their fortunes, they do point toward important differences that can be studied more systematically with other data.

Public roster estimates of who are wealthy and how much they own do provide important clues into the wealth mobility process. Like in-depth studies of wealthy families, public rosters are useful for identifying the wealthy and understanding how and why they came to be wealthy. They provide useful detail into the processes that lead to wealth accumulation that cannot be determined from survey data. For this reason, I begin my exploration of wealth by pointing to these studies. However, because these estimates do not provide a systematic glimpse of the whole population and movement among positions in the wealth distribution, it is important to use caution when drawing lessons from them.

Lessons From In-depth Studies of Wealthy Families

A related source of evidence about who is wealthy and why that is common in both academic research and popular writing is the in-depth study of a wealthy individual or, more often, a wealthy family. Among the more analytic of such studies is Chandler and Salsbury's (1971) exploration of the role Pierre S. du Pont played in the creation of a new organizational form: the corporation. Chandler and Salsbury document the decisions that Pierre du Pont made regarding financing, domestic versus international marketing, and the use of Frederick Taylor's scientific management. These decisions made Mr. du Pont wealthy, built the corporate empires of Du Pont and General Motors, and were instrumental in establishing the corporate form as the dominant form of organizing a business in the United States. More typical of the work in this genre are studies that document genealogical connections and explore the personal lives of members of the du Pont family (Colby 1984; Mosley 1980; Winkler 1935). Similar in-depth studies of wealthy families include, of course, an abundance of efforts to understand families such as the Astors

(Cowles 1979; Wilson 1993), the Hunts (Hurt 1981), Rupert Murdoch (Korporaal 1987; Munster 1985; Tuccille 1989), the Kennedys (Adams and Crimp 1995), the Vanderbilts (Auchincloss 1989; Hoyt 1962), and others (Aldrich 1988; Allen 1987). Such works are often a combination of biography, history, and social science, and can provide insight into the paths taken by the wealthy.

In-depths studies are problematic because they commit the important error of sampling on the dependent variable. By selecting wealthy families and not comparing them to comparable (in other ways) non-wealthy families for very obvious and practical reasons, these studies tell us only about families that are clear outliers. While it is difficult to generalize from in-depth studies of wealthy families, these works are instructive in a number of ways. For instance, in-depth studies describe, often in considerable detail, the paths wealthy people have taken to achieve wealth. Used in conjunction with more representative data, they can be useful in documenting the process by which the wealthy do such things as deliberately exclude others from their circles. A somewhat legendary story about relations between the Astors and the Vanderbilts illustrates both types of maneuvering. Those who have studied these two families write that Mrs. Caroline Astor saw herself as a gatekeeper of New York Society in the years prior to the turn of the twentieth century. As I described above, she and Ward McAllister largely decided who was "In" and who was "Out" in that city. Mrs. Astor apparently had a particular interest in maintaining a distinction between old wealth and new upstarts, and she had little interest in the nouveau riche or businessmen in her circles.

Cornelius "Commodore" Vanderbilt was among the businessmen who did not mix with the Astor-appointed elite. Commodore, his wife, their son William, and William's wife had little interest in exerting the energy necessary to break through the walls of Mrs. Astor's castle. Commodore's grandson, William K. Vanderbilt, and particularly his wife, Alva Smith Vanderbilt, were different. They decided to make their entry into upper social circles, and they had the wealth and determination to do so. Alva began her quest to enter the elite by building a home on Fifth Avenue in Manhattan that was much grander and more elegant than Mrs. Astor's home. She then planned

Table 2.3. *Historical Mobility Rates in the United States, 1828–48*

	Rich Parents	Middle-Class Parents	Poor Parents
New York	95%	3%	2%
Philadelphia	92	6	2
Boston	94	4	2

Source: Pessens 1974, p. 85.

an elaborate housewarming ball that New York Society began to anticipate as the party of the year. Everyone on the Four Hundred list was invited except Mrs. Astor, who had not properly called on the Vanderbilts. To add to the pressure, Mrs. Astor's daughter was in a dance group that was supposed to perform at the ball, but since her family was not invited, the daughter was not going to be able to perform. Under pressure from her friends, and now her daughter, Mrs. Astor finally called on Mrs. Vanderbilt. Mrs. Vanderbilt invited the Astors to the party and took their place on the list of New York's 400 most influential families.

Accounts such as these studies do neglect the big picture and are not systematic, yet they are useful in understanding the mechanisms by which mobility does (or does not) occur. The Vanderbilt experience, for example, provides clear evidence that part of the barrier to mobility is a deliberate effort by some to retain their positions and to exclude others. I will draw on these studies in the remainder of this book, but only as evidence that a certain mechanism is relevant to other, more systematically derived findings.

Mobility through History

In addition to evidence from public rosters and in-depth studies of wealthy families, limited evidence of general trends in mobility throughout U.S. history is available. Pessen (1974) identified the family origin of those who were wealthy between 1828 and 1848, dividing the rich into three classes given their parents' standing: rich/eminent, middling, or poor/humble. Table 2.3 summarizes his results for New York, Philadelphia, and Boston. As we would expect,

Table 2.4. *American Career Mobility, 1820–1910*

	Philadelphia	Boston	Poughkeepsie	Waltham	Warren	Seattle
Proportion of mobile individuals						
1820–30	14	–	–	–	–	–
1830–40	19	11	–	–	–	–
1840–50	15	10	–	–	–	–
1850–60	20	16	22	17	–	–
1860–70	–	–	24	22	–	–
1870–80	–	–	23	17	–	–
1880–90	–	21	–	–	–	28
1890–00	–	–	–	–	22	–
1900–10	–	–	–	–	–	9

Source: Kaelble 1985.

the vast majority of the rich in those cities, more than 90 percent in each case, were born to rich parents. Fewer than 10 percent were born to either middle class or poor parents. In a related study of career mobility, Kaelble (1985) demonstrated that there was very little career mobility in the United States between 1820 and 1910. Table 2.4 summarizes Kaelble's findings for six cities, omitting information for cities or years that was not available. While both of these studies suggest that our understanding of mobility in early eras of U.S. history is limited, both tables also demonstrate that existing evidence supports the idea that there was very little mobility prior to 1900.

MODERN MOBILITY: FROM SIMULATIONS TO SURVEYS

The bulk of what we know about general wealth mobility patterns comes from survey data and simulation models that often draw on the same survey data. Survey data provides the most reliable estimates of wealth mobility, but until recently, longitudinal data on wealth ownership has been rare. In the absence of adequate data, researchers have used simulations that draw on cross-sectional surveys to estimate wealth mobility (Davies and Kuhn 1988; Gokhale et al. 2001; Keister 2000c). Keister (2000c), for example, synthesized data from a number of surveys in a large scale microsimulation model to explore issues of wealth inequality and mobility. The simulation model in that study synthesized data from multiple basic sources, including household survey data, estate tax data, and aggregate data on the total assets and debts of household, to recreate historical trends in wealth accumulation and mobility. More precisely, the model relied on cross-sectional household survey data to estimate distributional patterns between 1962 and 1995 for an initial sample from the 1960 census. The model aged the sample on numerous demographic and behavioral dimensions, including wealth ownership, to recreate a population that resembled the actual U.S. population over a 30-year period. Finally, the model estimates were aligned every three years with data from estate tax records for the wealthy, other cross-sectional estimates of wealth ownership for the rest of the population, and aggregate data on total wealth household ownership.

In the absence of high-quality longitudinal survey data, simulation models have a number of advantages in estimating wealth mobility. First, these models use individuals and families as their units of analysis, a basic requirement for estimating mobility patterns. Second, the models capture much of the complexity of the multiple processes that interact to create wealth mobility. Third, simulation models make it possible to investigate the role numerous individual and family-level processes play in determining distributional wealth outcomes. Experiments conducted with simulation models can investigate questions about the interactions of multiple processes affecting mobility through time, over the life course and across the full population of families. In fact, simulation experiments can explore a number of questions. Of course, the downside is that although simulation models of this sort are empirically grounded, they are not necessarily empirically accurate.

Estimates of mobility patterns from simulation models can be quite similar to estimates from survey data as Table 2.5 suggests. The cells in the table indicate the percentage of households in the specified row percentile in 1983 and the corresponding column percentile in 1989. For example, those who were in the bottom 25 percent of the wealth distribution in both 1983 and 1989 were among the 67 percent in the bottom 25 percent in both years. Because the table

Table 2.5. *Wealth Mobility Using Surveys and Simulations*

| 1983 Percentile | 1989 Net Worth Percentile | | | | | | | | Total |
| | Bottom 25 | | 25–74 | | 75–94 | | Top 5 | | |
	Survey	Simulated	Survey	Simulated	Survey	Simulated	Survey	Simulated	
Bottom 25	67	65	31	30	2	5	0	0	100
25–49	25	25	69	70	6	5	0	0	100
50–74	7	7	66	67	25	24	2	2	100
75–89	1	1	42	41	52	54	5	4	100
90–94	3	3	31	30	50	51	16	16	100
Top 2–5	0	0	23	22	26	26	51	52	100
Top 1	0	0	5	4	11	9	84	87	100

Note: Survey estimates are author's calculations from the 1983–89 panel of the Survey of Consumer Finances. Simulated results are from a simulation model. Cells are the percentage of households that were in the specified row percentile in 1983 and the corresponding column percentile in 1989. The final column indicates that the other columns, both the survey and simulated columns, sum to 100 percent.
Source: Keister 2000c.

includes only endpoints of the 1982–89 time period, movement in the interim is not included in the table. For example, those in the bottom 25 percent of the distribution in 1983 who moved up to another percentile by 1985 but then returned to the bottom 25 percent by 1989 would still be counted among the 67 percent in the first cell. The simulated and survey estimates in the table are very similar because the survey data was an important input to the simulation.

The estimates in Table 2.5 suggest that there was considerable persistence in wealth status between 1983 and 1989. Indeed, 67 percent of wealth owners in the bottom quartile of the wealth distribution remained in the bottom. Thirty-one percent of those who started out in the bottom moved up to either the second or third quartile, and only 2 percent moved farther. This pattern was typical throughout the distribution: families tended to be in the same segment of the distribution in both periods, with some relatively small amount of movement, to either a higher or lower segment. There was no movement from one extreme of the distribution to another (e.g., between the bottom quartile and the top 5 percent), and very little movement occurred between near extremes (e.g., between the second quartile and the top quartile). Even the movement that does seem to be apparent in the table might be deceptive. It might be that they just moved a small amount. In many cases, movement between two quintiles may represent only a slight increase in wealth, one that carried a person from the top of one quintile to the bottom of the next highest quintile. The persistence in a segment of the distribution that appears in this table is not overly surprising given the short period of time included.

However, estimates of this sort likely over-estimate the amount of persistence that likely obtains across the life course. These estimates are for a short six-year period, and large changes in wealth ownership are unlikely in such a short period of time. Yet findings such as these suggest patterns that ought to emerge in longitudinal survey data. There is evidence that age, race, education, income, and family structure all affect the odds of becoming rich (Keister 2000c). Older people, naturally, have had more time to accumulate wealth. Likewise, education and income are known to improve mobility. In contrast, there is evidence that minorities and those from large families are disadvantaged in accumulation and, therefore, less likely to be mobile. In contrast, baby boomers are more likely than others to move into the top of the distribution of household wealth (Keister and Deeb-Sossa 2000). Finally, simulation models also provide evidence that having parents who were upwardly mobile increases the odds of mobility for offspring, that nonwhites are much less likely than whites to escape poverty, and that higher education is an important means of movement into the middle class (Davies and Shorrocks 1999; Keister 2000a, 2000b, 2000c).

INTERGENERATIONAL CORRELATIONS

Recent improvements in survey data now allow researchers to begin estimating wealth mobility patterns more systematically. The limited research that has been done on wealth mobility using surveys can be grouped into two broad approaches based on the methods used to compare generations. The first approach emphasizes correlations between members of different generations, usually parents and their children, to look at intergenerational persistence in a status. Mulligan (1997) includes an excellent review of the literature using this method. The second approach, which I will refer to as transition studies, tends to focus more on the individual members of a cohort and explore how much mobility they experience and what individual and family traits account for this. Grouping studies in this way is somewhat arbitrary because there is considerable overlap between the two groups, but mobility studies tend to cluster along these lines. Moreover, the methods are different enough, so that considering the findings that each produces is worthwhile. I will discuss research on intergenerational preference and provide some new estimates using this method first. I discuss transition studies in the next section.

Studies of intergenerational persistence use a single metric, the intergenerational correlation coefficient ρ, to represent the amount of variation in one generation's well-being that is associated with the same measure in the previous generation. In this research, the persistence of economic status is measured as

$$y_o = (1 - \beta_y)\bar{y} + \beta_y y_p + \varepsilon_y$$

where o is the offspring and p is the parent, y_o is an individual's status (such as wealth), y_p is the parent's status, $\bar{y}$ is the mean of y_o and is adjusted to equal y_p, β_y is a constant, and ε_y is an error term that is not correlated with y_p. Regression to the mean across generations, or the tendency for status to become more "normal" and less a function of parental status, is measured by $1 - \beta_y$. The intergenerational correlation is

$$\sigma_y = \beta_y \frac{\sigma_{y_p}}{\sigma_{y_o}}$$

where σ_y is the standard deviation of y. Bowles and Gintis (2001) provide an accessible description of this research in which they explain that early studies argued that intergenerational persistence was minimal. Blau and Duncan (1967), for example, estimated the intergenerational correctional for income or earnings among American men to be about 0.15 and concluded that parental advantages disappear rather quickly in the United States. However, errors

Table 2.6. *Intergenerational Persistence Estimates from other Sources*

	Persistence(Mean)	Number of Estimates	Range
Family wealth (log)	0.50	9	0.27–0.76
Education	0.29	8	0.14–0.45
Earnings or wages (log)	0.34	16	0.11–0.59
Family income (log)	0.43	10	0.14–0.65
Consumption (log)	0.68	2	0.59–0.77

Source: Mulligan 1997.

in reporting parents' income and high levels of error in incomes for both generations made the correlation coefficients artificially low.

In recent years, a sizable literature, using better data and more reliable measures, has begun to explore intergenerational persistence of a number of adult outcomes including education, earnings, wages, and even consumption (Mulligan 1997). These estimates suggest that there is persistence across generations in a number of status measures. Table 2.6 summarizes the findings from this literature. As the table indicates, there is considerable variation in studies of intergenerational persistence, but on average there appears to be considerably less mobility than early studies suggested. Average estimates for persistence in education and individual earnings or wages are approximately comparable, while persistence in family income is even greater. Mulligan's own estimates are the only estimates of persistence in consumption, and these suggest that the intergenerational correlation of parental and offspring consumption is even higher than correlations for other status measures.

Although research on persistence in education, earnings, and wages is now relatively common, studies of intergenerational persistence of wealth ownership are still rare. Yet research that has attempted to estimate intergenerational persistence in wealth ownership reports relatively low levels of mobility. Menchik (1979), for example, obtained the probate records of 1,050 parents who died in Connecticut in the 1930s and 1940s and who left a net estate of $40,000 or more in current dollars. He then located the probate records of their children who died in Connecticut by 1976. He found that the correlation between their estates was 0.76. Similarly, Harbury and Hitchens (1979) studied wealth mobility in England by collecting information on fathers who died in 1902 and then tracking as many of their sons as possible until they too died. This study estimated the intergenerational correlation of wealth to be 0.46. Kearl and Pope (1986) found somewhat less intergenerational persistence in their study of Utah Mormons between 1850 and 1870. Looking at sons only, this study found a correlation in wealth owner-ship of 0.27. As Mulligan points out (1997, pp. 208–9), all three of these are unusual samples. Both Menchik (1979) and Kearl and Pope (1986) only included fathers and sons who died in the same state. Harbury and Hitchens (1979) and Menchik (1979) included only very wealthy families, and Harbury and Hitchens (1979) lim-ited their research to Britain. Moreover, none of these studies adjusted for possible measurement error.

Table 2.4 compares estimates of persistence in wealth to persis-tence in other status measures. With the exception of consumption, wealth is the most persistent status measure in this group. Of the nine estimates of wealth persistence in this table, six are Mulligan's own estimates that he produced using the Panel Study of Income Dynamics (PSID). His objective was to use a single representative data set to estimate persistence on multiple status measures and, si-multaneously, to improve on previous flawed estimates. Mulligan's six estimates use different subsets of the sample and correct in var-ious ways for measurement error. In addition to Mulligan's six esti-mates, two additional estimates are from an unpublished dissertation that also used the PSID, and the remaining three are from Menchik (1979), Harbury and Hitchens (1979), and Kearl and Pope (1986). Although the average persistence of 0.50 is weighted heavily by es-timates from the PSID, removing all or most of the PSID estimates produces very similar results. In short, these estimates indicate that there is clearly intergenerational persistence in wealth ownership; in fact, there is more persistence in wealth ownership than in other measures of well-being. Yet parental wealth is by no means a perfect predictor of offspring wealth. That is, there is indeed enough mobility to warrant explanation.

TRANSITION STUDIES

The second broad group of studies that use survey data to study mobility focus on individuals within a generation (as opposed to the entire group of people in a generation) and tend to use transition matrices to study upward and downward mobility. Although studies that use a single number to indicate intergenerational transmission such as the intergenerational correlation coefficient convey important information about mobility, they neglect the details and variation that underlie the single correlation. Individual paths vary, household paths vary, and the processes that lead to outcomes can be quite unique. At the top of the distribution, for example, inheritance may account for transmission, while at the bottom of the distribution, discrimination may be operative. Transition matrices facilitate identification of these different processes more easily than single metric estimates of mobility. For this reason, transition matrices are also more easily exploited in efforts to understand the factors that lead to mobility. Intuitively, this approach is attractive because mobility implies movement between categorical groups, and the transition matrix captures such changes. Indeed, sociologists have a history of studying mobility categorically and have used transition matrices to study occupational (Biblarz, Raftery, and Bucur 1997; Blau and Duncan 1967), income (Breiger 1990; Singer and Spilerman 1979), career (Abbott and Hrycak 1990; Stovel, Savage, and Bearman 1996), and even geographic (Quillian 1999) mobility.

The transition matrix, or mobility table, used in this research typically arrays individuals within groups (e.g., occupations, quintiles, regions) in a start year and indicates the proportion of the sample who moved to other groups or stayed in the same group in a finish year. That is, the elements of the transition matrix, u_{ij}, represent the probability that an individual in group i in period t will be in group j in time $t + 1$. If there were perfect mobility, the main diagonal would include all 1's, and the off-diagonal cells would include 0's. Clearly there are also drawbacks to transition matrix approach. Creating a transition matrix requires specialized data that is difficult to collect. It is also difficult to determine from a transition matrix the degree of immobility in a sample or whether movement upward or downward was between adjacent or more separated cells. However, it is useful to explore the information that is available in wealth mobility tables.

Historical estimates suggest that mobility has changed in important ways in the past century. Steckel (1990; see also Steckel and Krishman 1992) used a national sample from census records from 1850–1860 to estimate patterns of mobility in the nineteenth century. He compared these with estimates of modern mobility patterns from the National Longitudinal Surveys (NLS) of older men and women. Steckel selected 10-year time intervals in the NLS data starting in 1966 for the men and in 1967 for the women. He found that more than 58 percent of households in the top 10 percent of the wealth distribution in the first period (in the 1960–70 data) remained in that position in the second period. He also found that those who left the top of the distribution typically moved only a short distance. Fewer than 10 percent of those who moved out of the top decile fell to positions in the lower half of the distribution, and fewer than 2 percent fell into the very bottom of the distribution. By contrast, nineteenth-century households were less likely to remain in the top wealth group; that is, they were more mobile than similar households in the 1960s and 1970s. However, those who moved from the upper portions of the distribution in the nineteenth century moved farther than their modern counterparts. Steckel also found that households at the lower end of the wealth distribution in the nineteenth century were less mobile than those in the modern sample.

Wealth mobility continued to vary across the wealth distribution into the 1980s. Steckel (1990) ended his comparison in 1976, the most current data at the time he conducted his research. Table 2.7 includes my own estimates of mobility for the male sample from the NLS older men's survey, extending the estimates to 1981 (see Appendix for data details). I measured wealth as the value of the home, farm assets, investment in real estate, businesses, savings and checking accounts, stocks, bonds, mutual funds, and personal loans minus total debt. These estimates are for those households that survived between 1966 and 1981 and reported usable wealth information in

Table 2.7. *Intragenerational Mobility, 1966–1981*

Early Adulthood Quintile	Later Adulthood Quintile				
	Quintile 1	Quintile 2	Quintile 3	Quintile 4	Quintile 5
Quintile 1	62.33	25.75	7.62	4.41	1.80
Quintile 2	23.80	37.42	23.11	13.80	2.00
Quintile 3	9.13	23.00	34.51	22.81	10.11
Quintile 4	3.00	7.12	25.82	37.53	25.30
Quintile 5	1.74	6.71	8.94	21.45	60.79

Note: Cells indicate the percent of people in adult quintiles who originated in each early adulthood quintile.

Source: Author's estimates from the National Longitudinal Survey of Mature Men. Later adult quintiles are based on 1981 net assets. Early adulthood quintiles are based on 1966 net assets.

both years. Death is an important cause of attrition for this group given their ages. If death were the only cause for attrition, the sample would continue to represent the population from which this cohort was selected. However, there was attrition from the sample for other reasons, and death was not evenly distributed by wealth ownership. Wealthier households were more likely to refuse interviews and to provide usable wealth data (Jianakoplos and Menchik 1997). In addition, mortality rates among poorer respondents in this sample were higher than for other segments of the population (Jianakoplos, Menchik, and Irvine 1989). Although I used sampling weights to correct these problems and to adjust for the oversample of black males included in the original sample, the sample is likely to underrepresent wealthiest respondents.

The estimates in Table 2.7 suggest that there is indeed persistence over time among the men in this sample but that there is still considerable movement among segments of the wealth distribution. More than 62 percent of those in the top quintile in 1966 remained there in 1981. Likewise, more than 60 percent of those in the bottom quintile in the first period were still there in the second period. Of those who moved, nearly 80 percent moved to an adjacent quintile. Very few moved into the extremes of the distribution: fewer than 2 percent moved between the lowest and highest quintiles in either direction. Yet there is a considerable amount of overall movement. Indeed,

Table 2.8. *Minimum Wealth Needed to Rank in Each Net Worth Segment*

	1985	1990	1996	2000
Top 1%	$226,500	$1,067,300	$1,153,100	$1,855,000
Top 5%	88,500	275,000	422,500	590,400
Quintile 5	23,800	74,300	136,100	195,200
Quintile 4	8,300	26,300	57,500	80,100
Quintile 3	2,700	7,300	20,100	23,700
Quintile 2	0	260	1,900	5,300
Quintile 1	−188,800	−530,200	−275,300	−793,000

Note: Cells indicate the minimum dollar value needed to be in each quintile (2000 dollars).
Source: Author's calculations from the National Longitudinal Survey of Youth, 1979 Cohort.

more than 60 percent of those who started in one of the three middle quintiles experienced some movement, and nearly 40 percent of those who began in the bottom or top quintiles moved. Jianakoplos and Menchik (1997) report similar findings in their analysis of these data. They also report that mobility among blacks in this sample is significantly less than for whites and that these general trends hold for different definitions of wealth (i.e., augmented wealth which includes, in addition to the wealth value I use, the capitalized value of future expected pension and Social Security income). To account for reporting errors in the data, Jianakoplos and Menchik also computed a number of mobility measures using average wealth over the two surveys. They found that in five of the six comparisons, the measures using average wealth suggested that there was somewhat less mobility than with the reported wealth, but that overall the patterns were quite similar.

In order to investigate even more recent mobility patterns, it is useful to turn to a different data set that has followed respondents until 2000. In particular, the National Longitudinal Survey of Youth, 1979 Cohort (NLS-Y) is useful because it followed respondents through 1998 (see Appendix for data details). The estimates in Table 2.8 indicate the minimum wealth needed to rank in each segment of the wealth distribution, and the estimates in Table 2.9 represent wealth mobility patterns between 1985 (the first year wealth was reported in this survey) and 2000 (the most recent wave currently available). Here I measured wealth consistent with the mature men's

Table 2.9. *Intragenerational Mobility, 1985–2000*

Early Adulthood Quintile	Later Adulthood Quintile				
	Quintile 1	Quintile 2	Quintile 3	Quintile 4	Quintile 5
Quintile 1	30.78	29.42	17.03	12.30	10.47
Quintile 2	24.24	29.61	18.76	15.11	12.27
Quintile 3	18.55	18.45	25.00	20.73	17.26
Quintile 4	13.96	13.29	22.56	26.48	23.71
Quintile 5	11.45	7.08	18.72	25.99	36.76

Note: Cells indicate the percent of people in adult quintiles who originated in each early adulthood quintile.
Source: Author's estimates from the National Longitudinal Survey of Youth, 1979 Cohort. Later adult quintiles are based on 2000 net assets. Early adulthood quintiles are based on 1985 net assets.

sample as possible. In this case, wealth is the sum of the primary residence, businesses, farm assets, investment in real estate, stocks, bonds, checking and savings accounts, trust accounts, Individual Retirement Accounts, 401K plans; and Certificates of Deposit less total debts. As with the estimates in Table 2.7, these estimates are for those households that survived between both years and reported usable wealth information in both years. Again, there was some attrition because of mortality of the respondents, but this problem was less severe than in the mature men's sample as the respondents are younger in the NLS-Y. There is also evidence in this sample that wealthy households were less likely to respond and to report their wealth, although those problems seem less severe than in the mature men's sample. Again, I used sampling weights to correct for these problems and to adjust for the oversample of minorities and poor whites included in the original sample. However, it is still likely that the sample underrepresents the wealthiest respondents.

In the NLS-Y sample, there was greater mobility than in the mature men's sample, and mobility was even more evident at the top of the distribution. Only 36 percent of those who started in the top quintile in this younger sample ended in the top quintile, while approximately 12 percent of those who started in the top quintile actually ended in the bottom quintile. There was considerably more movement out of the bottom of the distribution, where a full 70 percent of those who started in the bottom quintile in 1985 had moved up by 2000. Similarly, more than 70 percent of those who started in the middle quintiles left those positions by 2000. This sample is large; in fact, the survey started with nearly 13,000 respondents and nearly 10,000 of these were successfully interviewed regularly through 2000. The sample was also representative of the population of youth in 1979. Thus the mobility patterns evident in Table 2.9 are likely typical of the population of people aged 31–38 years in 2000. However, some of the difference in mobility compared to the mature men's sample is certainly accounted for by life cycle. The participants in the NLS-Y were just beginning to accumulate significant wealth when the survey was completed in 2000. Many had just begun to work in permanent jobs, to save money, and to acquire assets such as a home. Moreover, many respondents were either still paying off debts, such as college loans, that are more common early in life. Although less critical, it is also the case that 1985–2000 was a period of increasing wealth inequality and economic growth, whereas the mature men were observed during a period of relatively stable inequality and growth (Keister 2000c). Once later waves of this survey are collected, patterns comparable to those in the mature men's survey will be observable.

Although both the mature men and youth samples provide important information about mobility during the lives of the respondents (intragenerational mobility), none of the estimates I have provided so far address mobility between generations (intergenerational mobility). Intuitively, looking at intergenerational mobility is appealing because it speaks to the degree to which advantage at birth accounts for well-being across the life course. Not surprisingly, most mobility research focuses on intergenerational mobility for this reason. However, systematic, reliable data on intergenerational patterns are also among the most difficult types of social data to collect. Although the NLS-Y does not include parents' wealth directly, it is possible to estimate the socioeconomic status of respondents' families to explore intergenerational mobility among the youth respondents. To do this, I identified those respondents who were still living with their parents in 1979, the first year the survey was administered. I then used total household income in 1979, parents' educations, parents'

Table 2.10. *Intergenerational Mobility, 1979–2000*

Childhood Quintile	Adult Quintile				
	Quintile 1	Quintile 2	Quintile 3	Quintile 4	Quintile 5
Quintile 1	45.43	26.66	10.66	8.78	8.47
Quintile 2	23.90	35.27	20.06	13.94	6.83
Quintile 3	10.54	20.21	35.08	21.16	13.01
Quintile 4	7.42	11.40	23.21	32.96	25.01
Quintile 5	4.94	6.14	9.19	24.63	55.11

Note: Cells indicate the percent of people in adult quintiles who originated in each childhood quintile.

Source: Author's estimates from the National Longitudinal Survey of Youth, 1979 Cohort. Adult quintiles are based on 2000 net assets. Childhood quintiles are based on estimated wealth, predicted from family traits (e.g., income, parents' education, household structure, race) in 1979.

occupations, family structure, family religion, and total inheritances received through 2000 to estimate wealth and to categorize respondents in quintiles. Table 2.10 is a mobility table that uses these quintiles as the start period and looks at mobility through 2000. For 2000, I measured respondents' own wealth as their adult household wealth (the same value I used in Table 2.9 for 2000). Omitting respondents from these estimates because they were no longer living with their parents in 1979 biases the results against the older part of the cohort, increasing the amount of mobility that we should find.

Again, the results suggest that there is persistence in status across generations but there is still considerable movement among segments of the wealth distribution. Between childhood and adulthood, more than half of the respondents who started in the top quintile remained there. Similarly, 45 percent of those who started in the bottom quintile were still there in 2000. Yet more than half of respondents who started in the bottom quintile moved up over their lives, and nearly half of those who were in the top quintile as adults had moved up from lower ranks.

There is clearly a great deal of persistence in wealth ownership both across generations and across individual lives. However, not all people stay in the same positions; indeed, the same estimates that demonstrate persistence above can be read to illustrate a fair

Table 2.11. *Changes in Mobility Over Time: Percent Whose Position Changed in Mobility Tables*

	1966–1981 (Table 2.7)	1985–2000 (Table 2.9)	1978–2000 (Table 2.10)
Quintile 1	37.67%	69.22%	54.57%
Quintile 2	62.58	70.39	64.73
Quintile 3	65.49	75.00	64.92
Quintile 4	62.47	73.52	67.04
Quintile 5	39.21	63.24	44.89

Note: Cells indicate the percentage of people who were in a different quintile in the end year (2000 or 1981) than they were in the start year.

amount of mobility. There are definitely caveats associated with each of the estimates, but the story that emerges from the different data sets is that mobility does occur both upward and downward. The estimates in Table 2.11 summarize the findings from the Tables 2.7, 2.9, and 2.10, isolating the amount of mobility that occurs out of each quintile. The tables illustrate that between 39 and 63 percent of people starting in the top quintile left that quintile by the subsequent period represented in the respective table. Mobility out of the each quintile was greatest for the 1985–2000 sample. This is likely because this group was in a life stage that typically includes considerable change. Yet, Table 2.11 demonstrates across years and samples that wealth mobility is possible.

One of the most difficult questions to answer about mobility is whether it has changed over time. Yet this question is among the most central questions in mobility research. How have opportunities and constraints changed across adjacent generations? How have they changed over longer periods of time, such as across centuries? There is some evidence that things have changed, but the nature of that change is somewhat difficult to identify. The evidence I presented in Tables 2.1 and 2.2 suggests that the source of great fortunes has changed. Over the past 200 years, transportation, banking, and natural resources accounted for the bulk of the fortunes of the wealthy. Looking over the past 20 years, however, service-oriented endeavors have taken a much more prominent role in the creation of wealth. Broom and Shay (2000), and others that they cite, argue that sectoral changes are very important in understanding changes in wealth accumulation and differences in patterns of mobility over time. Because wealth is largely at the mercy of the sector in which it is earned or invested, when economic sectors experience expansions, declines, and other changes, so do fortunes. This is clearly evident in Tables 2.1 and 2.2. Steckel's (1990) comparative research looked more directly at mobility patterns over time. Like most research that compares mobility patterns over long periods of time, Steckel had some difficulty matching data sets. Yet his evidence is suggestive of some important differences between the mid-1800s and the mid-1900s. As I discussed above, Steckel concluded that those in the lower segments of the wealth distribution in the nineteenth century were less mobile than those in the modern sample. Yet, he also showed that households at the upper end of the wealth distribution in the early period were more mobile than similar households in the 1960s and 1970s.

The evidence included in Tables 2.3 and 2.4 suggests that there was enormous persistence in wealth mobility in the 1800s. Combined with anecdotal evidence from public rosters and in-depth studies of wealth families, these estimates suggest that mobility in America's early history was very limited. Of course, issues of data reliability advise caution in interpreting these estimates. Yet even if only the general pattern in the historic estimates is to be believed, a comparison with modern estimates such as those in Tables 2.5 through 2.11 suggests enormous increases in wealth mobility over time. Additional discussion of historic trends are beyond the scope of this book, but the topic is certainly worthy of additional research.

Conclusion

In this chapter, I verified findings from previous empirical research and the expectations from social and economic theory that there is considerable persistence in wealth ownership both across and within generations. However, I also provide evidence that considerable wealth mobility does occur in the United States. There is clearly less wealth mobility than we would expect if every person faced the same opportunities and constraints throughout life. I presented evidence from simulation models that showed that there was a great deal of persistence in wealth ownership over relatively short periods of time. I then explored the use of intergenerational correlations to identify patterns in mobility in survey data. These results also suggested that persistence in wealth ownership is substantial across generations. Indeed, compared to education, earnings, and total family income, wealth was relatively highly correlated across generations. Yet there was evidence even in intergenerational correlations that substantial mobility does occur, and evidence from transition studies confirmed this. I drew on estimates from previous research and my own calculations to show that, through the late 1990s, there has been considerable movement in all segments of the wealth distribution. An important caveat is that a great deal of this movement is to adjacent cells of transition matrices. That is, much of the mobility that does occur does not constitute movement across great spans of the distribution.

Previous research on wealth accumulation and mobility relied largely on public rosters such as social registers and in-depth studies of wealth families to draw vague conclusions about wealth ownership. These approaches provide some clues into the nature of mobility in the United States, but they are naturally limited in that they provide little information about how typical these patterns are. My aim in this chapter was to begin to unravel these issues by exploring what we know from previous research on the wealthy and then to provide more systematic estimates of how much wealth mobility Americans experience. Logically, it then makes sense to ask what factors account for differential patterns of mobility that are evident across households. This is the task of the remaining chapters of this book.

CHAPTER THREE

THE NEW RICH

As I demonstrated in Chapter One, basic facts about the distribution of wealth are well known but the processes that account for wealth inequality are still unclear. Understanding individual and family-level wealth accumulation and mobility – who gets rich and how – is an important piece of the puzzle. Chapter Two explored how much wealth mobility occurs, and in this chapter I begin to investigate the processes that underlie patterns of wealth accumulation. The specific goal of this chapter is to understand who the wealthy are. I present a basic portrait of the people and their wealth. I then show that the wealthy are an educated group. This chapter provides a preview to the more detailed explorations of the origins of the wealthy that are the object of the remainder of this book.

WHO ARE THE RICH?

One way to think about who is rich is to consider specific wealthy people, and the Forbes 400 is a logical place to begin. As I detail in the Appendix, *Forbes* magazine produces annual lists of the Four Hundred wealthiest Americans and augment the lists with information about the source of the person's wealth. Table 3.1 lists the top ten wealthiest individuals in 1996, during the rapid economic growth that characterized that period. The table also identifies the source of the persons' wealth and the size of their fortune.

William Henry (Bill) Gates III was the wealthiest person in the country in 1996, and he has maintained that position ever since. Gates first appeared on the Forbes' list in 1986 and rapidly moved to

Table 3.1. *The 10 Richest People in the United States, 1996*

	Source of Wealth	Net Worth[a]
1. William H. Gates, III[b]	Microsoft Corporation	$18.5
2. Warren Edward Buffett	Stock market	15.0
3. du Pont (Pierre Samuel II) family	Inheritance	10.5
4. Paul Gardner Allen[b]	Microsoft Corporation	7.5
5. John Werner Kluge[b]	Metromedia Company	7.2
6. Rockefeller family	Inheritance	6.5
7. Lawrence Joseph Ellison[b]	Oracle Corporation	6.0
8. Mellon family	Inheritance	5.8
9. Philip Hampson Knight	Nike, Inc.	5.3
10. Jim C. Walton	Inheritance	4.8

[a] Net worth is in billions of 1996 dollars.
[b] Names in high-tech industries.
Source: Forbes magazine.

the number one position. While many of the details of Bill Gates'
life are relatively well known, they are still important. In particular, Gates' wealth is self-made. That does not mean that he grew
up poor, of course. In reality, he was probably already upper class
as a child. Gates' father is a lawyer, and the family was relatively
well-off throughout Bill Jr.'s life. Nonetheless, the fortune that earns
Bill Gates Jr. the position of the richest American is all his own. A
talented student at Harvard, Gates quit to cofound the Microsoft Corporation with his friend Paul Allen in 1975. The company bought an
early version of the MS-DOS computer operating system, improved
on it, and re-released it shortly after. Now every time a copy of MS-
DOS is sold, Gates gets richer. His fortune has also grown as the
Internet expands. He was an early skeptic of the Internet, but he has
since reversed that opinion and currently has stakes in many Internet
ventures.

Three other members of the 1996 list of the ten wealthiest people also owe their fortunes to the growing importance of technology
during that decade. Paul Allen, cofounder of Microsoft, appears at
number four; John Kluge, of Metromedia, appears at number five;
and Larry Ellison, of Oracle, is number seven. Like Bill Gates, Allen
was also a successful student who dropped out of college to start

Microsoft. Also like Bill Gates, the fortune to which Allen can attribute his wealth is self-made. He left Microsoft in 1983 when he was
diagnosed with Hodgkin's disease, but he is still a major shareholder
in the corporation. Larry Ellison also built his fortune in computer-
related activities, including the Oracle Database, and he was also a
successful-student-turned-college dropout in response to the expansion of opportunities in the computer industry. Ellison continues as
CEO of the Oracle Corporation, and his fortune continues to grow
as the Internet expands and Oracle changes to provide related software. In contrast to these relatively young entrepreneurs (Gates and
Allen are 46 and 49 years old, respectively; Ellison is 58), John Kluge
is considerably older and a more traditional story of upward mobility. Yet Kluge's wealth is also self-made and also technology related.
Kluge was born in Germany and raised in a Detroit tenement house.
He finished his bachelor's degree at Columbia University and subsequently made his fortune in the Metromedia Corporation, which
provides numerous products and services in cable television, radio,
telephone, cell phone, and related industries.

Additional self-made billionaires on the list of the ten wealthiest Americans in 1996 are Warren Buffet, who made his fortune
in finance and various investments, and Larry Knight, who made
his fortune as founder of the Nike Fortune. Both Buffet and Knight
graduated from college, both have master's degrees, and both continue to appear on the list of the wealthiest Americans through 2002
(although Knight dropped to the thirty-first position). An important
difference between these two entrepreneurs is that whereas Knight's
fortune can largely be traced to a single corporation, Buffet became
rich investing in several different companies. His current financial
interests include significant stakes in Berkshire Hathaway, Geico
Insurance, Wells Fargo, American Express, and Coca-Cola.

Of course the list of wealthiest Americans also includes a number of rich who inherited their wealth. In 1996, four of the top ten
entries inherited their fortunes. Pierre du Pont, for instance, the
third richest person in the country that year, inherited part of the
fortune amassed initially by Samuel du Pont. Descendents of John
D. Rockefeller, America's first billionaire and well-known oil baron,

appear at number six. Similarly, Andrew Mellon's descendents appear at number eight. Finally, the tenth position in 1996 is held by Jim C. Walton, who inherited part of the fortune of Sam Walton. Notably, positions eleven through fourteen of this list are occupied by Walton's other heirs. While this group is relatively new to the group of wealthiest Americans (relative to the du Ponts and Rockefellers, that is), combining their current fortunes would place them above Bill Gates in the list.

While the list of the wealthy in a given year is interesting and useful, it is perhaps more useful to explore how membership in such lists changes over time. Tables 3.2a and 3.2b replicate the list of the top ten wealthiest Americans for 2000, just after the peak of the economic expansion of the 1990s, and 2002, after the subsequent economic downturn. In Tables 3.1a and 3.2b, those billionaires whose fortunes are clearly the result of technology-related ventures are highlighted. There is a clear trend in the presence of technology-created rich in the Forbes list. In 1996, the overall wealth was low relative to its level in 2000, and as Table 3.1 indicates, only four of the ten richest Americans generated their fortunes through technology-related pursuits. By 2000, six of the top ten wealthy individuals had fortunes that originated in a high-tech industry, primarily computer software. Gordon Moore of the Intel Corporation, Philip Anschutz of Qwest Communications, and Steven Ballmer of the Microsoft Corporation joined Gates, Ellison, and Allen in the top ten. Also notable is the fact that John Kluge had fallen to number fifteen by 2000. While his fortune was still vast, its growth did not keep pace with the growth experienced by those who more heavily invested in computer technology. What these tables do not indicate is the extent to which technology-based wealth became more evident between 1996 and 2000. There were 32 new entrants to the Forbes 400 in 2000, and the majority of these got rich via fiber optics or Internet software.

Following the trend of the wealthiest Americans for another two years – through 2002 – demonstrates the effect of a sudden change in the economic climate on the composition of the Forbes list. Table 3.2b shows that in 2002, after the economic downturn that was occurring at that time, the value of technology-related wealth

Table 3.2a. *The 10 Richest People in the United States, 2000*

	Source of Wealth	Net Worth[a]
1. William H. Gates, III[b]	Microsoft Corporation	$60.0
2. Lawrence Joseph Ellison[b]	Oracle Corporation	58.0
3. Paul Gardner Allen[b]	Microsoft Corporation	36.0
4. Warren Edward Buffett	Stock market	28.0
5. Gordon Earle Moore[b]	Intel Corporation	26.0
6. Philip F. Anschutz[b]	Qwest Communications	18.0
7. Steven Anthony Ballmer[b]	Microsoft Corporation	17.0
8. Alice L. Walton	Inheritance	17.0
9. Helen R. Walton	Inheritance	17.0
10. Jim C. Walton	Inheritance	17.0

[a] Net worth is in billions of 2000 dollars.
[b] Names in high-tech industries.
Source: Forbes magazine.

Table 3.2b. *The 10 Richest People in the United States, 2002*

	Source of Wealth	Net Worth[a]
1. William H. Gates, III[b]	Microsoft Corporation	$43.0
2. Warren Edward Buffett	Stock market	36.0
3. Paul Gardner Allen[b]	Microsoft Corporation	21.0
4. Alice L. Walton	Inheritance	18.8
5. Helen R. Walton	Inheritance	18.8
6. Jim C. Walton	Inheritance	18.8
7. John T. Walton	Inheritance	18.8
8. S. Robson Walton	Inheritance	18.8
9. Lawrence Joseph Ellison[b]	Oracle Corporation	15.2
10. Steven Anthony Ballmer[b]	Microsoft Corporation	11.9

[a] Net worth is in billions of 2002 dollars.
[b] Names in high-tech industries.
Source: Forbes magazine.

declined and its owners moved down the list of wealthy Americans. Bill Gates still occupied the top position on the Forbes list in 2002, and Larry Allen was close behind at number three. However, Larry Ellison and Steven Ballmer had fallen to numbers nine and ten, respectively, and the Walton heirs moved to positions four through eight. Of course, ranking at numbers nine and ten among the wealthiest Americans means that Ellison and Ballmer still had absolutely

Table 3.3a. *The 10 Richest People in the World, 2000*

	Country	Source of Wealth	Net Worth[a]
1. William H. Gates, III[b]	United States	Microsoft Corporation	$60.0
2. Lawrence Joseph Ellison[b]	United States	Oracle Corporation	47.0
3. Paul Gardner Allen[b]	United States	Microsoft Corporation	28.0
4. Warren Edward Buffett	United States	Stock market	25.6
5. Theo & Karl Albrecht	Germany	Retail	20.0
6. Prince Alwaleed Bin Talal Alsaud	Saudi Arabia	Inheritance	20.0
7. S. Robson Walton	United States	Inheritance	20.0
8. Masayoshi Son[b]	Japan	Softbank Corporation	19.4
9. Michael Dell[b]	United States	Dell Corporation	19.1
10. Kenneth Thomson[b]	Canada	Thomson Corporation	16.1

[a] Net worth is in billions of 2000 dollars.
[b] Names in high-tech industries.
Source: Forbes magazine.

Table 3.3b. *The 11 Richest People in the World, 2003*

	Country	Source of Wealth	Net Worth[a]
1. William H. Gates, III[b]	United States	Microsoft Corporation	$40.7
2. Warren E. Buffet	United States	Stock market	30.5
3. Theo & Karl Albrecht	Germany	Retail	25.6
4. Paul Gardner Allen[b]	United States	Microsoft Corporation	20.1
5. Prince Alwaleed Bin Talal Alsaud	Saudi Arabia	Inheritance	17.7
6. Lawrence J. Ellison[b]	United States	Oracle Corporation	16.6
7. Alice L. Walton	United States	Inheritance	16.5
8. Helen R. Walton	United States	Inheritance	16.5
9. Jim C. Walton	United States	Inheritance	16.5
10. John T. Walton	United States	Inheritance	16.5
11. S. Robson Walton	United States	Inheritance	16.5

[a] Net worth is in billions of 2003 dollars.
[b] Names in high-tech industries.
Source: Forbes magazine.

huge fortunes, but the change in the list does demonstrate how critical aggregate economic trends are to determining the composition of such lists.

Similar patterns and changes are evident in the list of the ten richest people in the world. Tables 3.3a and 3.3b include the world's wealthiest individuals in 2000 and 2002, respectively. Again, I include these two years to demonstrate the relatively current composition of these lists and to show how the lists change over time in response to economic fluctuations. As the lists demonstrate, most of the world's richest people were Americans in 2000 (60 percent), and most of the rich (60 percent, though not the same 60 percent) were rich because they had invested in industries that boomed during the technology-based expansion. Four of the world's richest people were on this list, Bill Gates and Paul Allen of Microsoft, and Larry Ellison of Oracle, and Michael Dell of the Dell Corporation. In addition to these Americans, Masayoshi Son, head of the Japanese Softbank Corporation that makes computer hardware and software, and Kenneth Thomson, head of Canada's Thomson Corporation that specializes in early-stage information technology, also made it to the list. By 2002, the list had changed dramatically, and as with the list of richest Americans, the list of the world's richest people contained fewer technology-created fortunes.

Forbes lists are useful to understanding how the wealthy got rich because they include rather reliable lists of the very rich and details about their backgrounds. Yet there are problems with relying exclusively on these lists. In Chapter Two, I explained why it would be unwise to rely exclusively on such lists to understand how much mobility there is. For similar reasons, it would be imprudent to rely only on these lists to understand the causes of wealth accumulation and mobility.

There are several problems with relying solely on Forbes lists. First, the content of these lists varies rather dramatically with changes in aggregate economic trends. Of course, aggregate trends do influence wealth accumulation, but the degree to which the lists vary in response to economic booms and busts is rather extreme. The lists also need to be read with some caution because decisions by the compilers at Forbes about how to list individuals and families also affects the composition of the lists in important ways. For example, grouping the Rockefellers and Mellons as families and including the Waltons separately shapes the content of the lists in each of the years replicated earlier. The decision to list these families either as a unit or separately makes some sense given the financial relationships among the heirs to these great fortunes, but it does shape who else is – and is not – included in the lists. Moreover, the additional information available about those included in the lists is rather limited. There is basic information available on their investments and career paths, and there is even some information about their families. Yet, the factors that shape wealth accumulation and mobility are likely to be rather complex, and the fairly basic information available about the Forbes 400 is not nearly comprehensive enough to help understand the relative importance of competing influences on these processes.

Finally, and perhaps most important, *the Forbes 400* – the entire 400, not just the top ten – *accounts for only two percent of total household wealth in the United States* (Kennickell 2003). So although these lists are important, they are not at all representative of even the U.S. wealthy, much less the entire population of the country. To understand the determinants of wealth accumulation for a more representative group of Americans, it is necessary to turn to survey data.

How Rich is Rich?

To really understand how people accumulate wealth, it is necessary to move beyond lists such as the Forbes that include specific wealthy people. Survey data is an important alternative to these lists. For the remainder of this book, I largely rely on survey estimates of the wealthy and the processes that explain how they got rich. Survey data is useful because it tends to contain much more detailed information about representative groups of respondents. An important first step is understanding how rich is rich.

In Table 3.4, I use data from the National Longitudinal Survey of Youth (NLSY) to provide estimates of family wealth for the rich and others in 2000. In the Appendix, I provide data details for the NLSY, compare estimates from the NLSY to estimates from other survey data sets, and explain that I rely on the NLS because it contains extremely detailed information about a very large number of respondents for over 20 years. The Appendix demonstrates that wealth estimates from the NLSY are somewhat lower than estimates from

Table 3.4. *The Wealth of the Rich, 2000*

In Thousands	Millionaires	$500K–999K	$300–499K	All Others
Net worth (mean)	2,172	680	384	66
Net worth (median)	1,600	650	380	40
Home (median)	400	260	220	65
Stocks, bonds (median)	200	200	1	0
Debt (median)	154	140	95	32

Note: Values are for those with nonnegative assets.
Source: National Longitudinal Survey of Youth, 1979 Cohort.

surveys that include more wealthy people. However, NLSY estimates are relatively comparable to other data and contain much greater detail about other life-course processes that are critical to understanding wealth accumulation. In Table 3.4 and subsequent tables, I include estimates for millionaires (i.e., those with net worth of at least $1 million), those with net worth between $500,000 and $999,999, those with net worth between $300,000 and $499,999, and all others.

The estimates in Table 3.4 underscore the degree to which wealth ownership is unevenly distributed, particularly at the top of the distribution. The mean wealth for each group is higher than the median (an indicator of a skewed distribution as the mean is dragged higher or lower by extreme values), but for the highest group the difference is particularly pronounced. Specifically, the mean net worth for millionaires was $2.1 million, while the median net worth was only $1.6 million. Of course, both the mean and the median are high, but the difference between the two highlights the presence of some individuals with exceptionally high wealth. At the lower end of the distribution, the mean is $64,000 and the median is only $40,000, reflecting the presence of some outliers. Of course the difference between the mean and the median for the remaining two groups is relatively small, at least in part because of the nature of the groups. Restricting the high and low values for the groups displayed necessarily prevents the inclusion of outliers. Yet the point that there are extreme outliers in the top category still holds.

The estimates included in Table 3.4 also suggest that the rich own different investments than others. Given that the categories used in this table are defined by net worth, it is not possible to determine exactly how different the portfolio behavior (ownership of components of wealth) is for the wealthy, but clear patterns do emerge. Differences between the wealthy and other families are clear in both the median value of real assets, such as the home, and financial assets, such as stocks and bonds. The median home value for millionaires is more than six times the median value for those who are not in one of the wealthy categories. Even more extreme, for this sample, the median value of stocks and bonds is zero, while millionaires own on average more than $200,000 in these financial assets. Those with between $300,000 and $499,999 in net worth have on average very little invested in stocks and bonds. This is a very clear difference between this group and the very wealthiest respondents included here. Another important pattern that emerges from this table is the amount of overall debt assumed by each group. It might be tempting to assume that the rich do not have debts, but the estimates in this table also demonstrate that they do. In fact, the millionaires in this sample had on average more than $150,000 in debt. This includes mortgage debt and other types of debt, but it is clear that the portfolios of even the very wealthy include some liabilities.

ASSETS OF THE RICH

To really explore the investments of the wealthy, Figure 3.1 compares the percentage of households owning particular components of wealth in 2000 (the values for this figure are given in the Appendix). The figure highlights the greater likelihood of the rich to own financial assets such as stocks and bonds. The rich are also more likely to own a home, although the difference here is less pronounced than it is in the ownership of stocks. Within the three groups of the rich, there are very few differences in the ownership of housing assets and cash accounts, such as checking and savings accounts. There is, however, a noticeable difference in the ownership of stocks. In particular, the wealthiest respondents are more likely to own stocks, suggesting that stock values do drive wealth ownership to some degree,

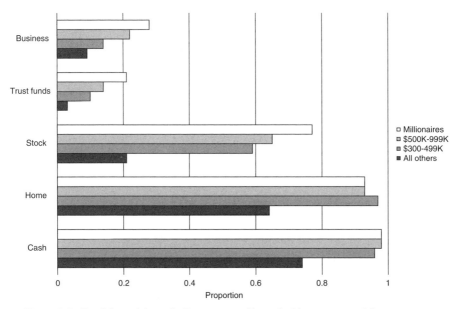

Figure 3.1. Portfolios of the rich: Percentage of households owning wealth components (2000). *Source:* National Longitudinal Survey of Youth, 1979 Cohort.

particularly among the groups of people who are likely to be owners
at all. Figure 3.1 also demonstrates that few families, even rich families, received trust accounts. While this does not provide definite
evidence of mobility, it is certainly consistent with the trends evident in Chapter Two. That is, upward wealth mobility is possible. If
all wealthy people were raised as wealthy children, we would expect
a greater proportion of them to have received a trust account.

The difference between the rich and the rest of the population
is even more evident in the percentage of total assets accounted for
by different wealth types, illustrated in Figure 3.2. Again, the values
for this figure are included in the Appendix. What is most notable
here is that whereas the home accounts for a very large proportion of
the portfolios of all families, the percentage is higher for the nonrich
than it is for the rich. In contrast, stocks account for a very significant
proportion of the portfolios of the wealthy. Again, trust accounts
account for less than 10 percent of the values of the accounts of any
respondent, suggesting that mobility is indeed possible.

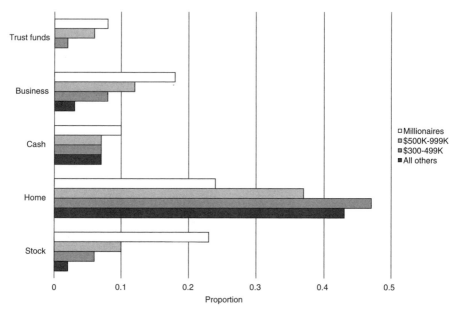

Figure 3.2. Portfolios of the rich: Percentage of total assets accounted for by wealth types (2000). *Source:* National Longitudinal Survey of Youth, 1979 Cohort.

Of course, these estimates of the wealth of the rich are simple descriptive statistics. They do not control for differences in background, life trajectories, or other relevant processes. I explore those differences in later chapters. I simply show these patterns to provide a first glance at how the wealthy differ from the remainder of the population.

The Educated Rich

One trait that stands out in the Forbes' lists of the wealthy is that the rich are highly educated. Indeed, it is unusual to find members of the list who are not well educated. Bill Gates and Paul Allen stand out because they dropped out of college, but a mention of this fact is usually accompanied by a note that the two were excellent students who dropped out of equally excellent universities. More typically, members of the Forbes 400 have at least a bachelor's degree, and often they have a master's degree as well.

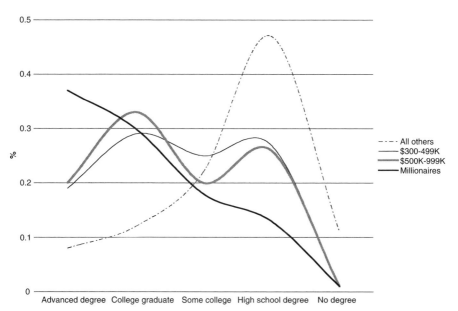

Figure 3.3. The educated rich (2000). *Source:* National Longitudinal Survey of Youth, 1979 Cohort.

Survey data uphold the impression that the rich are well educated. Figure 3.3 shows that the rich are well educated (values are included in the Appendix). This figure graphs the highest level of schooling completed by those in the top segments of the wealth distribution in 2000 and compares their educational attainment to that of other respondents to the NLSY. Nearly 40 percent of millionaires had advanced degrees, thirty percent had at least a college degree, and another twenty percent had completed some college but had not graduated. Altogether 75 percent of these millionaires had at least begun college, and the majority had finished. A mere 13 percent of the millionaires had only a high school degree, and virtually none had no degree. Similar patterns are evident for those whose net worth was between $300,000 and $499,999 and for those whose net worth was between $500,000 and $999,999. In each of these groups, nearly three-quarters had at least some college, about one-third had graduated from college, and about 20 percent had completed a college degree. The overall attainment for the second two groups in

Table 3.5. *Demographic Characteristics of the Wealthy, 2000*

	Millionaires	$500K–$999K	$300–$499K	$0–$299K	Negative	All
Education	15.9	15.0	14.8	13.1	12.7	13.3
Age	40.0	39.8	39.6	39.3	39.2	39.5
Children	1.6	1.8	1.8	1.9	1.9	1.8

Note: Age and education are in years. "Children" is number of people aged 18 years or less and living in the home. Millionaires are those with net worth greater than or equal to $1 million. *Sources:* The 2000 National Longitudinal Survey of Youth, 1979 Cohort, and the 2001 Survey of Consumer Finances.

Figure 3.3 is slightly less than it is for the millionaires, but it is still very high compared to other respondents. Only about 8 percent of the remaining respondents had advanced degrees, and only 12 percent had completed college.

These patterns translate into about 16 years of total education on average for millionaires, and 15 years on average for other rich. Consistent with the U.S. population, most of the respondents in the NLSY, 47 percent, had only a high school education. Moreover, as Table 3.5 shows, those with negative net worth had only 12.7 years of education on average. This table includes estimates of average educational attainment, respondent age, and number of children ever born by net worth category in 2000. The estimates are from the NLSY, and the education averages are quite consistent with estimates from the Survey of Consumer Finances (see Appendix for details).

There is some evidence that the rich are more educated than they were in the past. In a provocative exploration of the nature of today's elite, David Brooks (2000) argues that the information age has changed the requirements for becoming wealthy. It used to be that natural resources and financial capital, materials that can be bequeathed from generation to generation, were the tickets to great wealth. Brooks reasons that in the technology-dominated economy of the late twentieth and early twenty-first centuries, ideas and knowledge are more vital to economic success. He observes related cultural trends such as the use of phrases such as "intellectual capital" and "the culture industry," which mesh notions of intelligence and money (p. 10). He refers to the highly educated people who are both creative and financial successful as bourgeois bohemians (or bobos), and he argues that they define our age. He provides a host of largely anecdotal evidence to support this claim. He shows, for example, that the *New York Times* wedding pages have changed from emphasizing breeding to emphasizing education and related accomplishments. His evidence reveals that the majority of the educated elite who are married now were born into upper-middle-class households and that 84 percent of them have a parent who is a professional. He shows that this group marries late (29 for brides, and 32 for grooms) and has a penchant for occupational homophily (p. 15). In the 1950s, the wedding pages emphasized membership in such organizations as the Junior League and date of presentation to society for brides. For grooms, information about attendance at a military academy was common. In more recent years, this information has been replaced with information about the college and professional schools the couple attended and the law firms for which they work (Chapter One).

Perhaps most interesting, as Brooks points out, is the fact that there have been genuine changes in the educational accomplishments of the elite in recent decades. In 1952, the majority of Harvard freshmen had graduated from New England prep schools such as Andover and Exeter (which contribute 10 percent of that year's first-year students), and 90 percent of applicants whose father was a Harvard graduate were admitted (Brooks 2000; see also Herrnstein and Murray 1994). In 1952, the average verbal SAT score for Harvard freshman was 583, and the average across the Ivy League was about 500. However, as early as 1960, the average verbal SAT score for Harvard freshmen was 678 and the average math score was 695. In fact, as Brooks points out, the typical freshman at Harvard in 1952 would have been in the bottom 10 percent of the Harvard freshmen in the class of 1960. It was also more common by 1960 for intelligent students from around the country, not just from New England prep schools, to apply to Harvard and to be admitted. These findings are consistent with arguments that during the 1960s, class hierarchies were changing dramatically as college admissions committees opened the doors of universities to talented students regardless of class background (Baltzell 1964).

There is also some evidence of a relationship between informal education and wealth accumulation. The book *Rich Dad, Poor Dad: What the Rich Teach Their Kids about Money that the Poor and Middle Class Do Not* (Kiyosaki and Lechter 2000) popularized the idea that there is a qualitative difference between the education that goes on in rich and poor or middle-class homes. Written by a business owner and investor and a businesswoman, the book is less an empirical exploration of trends in informal education and more a how-to-get-rich manual. The authors draw on their own experiences as financial consultants to identify lessons that the wealthy learn from their parents. These lessons include solid financial advice about reducing debt, streamlining consumption, and paying taxes wisely. The basic notion that rich families teach their children different lessons than do poor families is also consistent with studies in the social sciences on the role that family structure plays in shaping parent–child interactions and thus adult outcomes (Chang 2002; Chiteji and Stafford 1999; Downey 1995a; Keister 2003). These studies show that children learn about finances from their parents, and it follows that parents who are wealthy have lessons to teach that are more likely to help their children become wealthy as well. Of course, it is extremely difficult to test these ideas directly because obtaining data on the casual interactions between parents and children is a tall order, and because much of the education involved in this type of interaction occurs nondeliberately. Yet the idea that informal education is different for the rich is an important point.

These trends definitely suggest that the rich are more educated and that there is a relationship between informal education and wealth. Yet the evidence on which these claims are made is to a large degree anecdotal. The supporting claims are certainly conceptually appealing. The information age does require a different set of skills than previous ages, and college admissions did change during the 1960s and 1970s. Moreover, it makes a great deal of sense that processes that occur in families affect the educational and occupational trajectories on which children embark, and these are likely to translate into adult wealth (or lack of wealth). These ideas are also consistent with empirical trends in the current educational attainment of the rich as we saw in Figure 3.3. What is not readily evident is whether this is a general trend among the wealthy (after all, a convenience sample of the *New York Times* wedding pages is not a representative sample of the population). Nor is it evident that it is education that leads to wealth accumulation or whether the wealthy are simply able to buy more education for their children. Disentangling these issues is the subject of later chapters of this book.

While I will explore the demographic traits of the wealthy in more detail in later chapters, it is worth noting at least a few more key characteristics. Table 3.5 includes the number of children ever born to respondents. There is little variation across the wealth distribution on this dimension. The wealthy tended to have 1.6 to 1.9 children, while all respondents in the sample had an average of 1.8 children. Although family size does not vary across wealth groups currently, there are important differences in current family size of the wealthy and family size from previous decades. In the first decades of the twentieth century, for instance, millionaires had an average of about 4 children (Sorokin 1925). Table 3.5 also includes average age and average number of children for respondents in various segments of the wealth distribution. Age is highly consistent across the wealth levels because the NLSY data restricts the age of respondents (see Appendix for details). In a more age-representative sample, millionaires would be closer to 60 years old on average, and the total adult sample would be approaching 50 years. The Appendix also includes comparisons of the NLSY demographic traits with traits from the Survey of Consumer Finances. It is worth bearing in mind that the behaviors and patterns of the NLSY sample are likely to continue to change, and their wealth is also likely to change as they age. Future research will be able to identify how the patterns I describe are affected by the aging of this sample.

CONCLUSION

This chapter provided a glimpse of who the rich are and is a preview to later chapters that will explore in more detail the processes that account for wealth accumulation and mobility. I used *Forbes* lists and simple bivariate statistics from survey data to briefly present a portrait of the rich and their wealth. I also showed that the wealthy are a relatively well-educated group, and I presented evidence that they are more educated than the rich of previous generations. Of course the basic statistics I presented in this chapter do not control for the multitude of other behaviors and processes that explain wealth accumulation and mobility. For that reason, it is impossible to draw conclusions about whether the rich are more able to afford education or whether the educated are more likely to get rich. I will control for other influences in later chapters in an effort to answer this question and to parse out the relative importance of the other factors that shape wealth ownership. But before I begin untangling the processes that create wealth, let's take stock of what processes are likely involved in wealth accumulation.

CHAPTER FOUR

GETTING RICH

There is little doubt that the process by which people get rich is complex. It begins in childhood with interactions, experiences, and events that do not all appear to be related to adult wealth ownership. It then extends through adolescence and early adulthood. Over the life course, multiple interacting processes and events shape the trajectory that an individual follows. Individual choice is important, and of course, choice occurs within important constraints that make choice more or less free.

Understanding who gets rich is closely related to efforts to understand who is upper class in the United States. This intensely debated issue has attracted attention for decades. Class, or Marxist, theorists argue that the United States is ruled by a small, fairly stable upper class that is largely defined by wealth and the power that accompanies wealth ownership (Domhoff 1983). According to this camp, a cohesive upper class dominates government, controls powerful positions in business, and shapes the social and cultural climate in the United States. A more modest version of this perspective holds that the capitalist class does not control political organizations and that there is autonomy among politics, business, and social spheres. However, this moderated class approach retains elements of the Marxist perspective. They suggest, for example, that the pervasive ideology among both the upper class and everyone else is an ideology that originates from the upper class and serves upper-class interests (Lerner, Nagai, and Rothman 1996). Although class theorists are not usually interested in explaining wealth mobility in particular, their ideas do imply that movement into the upper economic class is at best very limited.

Another group of researchers, elite theorists, agrees with the Marxist school that there is a dominant ruling class. Yet they argue that a group of elites – either one elite or multiple elites – holds power (Dye 1995; Mills 1956). In terms of mobility, then, the conclusion of elite theory would largely be the same as that drawn by Marxists. Specifically, while this perspective implies that there is a possibility of mobility into and out of the controlling group, the underlying assumption in elite theory is that there is an inner group of power-ful individuals that controls most aspects of political, economic, and social life.

While there is some appeal to the idea that movement into the upper echelons of society is impossible, there is evidence that upward wealth mobility is not only possible but relatively and increasingly common. The findings I presented in the previous chapters of this book, for example, demonstrate that there is considerable upward wealth mobility. Given this reality, the pluralist perspective on who is upper class provides an appealing starting point for a conceptual explanation of mobility. In contrast to both class and elite theorists, pluralists argue that the notion of a ruling class is simply not based on fact. These critics of ruling-class views observe that there are powerful people in all organizations, but there are so many levels and inter-secting spheres of social, political, and economic organization that it is impossible for a single group to control all areas (Keller 1963; Rose 1967). Pluralists do not propose that there is no overlap be-tween business and politics, but they allow for more separation given the complex relations that occur among organizations. Like class theorists and elite theorists, pluralists are typically concerned with explaining interactions between those who hold economic and po-litical power, but again their ideas speak to understanding wealth mobility. If, as the pluralists have shown, the upper class is not a unified group, it is much more likely than class theorists would al-low that upward social movement is possible. This perspective is consistent with the evidence that there is, in fact, considerable wealth mobility.

In the remainder of this chapter, I start from the basic notion that upward mobility is possible, and I explore the factors that affect who experiences this mobility. I no longer address issues of how many people get rich each year and whether there is more or less wealth mobility than we would expect. I now turn to exploring the factors that account for the paths taken by those who are fortunate enough to get rich during their lives. Figure 4.1 summarizes the arguments I make about how various contributing factors interact to produce adult wealth. The model I propose incorporates processes from childhood, adolescence, and adulthood that contribute to wealth ownership, in general, and upward wealth mobility, in particular. I elaborate on the details of the model below.

FAMILY BACKGROUND

Family background can be among the most critical determinants of success in life, including upward social and economic mobility. Social scientists have shown that childhood family structure shapes adult educational attainment, occupation and employment outcomes, and socioeconomic well-being in important ways (Biblarz and Raftery 1993; Biblarz, Raftery, and Bucur 1997; Eggebeen and Lichter 1991; Hao 1996). Family background refers to all aspects of the childhood family, including parents' educations and occupational attainment, family income and finances, family size and structure, religion and other cultural factors, and parents' marital status.

One of the characteristics of family background that has attracted a great deal of attention from sociologists is *parents' achievement* (Warren and Hauser 1997). Parents' educations and occupations affect their children's educations, income, occupations, and various other aspects of adult well-being. Children whose parents are successful are much more likely to have high levels of education, earn high incomes, and be successful in their jobs. While there is little previous research on the effect of parents' success on their children's adult wealth, it is likely that children whose parents have done well will have more wealth than those whose parents were less successful. Thus those whose parents have been high achievers also stand to inherit more than those with less successful parents.

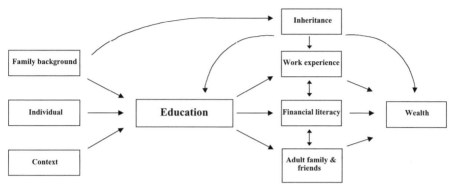

Figure 4.1. Getting rich.

As Figure 4.1 suggests, there are two primary paths through which parents' success translates into children's success: direct transfers of wealth from parent to child and education. Parents can transfer money directly to their children during life (as *inter vivos transfers*) and after death (as *inheritance*). Inter vivos transfers include direct transfers of money and other transfers such as payments for college, purchases of automobiles early in life, and assistance in buying a home later in life. Not all intergenerational transfers are substantial enough to necessarily make the recipient wealthy. Indeed, the majority of these are rather small and need to be considered in the context of other life-shaping events. Moreover, children who receive large sums of money from their parents either as inter vivos transfers or inheritance are generally not upwardly mobile; rather, they are simply rich. It is possible to be raised in a family with little wealth and then to inherit, but this is also quite rare.

Successful parents may give money to their children directly, and that has a clear effect on the children's wealth. Yet successful parents also tend to provide relatively high quality education to their children, and education is a critical component of the wealth accumulation process. As Figure 4.1 suggests, education translates into wealth via work experiences, financial literacy, and other adult behaviors. I explore these interceding factors in more detail later in this chapter. Parents' success also affects other aspects of family structure, but, as I argue below, education is the crucial factor that intercedes between family background and children's wealth.

Family Structure

Another important element of family background is family structure. An abundance of research demonstrates that *parents' separation* or *divorce*, for example, decreases children's well-being both during childhood and into adulthood (Baydar 1988; Cooksey 1997; Demo and Acock 1988; McLanahan and Sandefur 1994). Experiencing divorce or separation decreases performance in school, reduces educational attainment (Downey 1995a; Houseknecht and Spanier 1980), and ultimately decreases occupational attainment and mobility (Biblarz and Raftery 1993). Children whose parents divorce or separate are less healthy both physically (Horwitz, White, and Howell-White 1996) and mentally (Cherlin, Chase-Lansdale, and McRae 1998) than those from intact families. There are also economic costs of experiencing marital dissolution. Divorce increases poverty rates (Duncan and Hoffman 1985; McLanahan and Sandefur 1994; Nestel, Mercier, and Shaw 1983) and decreases per capita income (Cherlin 1981; Mott and Moore 1978; Peterson 1996), labor force participation (Cherlin 1979), and the ratio of income to needs (Corcoran 1995), particularly for women (Holden and Smock 1991; Stirling 1989).

Because divorce and separation reduce school performance, educational attainment, occupational mobility, and health, there is likely to be an indirect effect of divorce and separation on wealth through these other processes. Divorce and separation are also likely to decrease direct transfers of assets from parents to children. Financial resources will be spread across two households following the separation. If either parent does not remarry or remarries a person with few independent financial resources, the resources available to that parent will be diluted. Resources may also be strained by settling financial disputes between parents, which can further reduce the resources that are devoted to raising children or transferred directly to them as financial assets. In addition, parental divorce and separation are likely to take an emotional toll on children, which may decrease adult attainment, including wealth accumulation. Finally, family disruption may reduce the time parents have available to nurture children, to create stimulating educational experiences, or to intervene when they have problems (Mechanic and Hansell 1989). In other words, experiencing parents' divorce or separation as a child is likely to decrease adult wealth.

FAMILY SIZE

Family size is among the elements of family background that influence adult characteristics most strongly. Even when their parents are equally successful, people from larger families fare worse in adulthood than people from smaller families. The negative effect that family size has on adult educational performance in particular has been well established (Downey 1995b; McLanahan 1985; Sandefur and Wells 1999). This relationship is largely attributable to the resource dilution that occurs as families grow (Downey 1995b; Thomson, Hanson, and McLanahan 1994).

Additional siblings reduce overall adult well-being because they dilute three critical resources: material resources, opportunities, and parental attention and intervention (Blake 1981; Hill and Stafford 1978; Stafford 1996). The negative effect of family size on the availability of material resources is relatively direct, and the effect on the child is evidenced both immediately and over time (Blake 1981; Teachman 1987). Parents have finite material and nonmaterial resources, and additional siblings dilute the amount that can be devoted to each child. Larger families have fewer resources available for education, home improvement, books and newspapers, dance and music lessons, foreign travel, and other experiences that contribute to intellectual development (Blake 1989). As family size increases, each child enjoys a smaller proportion of the financial resources that are devoted to education and other childhood activities, and inheritances are also spread more thinly when there is money to be transferred across generations. Similarly, nonmaterial resources are diluted in larger families. Parental involvement, encouragement, intervention, and opportunities to engage the world are all vital to well-being, and these are less available to children in larger families than to those in smaller families.

Family size is likely to decrease adult wealth and reduce chances of upward wealth mobility for many of the same reasons that siblings diminish other elements of adult success. As Figure 4.1 suggests, siblings reduce adult wealth by affecting inheritance and education.

FAMILY SIZE AND INHERITANCE

Siblings reduce adult wealth by reducing the resources that parents can transfer directly to their children as inter vivos transfers or inheritance. Siblings reduce inter vivos transfers, making it more difficult for each child to attend and complete college, to begin saving, to become a homeowner, and to make other life transitions. Siblings also reduce inheritance where parents have resources to bequeath after death (Blake 1989). As sibship size increases in families with resources available to make intergenerational transfers, each child will subsequently be less likely to inherit because additional siblings reduce parental savings and thereby reduce the wealth that can be bequeathed. If there are sufficient resources remaining, children in larger families will inherit a smaller amount because inheritance in the United States is typically divided equally among offspring. A smaller or completely diminished inheritance changes the point at which the child begins to accumulate wealth. Any direct transfer of financial resources from parents to children has the potential to provide a base savings that can grow, even if additional savings are never added. A reduced inheritance postpones the age at which wealth accumulation can begin and, because long-term compounding adds significantly to net worth, the long-term rate of accumulation may be significantly decreased when inheritance is lower.

FAMILY SIZE AND EDUCATION

As family size increases, there are fewer resources, both material and nonmaterial, available during childhood to enhance children's

intellectual development and education. That is, family size reduces
(1) financial resources that would allow children to attend higher
quality schools, have access to educational materials and experiences, and enhance other educational opportunities; (2) nonmaterial resources such as parents' time, energy, and encouragement; and
(3) the time parents spend teaching their children how to save, which
shapes the children's own saving behavior as adults.

Financial resources improve educational opportunities directly and
increase the availability of educational resources that improve educational attainment indirectly. Young children are able to attend
higher-quality schools when their parents can afford to pay tuition
for elementary and secondary school. Older children are more likely
to attend college, to attend an elite college or university, and to
continue onto graduate school when their parents have sufficient
resources. Financial resources also increase access to newspapers and
books, computers, music and dance lessons, foreign travel, and other
educational experiences such as theater performances and museum
trips (Blake 1989; Downey 1995b). These experiences improve children's intellectual development and ultimately enhance educational
attainment indirectly.[1]

Family size reduces the *nonmaterial resources* that affect children's
educational attainment (Blake 1981, 1989). In larger families, the
time parents have available to assist children with homework, to
create educational opportunities, to encourage them, and to otherwise nurture and provide positive reinforcement is reduced. Similarly,
when more children compete for attention, parents have less time
to intervene when any one child is rebellious, delinquent, or otherwise getting into trouble. Likewise, children's opportunities to engage
the world, that is, to interact with others and to become involved

---

[1] Some question this claim (Guo, Guang, and Leah K. VanWey. 1999. "Sibship
Size and Intellectual Development: Is the Relationship Causal?" *American Sociological Review* 64:169–87), but most previous research finds a strong connection
between material resources and intellectual development [Downey, Douglas B.,
Brian Powell, Lala Carr Steelman, and Shana Pribesh. 1999. "Much Ado About
Siblings: Change Models, Sibship Size, and Intellectual Development (Comment on Guo and VanWey)." *American Sociological Review* 64:193–8].

in meaningful activities that feed into later life outcomes, can be decreased in larger families. Researchers have shown that these non-material resources are critical for children's development and can contribute significantly to adult attainment. In their absence, attainment is likely to be reduced (Blake 1981).

In addition, family size also reduces the *time parents can devote to teaching their children to save*. Knowledge about the importance of saving, avenues available for saving, and saving strategies is at least partly gained through exposure to the parents' savings behavior (Chiteji and Stafford 1999). Because additional siblings reduce saving, children are less likely to be exposed to investment options and saving in general. In large families, parents also have less time to devote to deliberately teaching their children about saving. A more abstract, but perhaps even more important, component of this informal education is nondeliberate education. Those with a propensity to postpone consumption save more and have fewer children (Friedman, Hechter, and Kanazawa 1994). This is not a competing argument; rather, it is a critical mechanism relating sibship size to adult wealth. The strong positive relationship between educational attainment and wealth accumulation has been partially attributed to the preference for delayed consumption, and those who are upwardly mobile have a relatively strong preference to delay gratification (Dynan 1993). This increases educational attainment and directly increases wealth. In families that save, children learn to postpone consumption, and their adult wealth accumulation is thus greater. Parents who postpone consumption have more resources and fewer children, and they teach their children also to postpone. This is not a spurious relation, but it is part of the reason that these children save more as adults.

Family Culture and Religion

Another important component of family background that shapes adult wealth is family culture. Culture can be thought of as the formal "symbolic vehicles of meaning, including beliefs, ritual practices, art forms, and ceremonies" and the "informal cultural practices such as language, gossip, stories, and rituals of daily life" (Swidler 1986). Like political groups such as nations and geographic groups such as region within nations, family groups have cultures. Families have formal beliefs they hold and rituals in which they engage. They also have informal practices, rituals, and styles that affect how members of the family interact with each other and with the rest of the world.

Culture is generally difficult to measure, and thus it is difficult to study empirically. But one element of culture – religious beliefs and practices – is somewhat more amenable to empirical investigation. Religion can be among the most significant defining traits of a family, and a rich tradition of research demonstrates clear religious differences in childrearing, marital stability, divorce, and fertility (Alwin 1986; Ellison, Bartkowsi, and Segal 1996; Lehrer 1996b; Sherkat and Ellison 1999) and other outcomes such as earnings and female employment rates (Darnell and Sherkat 1997; Lehrer 1999; Wuthnow and Scott 1997). Figure 4.1 suggests that the religious upbringing affects these processes and adult wealth *indirectly* by shaping educational attainment. While the model does not depict a *direct* relationship between religion and adult wealth, it is likely that religious upbringing does affect wealth ownership directly. In particular, religion shapes values and priorities, contributes to the set of competencies from which action is constructed, and may provide important social contacts.

Religion shapes adult wealth *indirectly* through its effect on education – and the outcomes of education such as fertility – that shapes asset accumulation. Previous research on the effect of religious affiliation and religious participation on economic behavior and attainment has largely focused on these indirect effects. Variations in fertility across faiths and even denominations within a single faith, for example, are important determinants of family resources and, ultimately, children's life attainment. It is likely, then, that people who are raised in religions where fertility is relatively low are going to accumulate more wealth over their lives. Similarly, religious differences in attitudes toward educational attainment and returns to education are important determinants of wealth ownership. Thus those from religious backgrounds that encourage educational advancement are likely to have an advantage in wealth accumulation over those who are affiliated with a religion that either does not incorporate ideas about education or that is either skeptical of or overtly hostile toward secular education. Similar arguments can be made about the relationship between religion and other family practices such as parental work behavior, union formation, and other critical determinants of wealth accumulation. These are certainly important determinants of economic behavior, and because of these differences, there are likely to be important differences in wealth ownership across people from different religious backgrounds.

Religion can also shape action *directly* by both defining the end values toward which behavior is oriented and providing a tool kit that people draw on to construct "strategies of action." One of the primary goals of churches is to distinguish desirable behavior from undesirable behavior and to delineate and even impose sanctions for noncompliance. A traditional view of culture suggests that religious affiliation and participation in religious ceremonies expose people to rituals, symbols, beliefs, and expectations that identify worthwhile objectives. In addition, Swidler (1986) argues that religious habits and practices transmitted by parents or during religious services during youth shape the set of competencies from which strategies of action are constructed. Similarly, exposure to religious ideals and views in adulthood may define the repertoire of capacities from which actions are formulated. From this perspective, strategies organize life and make particular choices and habits both sensible and useful. A similar frame is Bourdieu's notion that cultural patterns provide a structure against which individuals formulate and implement strategies or habits (Bourdieu 1977). The ideas are quite similar and both imply the same outcome for wealth accumulation. That is, people draw on the tools they learn from religion to develop consistent strategies for dealing with problems and for making decisions such as those about savings, investment, and consumption. In terms of wealth accumulation, for example, the frequent recourse to prayer and trust in God among conservative Protestants may reduce their inclination to invest.

In addition to shaping strategies, religious affiliation and participation affect wealth accumulation directly by providing social contacts that provide information, assistance, and referrals to those who can provide these important things. Like intergenerational influences in other domains, savings behavior reflects parental asset ownership and the asset ownership of others to whom people are exposed during childhood (Chiteji and Stafford 2000). Knowledge about the importance of saving, the avenues available for saving, and saving strategies is at least partly gained through exposure to the savings behavior of others. Wealth accumulation depends on having information about a number of financial instruments and their features. Because information barriers make it largely impossible for people to gather this information individually, information from social contacts is often used instead. Social contacts may also provide direct assistance in the form of capital transfers, such as capital for starting a business, making an initial financial investment, or making a down payment on a home. The information that contacts have will vary by religion, and their ability to assist more directly will also vary.

Of course, values, repertoires, and contacts vary by religious group. The following sections explore how Jews, conservative Protestants, mainline Protestants, and Roman Catholics likely accumulate wealth.

Jews

A host of unique demographic traits lead to high levels of attainment for Jews that are likely to increase wealth accumulation indirectly (Chiswick 1986, 1993; DellaPergola 1980; Wuthnow 1999). The "diaspora hypothesis" suggests that for historical reasons, Jewish family and community traditions have developed that encourage development of human capital as opposed to more fixed varieties of physical capital (Brenner and Kiefer 1981). Moreover, both fertility rates and rates of female employment when children are young are relatively low in Jewish families (Chiswick 1986; DellaPergola 1980). Together these create high levels of home investment in child quality and ultimately lead to high educational attainment and relatively high returns to educational investments (Chiswick 1988; Lehrer 1999). Because fertility rates are low, the dilution of material resources that are transferred in the form of inheritance is low and strains on resources in the adult family are minimal. High rates of homogamy among Jews also suggests that the influence of these demographic traits is likely to be enhanced by marriage to a person with a similar propensity for attainment (Kalmijn 1991; Thornton 1985). Generally high levels of attainment suggest that wealth accumulation among Jews is likely to exceed that of other groups by a considerable margin.

Yet there is also likely to be a direct effect of Jewish religious affiliation on wealth accumulation. In Jewish culture, accumulation is seen as an indicator of success, and Jews have been shown to have a highly positive cultural orientation to education and occupational status (Stryker 1981). Rather than having an orientation toward the after life and downplaying this world, Jewish families encourage this-worldly pursuits including actual accumulation of wealth and other activities that lead to wealth accumulation, such as high-income careers and investing. Expectations for children include success in this world, and the use of success-oriented strategies in Jewish families creates a tool kit for children that includes the skills necessary to accumulate resources. The diaspora hypothesis suggests a relatively high propensity for Jews to invest in financial assets and a relatively low propensity to invest in real, or fixed, assets.[2] Because financial assets tend to be higher-risk, higher-return investments, the return to investments is likely to be higher in Jewish families, leading to greater overall wealth. The pervasiveness of financial investments adds particular skills to the repertoire of skills developed in Jewish families, which suggests that Jewish children are relatively more likely to make an early transition to the ownership of financial assets, injecting their financial trajectories with high-return assets that will have extended time to accumulate. Because Judaism is also an ethnicity, the Jewish cultural repertoire is likely to be more salient than

---

[2] The diaspora hypothesis does not imply that today's adult Jews in America have a sense that their physical assets might be taken; rather, the hypothesis suggests that *family and community traditions that place a relatively high value on human capital and financial assets have developed.*

the repertoires established in other faiths, and the direct Jewish effect
on wealth accumulation is likely to be even stronger than it might
otherwise be.

Opportunities to build relevant social capital are also relatively
high in Jewish families. Social connections developed through
schools and universities can provide information about investment
strategies, actual investment opportunities, and access to capital for
investing (Sherkat and Ellison 1999). Family contacts and contacts
in the local Jewish community can also provide information, access to
investments, and support that make investing feasible at all, and particularly so for young people. For each of these reasons, I expect that
people who grew up Jewish or who are Jewish as adults will accumulate more wealth as adults than those who were not Jewish. Jews will
inherit more wealth because of the intergenerational transmission of
both wealth and the behaviors that increase wealth accumulation.
Jews will, however, accumulate more wealth even at similar levels
of inheritance than non-Jews. Similarly, while educational attainment, fertility, female employment patterns, and other demographic
differences will increase wealth accumulation for Jews, there will be
a direct effect of Jewish religious affiliation reflecting the importance
of the cultural repertoire that is transferred intergenerationally in
Jewish families.

CONSERVATIVE PROTESTANTS

In direct contrast to Jewish families, wealth accumulation among
conservative Protestants is likely to be relatively low. In recent
decades, Americans have generally become more accepting of egalitarian gender roles, divorce, smaller families, childlessness, and other
nontraditional family behaviors. Conservative Protestants have also
become more accepting of these behaviors, but change in this group
has been less pronounced and slower than among nonconservatives.
As a result, conservative Protestants have become relatively more
traditional than others (Lehrer 1999; Smith 1998; Wilcox 1998).
Traditional attitudes have translated into relatively high fertility
rates that are likely to decrease wealth accumulation by diluting

both material and nonmaterial resources during childhood, reducing inheritance, and making saving more difficult in adulthood (Lehrer 1999; Thornton 1985). Similar to Jewish families, female employment when children are young is also low among conservative Protestants (Thornton 1985). While this suggests that there is potential for greater investments in children in conservative Protestant families, the effect is likely offset by relatively high fertility rates (Lehrer 1999).

Reduced achievement among conservative Protestants is evident in low levels of educational attainment in these families. In addition to high fertility, hostility toward formal education and the scientific method, resulting from literal interpretation of the Bible, reduce educational advancement dramatically (Lehrer 1999). Because the aim of science is the pursuit of truth rather than the blind acceptance of God's word, secular education contests the beliefs of conservative Protestants (Darnell and Sherkat 1997). Parental expectations for educational attainment are thus low among conservative Protestants, children in these families are relatively more likely to be schooled at home, and parents are less likely to save for education (Darnell and Sherkat 1997; Lehrer 1999). Moreover, while both conservative Protestant mothers and Jewish mothers exit the labor force to take care of their young children, the typical level of education of a conservative Protestant mother is much lower than that of a Jewish mother. As a result, the stay-at-home mother who is a conservative Protestant is likely to have little effect on her children's educational development. For each of these reasons, children from conservative Protestant families achieve lower levels of education, and the rate of return to education is lower for individuals raised in conservative Protestant families, too. Because education is an important predictor of wealth accumulation, the lack of education is likely to reduce wealth accumulation.

While indirect factors are important, there is also likely to be a direct effect of a conservative Protestant culture on the accumulation of wealth. The strategies of action that become part of the repertoire of conservative Protestants, however, are unlikely to include skills necessary for asset accumulation. Traditional gender-role attitudes and corresponding family division of labor reduce female employment out of the home, which, in turn, reduces saving and contributes to the creation of patterns that do not include high savings (Sherkat and Ellison 1999). When saving is not common, strategies for investing naturally do not develop and social capital that might provide either information or financial backing is not present. Literal Bible interpretation can also lead to the conclusion that wealth accumulation should be avoided, and a steadfast devotion to tithing exacerbates this. Conservative Protestants "are not averse to worldly pursuits. However, they are admonished to avoid choices that might endanger their souls" (Darnell and Sherkat 1997). Few American religions discourage hard work, saving, or investment. Yet religious groups also seldom promote the idea that God favors the rich over the poor (Wuthnow and Scott 1997), and conservative Protestant religious doctrine includes more messages of this sort than other doctrine. Like Jews, Conservative Protestants are unlikely to marry people of other religions and thus unlikely to expand their repertoire of skills and strategies by marrying someone with a different tool kit (Kalmijn 1991; Thornton 1985). The result in the case of conservative Protestants, however, is that they are unlikely to increase their propensity to accumulate wealth.

As these patterns cumulate across generations, they are likely to result in lower rates of inheritance and lower overall wealth, even where there is an inheritance. Traditional values increase the likelihood that if saving is possible, funds will be channeled into home ownership rather than into financial investments, although relatively low overall saving suggests that total investments in housing are likely to be low for those who are able to become homeowners. These patterns are likely to create financial trajectories that never include savings or investment or that include only transitions to home ownership with a low subsequent likelihood of other types of saving.

MAINLINE PROTESTANTS AND CATHOLICS

Mainline Protestants and Roman Catholics were at one time distinct from each other and from the general population in the United

States. This distinctiveness, however, has diminished in recent years. Fertility patterns are instructive. Prior to the 1970s, Catholic fertility rates were relatively high, exceeding rates both in the general population and among mainline Protestants (Lehrer 1996a; Westoff and Jones 1979). During the baby boom, fertility increases were actually disproportionately high among Catholics, but Catholic fertility also declined more precipitously following the baby boom. In recent years, Catholic and mainline Protestant fertility rates are comparable (Westoff and Jones 1979; Lehrer 1996a). Convergence has also been documented in educational attainment (Lehrer 1999; Sherkat and Ellison 1999), female labor force participation and time allocation (Lehrer 1996b), union formation (Lehrer 1998; Sander 1995; Sherkat and Ellison 1999), and separation and divorce (Lehrer and Chiswick 1993). This convergence suggests that the processes, such as educational attainment and fertility, that indirectly affect the wealth of Jews and Conservative Protestants are likely to have little effect on the wealth of mainline Protestants and Catholics.

Because the convergence of these two groups with each other and with the rest of the population is relatively recent, there is likely to be some residual effect of the distinctiveness of prior generations. In particular, those who were raised as mainline Protestants are likely to inherit more wealth on average because their parents were part of a religious group that was relatively more affluent than it is today. Affiliation with a mainline Protestant church as an adult is not likely to have the same effect because of the diminishing distinctiveness. Likewise, the growing similarity between these two groups and their diminishing distinctiveness in general suggest that there is likely to be little other effect of affiliation with either religious group on patterns of wealth ownership.

RELIGIOUS PARTICIPATION

Values and the strategies that people draw on as they make decisions are also acquired during religious services and ceremonies. Lenski (1961) emphasized the communal aspect of religion, and Wuthnow (1999) later provided a number of examples of the mechanism by which the communal nature of religion shapes behavior. Wuthnow emphasized that participation in religious ceremonies instills an understanding of the importance of social relations, provides moral instruction, improves understanding of doctrine about the correct way to live, and provides the youth with practical skills and role models. The communal affirmation of values and strategies by a religious group, a group that the participant typically perceived of as worthy of emulating, is a powerful mechanism for instilling ideals and shaping habits. When people face problems and need to make decisions, they are likely to draw on both the skills they learned from their parents and those they learned during religious ceremonies and other religious activities. Because religious doctrine seldom discourages saving and nearly always encourages correct and conventional living, those who attend services are likely to behave in ways that lead to saving and wealth accumulation. There is evidence, for example, that high school students who attend religious services and activities devote more time to schoolwork, cut classes less often, and are more likely to graduate than those who do not (Sherkat and Ellison 1999). Similarly we should see a direct relationship between religious participation and other positive behaviors, and the result is likely to be greater wealth accumulation.

Likewise, attendance at religious services builds social networks. Social capital cultivates values and norms that encourage positive behaviors, promote the circulation of information, and encourage long-term investment in relationships (Sherkat and Ellison 1999). Not all social networks will increase asset accumulation, but religious participation does improve the possibility of having contacts who can provide information, capital, or other support that might lead to wealth ownership. Thus, it is likely that religious participation during childhood and adulthood will increase wealth accumulation, even for those who only participate occasionally.

Individual Traits

Of course, individual traits also shape many of these processes. Genetic endowments account for some of the variance across individuals in schooling, occupational attainment, and income (Gove 1994; Taubman 1982). Likewise, genetic traits are likely to affect wealth accumulation. In particular, individual abilities and motivation may shape wealth accumulation and mobility indirectly by shaping education, occupation, and income; aptitude may also affect wealth directly by shaping a person's capacity to save and invest. In addition to abilities, other individual traits – both ascribed and achieved – shape wealth.

RACE

Race is perhaps the most critical ascribed individual trait that affects adult wealth. Race may be considered a family characteristic, but given that an individual can be from multiple races, the individual's race may differ from that of the parents. Whether it is considered individual or family, its effect is unquestionable. A number of studies have documented racial differences in asset ownership, particularly home ownership. Blacks and Hispanics, in particular, own considerably less wealth than whites. In 1992, whereas median income for blacks was about 60 percent of the median income for whites, median net worth for blacks was only 8 percent of median net worth for whites. In that same year, 25 percent of white families had zero or negative assets, but more than 60 percent of black families had no wealth (Oliver and Shapiro 1995). Longitudinal estimates suggest that between 1960 and 1995, whites were twice as likely as minorities to have more wealth than income and nearly three times as likely to experience wealth mobility (Keister 2000a). Minorities are also underrepresented among the very wealthy. In 1995, 95 percent of those in the top 1 percent of wealth holders were white, while only 1 percent were black (Keister 2000b; Wolff 1998). The wealth position of nonblack minorities has attracted less attention, but there is evidence that the wealth accumulation of whites also exceeds that of Hispanics and Asians (Wolff 1998).

There are various explanations for racial differences in asset ownership. Again, my conceptual model proposes that education largely mediates the effect of race on wealth. There are considerable

differences in the levels of education attained by whites and minorities, and as a result, income and thus opportunities to save and
invest vary systematically by race. In addition, there is evidence that
there are racial differences in consumption that affect saving and investment behavior (Brimmer 1988; Keister 2000a; Lawrence 1991).
Moreover, because parents teach their children about how to save,
parents' wealth affects their children's patterns of saving. Children
from relatively poor minority families learn different lessons about
saving, and these may translate into different saving behaviors in
adulthood.

In addition to demographics and family background, other direct
structural influences also affect the portfolio behavior of black and
white families differently. Discrimination in lending and interest rate
differences may make some assets less attractive or unreachable to
some groups of people or in some regions – or even neighborhoods –
in the United States. Opportunities to invest (determined by such
factors as the location of banks) are structurally constrained and
thus may systematically influence the types of assets families own
(Oliver and Shapiro 1995). Not only do investment opportunities
vary by race, but the ability to save also varies systematically because families without savings must often pay more for basic financial services (Caskey 1994. As Caskey observed in his work on fringe
banking, a household that does not have savings is much less likely
to begin saving, simply because the cost is prohibitive. In addition,
families with little or no savings are often forced to assume additional
credit and may be unable to improve their debt-to-income ratios suffi-
ciently to gain access to mainstream financial instruments, including
both assets and liabilities. Caskey documented the prevalence of the
patterns and showed that banking conditions worsened during the
1980s and 1990s, exacerbating inequality that originated with stock
market booms and the stagnation of the housing market.

ADOLESCENT DELINQUENCY

In contrast to race, adolescent delinquency can be considered an
achieved characteristic of an individual, and delinquency also shapes
adult wealth in critical ways. Research on delinquency has begun

to demonstrate that deviance during adolescence can affect later-life outcomes in important, and usually negative, ways (Tanner, Davies, and O'Grady 1999). Research on education has shown that delinquency has a negative impact on school grades and retention (Davies and Guppy 1997). There is also evidence of a more direct effect of youth delinquency on occupational and later financial outcomes (Tanner et al. 1999). While there continues to be some disagreement in the delinquency literature regarding the relationship between youth deviance and adult outcomes (Monk-Turner 1989), evidence in favor of a negative association is mounting.

Again, the critical link between adolescent delinquency and adult wealth is education. Adolescents who engage in disruptive or illegal activities are likely to attain less education than their peers and to benefit less from educational experiences to which they are exposed. That is, adolescents who are delinquent are less likely to attend college, to attend an elite college or university, and to continue onto graduate school. There is also evidence of a more direct effect of youth delinquency on occupational and later financial outcomes (Tanner et al. 1999).

Delinquency also detracts from the time that parents have available to informally educate their children. As a result, when children are delinquent, parents have less time to assist children with homework, to create educational opportunities, to encourage them, and to otherwise nurture and provide positive reinforcement. Because these nonmaterial resources are critical for children's development and attainment, adult well-being will be reduced in their absence (Blake 1981).

Context

Context also matters. Birth cohort, economic trends, and geography, for instance, are important influences on wealth accumulation and mobility. Context can shape opportunities for education and employment, and it can directly affect wealth accumulation via such trends as stock market booms and busts.

A comparison of baby boomers and their parents provides an important example of how people face different opportunities depending on when they are born. The baby boom generation, which is that of those born following World War II, has put pressure on social and economic resources at every stage of their lives. This cohort strained educational resources in the 1950s and 1960s as they filled classrooms to capacity, caused crowding in colleges and universities in their late teens and early twenties, and contributed to slow wage growth in the 1970s and 1980s when they entered the labor force (Sabelhaus and Manchester 1995).

The notion that membership in a birth cohort affects individual behaviors and outcomes is orthodox among sociologists (Elder 1995; Morgan 1998). Features of a cohort as well as events that the cohort experiences combine to imprint members of a generation in ways that affect behavior and outcomes over the entire life course. The Great Depression, for example, affected the attitudes, behaviors, emotional health, and many later-life outcomes of the people who were children and young adults during the 1930s (Elder 1974; Elder and Liker 1982). While material loss during the Depression affected the middle and working classes more than the upper classes, the long-term effects of growing up during the Depression have been evident across all classes (Elder and Liker 1982). The parents of baby boomers, many of whom grew up during the Depression, have been relatively conservative investors and have a relatively high aversion to risk (Keister 2000b; Sabelhaus and Manchester 1995). In addition, the generation that grew up during the Depression has exhibited rather traditional gender roles and low levels of female labor force participation, high fertility rates, low divorce rates, and low levels of educational attainment compared to subsequent generations. As a result of work and family patterns, the Great Depression generation accumulated relatively few assets over their lives (Sabelhaus and Manchester 1995).

Like their parents, baby boomers have experienced events that contribute to their cohort's unique behavioral traits (Morgan 1998). The aspirations that baby boomers developed as children were influenced by their parents' conception that hard work ensured success, yet crowding may reduce payoffs to hard work (Easterlin 1987). Baby boomers responded to crowding by changing their demographic behavior in ways that have actually improved their financial well-being (Easterlin, MacDonald, and Macunovich 1990a, 1990b). These changes include achieving higher levels of education, which is arguably the critical change. Increased educational attainment has, in turn, affected other behaviors in this generation. In particular, baby boomers have also tended to postpone marriage, have fewer children, and have smaller families. Female baby boomers are more likely to work out of home and to make career advancement an important life goal than previous generations. As a result, baby boomers have enjoyed higher earnings than their parents. Increases in women's labor force participation and reduced fertility suggest that female baby boomers have also contributed to household earnings more than their mothers. Together these patterns explain why baby boomers have had more income to invest and to save for retirement.

Wealth values also, of course, tend to follow macroeconomic trends: values increase during good economic times and decline when the economy worsens. The direct relationship between economic booms and wealth values has largely been a function of stock market movement. In the 1990s, an increasing number of Americans began putting their savings into stocks and stock-based mutual funds (including Individual Retirement Accounts and pension plans), hoping to reap some of the benefits of a stock market that experienced record increases yearly, starting in the late 1980s. Moreover, the increasing availability of mutual funds in the 1980s and early 1990s made stock ownership more feasible, and by the mid-1990s, stocks surpassed housing wealth as the largest component of Americans' portfolios (Sloane 1995). The economic downturn of the early 2000s, of course, pushed stock values – and thus many portfolios – in the opposite direction. Trends in housing markets affect wealth similarly, although housing trends affect less wealthy families more, as these families tend to have more of the assets invested in housing real estate than stocks.

INHERITANCE

Inter vivos transfers and inheritance increase adult wealth by increasing the resources children have to save, decreasing the need to assume debt, and improving the financial trajectory on which children begin to accumulate assets. Parent's resources make higher education more feasible and can reduce the need for children to accumulate debt during college or graduate school. Other life transitions may also be easier for children whose parents have sufficient resources. If their resources are adequate, parents may aid their children in purchasing a first home, establishing a household after marriage, and preparing for and taking care of children.

Direct transfers of resources from parents to children may also alter the types of assets and debts the child owns as an adult, and this may alter long-term patterns of wealth accumulation and mobility. Assistance with home ownership, in particular, can be an important inter vivos transfer. Inherited wealth is often used to make a down payment on a home (McNamee and Miller 1998). Home ownership is a core component of a stable wealth portfolio. In addition, because investing in a home is the most typical first investment for Americans, homeowners are more likely to also own stocks, mutual funds, and bonds (Keister 2000b). Because even a relatively small inheritance can have a substantial effect on the likelihood of home ownership, inheritance can create a stable base for saving throughout the life course.

EDUCATION

I have been arguing that many of the forces that shape adult wealth ownership and that propel people upward in the wealth distribution operate through education. I have argued that family background, context, and even individual traits largely shape educational attainment and educational experiences and that this translates into wealth. But what is it about education that is so important? The answer is: quite a bit. Indeed, if we consider both formal and informal education (learning that occurs outside of schools), it is clear that education plays a pivotal role in determining who gets rich.

Formal education refers to learning and other experiences that occur in schools and colleges or universities. The number of years a person spends in school matters because, other factors held constant, more years in the formal schooling system implies more time to absorb the information available there. Yet there is more to education than time spent in the classroom. Willis (1981) made the important observation that working-class schools train their students to take working-class jobs. That is, working-class schools prepare students to be obedient, follow directions, and perform rote tasks. In contrast, upper-class schools train student to think critically and assume leadership roles. Indeed, the different effects that public and private schools have on their graduates suggests that there may be an added effect of a private formal education. Elite preparatory schools and undergraduate schools, in particular, are known to give students an edge in occupational pursuits, to yield them higher incomes, and to increase their odds of serving on the board of a Fortune 500 company (Cookson and Persell 1985; Kingston and Lewis 1990). *Informal education* is education that occurs outside the formal school system. Much of what people learn about finances and saving occurs in the home (Chang 2002; Chiteji and Stafford 1999; Kiyosaki and Lechter2000). Parents deliberately teach their children about saving, and they teach their children through their actions as well.

But why does education matter so much? Education matters because it improves occupational opportunities and financial decision making, provides important social contacts, and alters adult demographic behavior (e.g., marriage and fertility) that shape saving and wealth mobility. At all income levels, those who have completed more education save more, assume less debt, and make decisions regarding investments that yield larger overall portfolios. In addition, those with more education are likely to begin saving earlier in life, which allows them to accumulate assets more rapidly throughout their careers and into retirement.

WORK AND OCCUPATION

Occupation affects wealth by shaping income, savings plans, and pensions. People in *professional* and *managerial* occupations generally have higher incomes than those in *labor-* and *craft*-related occupations. It is also possible that professionals and managers typically have more opportunities to save and invest than people in other occupations. It is likely, then, that there are important differences in wealth accumulation by occupation. However, the degree to which occupation versus characteristics of a job account for wealth differences is a more complex question. Understanding the importance of other job traits may clarify the nature of the relationship between work and wealth.

At one end of the spectrum are occupations and jobs within occupations that may impede upward wealth mobility. Nonstandard work, for instance, is a work arrangement that has become much more common in recent years and that may affect how workers accumulate assets. Changes that began during the 1970s encouraged both firms and workers to seek more flexibility in employment (Houseman 2001b; Kalleberg 2000). Increasing global competition and resulting uncertainty encouraged firms to use nontraditional workers to reduce costs associated with recruiting, screening, and training. Labor laws that improved conditions for permanent workers created additional incentives for firms to draw on nonstandard labor to reduce the burden of paying full-time benefits. Technological advances made it possible for firms to specialize, to rely more on external suppliers, and to assemble temporary workers quickly for special projects (Cappelli 1999; Lee 1996). At the same time, a changing work force demanded greater flexibility in employment arrangements. Increasing numbers of married women and older workers in the labor force created a demand for part-time, temporary, and contract jobs. As a result, about 25 percent of all workers in the United States have some type of nonstandard job, and more than 30 percent of female workers hold nonstandard positions (Cassirer Forthcoming; Kalleberg 2000).

There is some evidence that nontraditional workers on average earn less and have fewer benefits, including employer-sponsored pension plans, than their counterparts in traditional jobs (Houseman 2001a; Kalleberg et al. 1997). Virtually no nonstandard workers have employer-sponsored pension plans. This implies that nonstandard workers, on average, will accumulate less wealth in pension assets than traditional workers. Moreover, part-time workers, agency temporaries, and direct-hire temporaries earn less than regular employees. Thus, because they earn less than traditional workers, part-time workers, agency temporaries, and direct-hire temporaries on average are likely to accumulate less in all categories of assets than traditional workers.

Of course there are nonstandard workers who might be more likely to be mobile, particularly because they are more like entrepreneurs than like other nonstandard workers. Consultants, self-employed contractors, and employees of contractors tend to have earnings that are comparable to those of regular workers (Houseman and Polivka 2000). In addition, these workers tend to be self-starters and more entrepreneurial. This suggests that consultants, self-employed contractors, and employees of contractors are likely to accumulate at least as much as, if not more than, regular workers in nonpension assets.

A related issue is the extent to which self-employment shapes wealth accumulation. *Entrepreneurs* are an important class of professional workers because they can have unique opportunities to accumulate wealth rapidly. Of course, not all entrepreneurs become wealthy, but the potential for wealth accumulation is great in entrepreneurial occupations. The families of entrepreneurs may also experience upward mobility, both immediately and over time. Many business owners, particularly those who create large firms, employ family members in their business ventures, and some pass on their businesses to their families, either during their lives or as part of an inheritance (Keister 2000b). Entrepreneurs who successfully accumulate financial assets are also able to invest in their children's human capital, and they may be able to expand their children's social capital and occupational opportunities as well. An important question related to entrepreneurship is whether entrepreneurs accumulate more wealth or whether wealthy people are more likely to become entrepreneurs. It is certainly difficult to determine causal direction with certainty. However, I will argue that it is likely that when all other factors are held constant, there is a positive relationship between becoming an entrepreneur and accumulating wealth, while the effect of family wealth on becoming an entrepreneur is mediated entirely by other intervening factors such as education.

FINANCIAL LITERACY

Financial literacy refers to knowledge regarding decisions of savings and consumption, and this knowledge can be a critical determinant of adult wealth ownership. Investing in high-risk, high-return financial assets, for example, as opposed to relatively conservative instruments, such as Certificates of Deposit, can have dramatic effects on total wealth accumulated over the life course (Keister 2000a). Likewise, the timing and ordering of financial decisions can shape wealth accumulation in important ways. Beginning to save in early adulthood can have significant advantages over postponing saving until later. Because there is a degree of path dependence built into saving and consumption decisions, people tend to follow paths through their lives that influence in important ways the amount of wealth they accumulate over time. For example, a traditional trajectory might involve buying a house first and investing in financial assets only later in life. In contrast, investing in financial assets early is likely to increase total accumulation across the life course because the returns on these assets tend to be relatively high and compounding can create a sizable portfolio with time. A positive early saving trajectory also tends to provide somewhat of a buffer against financial emergencies and economic downturns that could otherwise create a crisis and prevent additional accumulation.

ADULT FAMILY AND FRIENDS

Adult family structure also has important implications for adult wealth. Decisions about whether to have children, how many children to have, marriage and divorce, and the timing of these behaviors all interact to shape family finances and opportunities to save. Many of these influences have somewhat obvious effects on wealth: marriage, for example, generally increases wealth because two single households combine assets. Yet other adult influences are more complex, including the effect of social connections. Friends, or social contacts, may be an important part of the wealth picture: social contacts can provide direct assistance such as capital for starting a business, making an initial financial investment, or making a down payment on a home. Adult characteristics also, of course, interact with each other and with factors that originate earlier in life to shape wealth ownership. I explore these in more detail later in this book.

CONCLUSION

The processes that produce adult wealth ownership are indeed complex, as this chapter suggests. It is tempting to attribute wealth almost exclusively to market fluctuations, perhaps combined with inheritance. There is little doubt that these factors matter. Yet other life experiences, including childhood, adolescent and early adult situations, experiences, and events do contribute as well. The remainder of this book explores in more detail, and using empirical evidence, the role of the factors identified here in producing wealth.

PART TWO

CHAPTER FIVE

Family Background: Parents, Structure, and Siblings

Efforts to document mobility in the United States demonstrate that although there is considerable persistence in wealth ownership both intergenerationally and intragenerationally, upward mobility is relatively common. Efforts to explain who is mobile and why are even more rare than efforts to document mobility levels, but it is definitely possible to explain who moves up in the wealth distribution. New large-scale longitudinal data sets make this more possible than ever before. In Part Two of this book, beginning with this chapter, I explore the factors that affect wealth mobility. In particular, in this chapter, I isolate the effects of family background on wealth accumulation and mobility, emphasizing the role of such factors as inheritance, parents' achievement, and family size and structure during childhood. In the first sections of the chapter, I focus on the independent effect that these inputs have on adult wealth position. That is, I present separate estimates showing the relationship between parents' attainment and adult wealth, inheritance and adult wealth, siblings and adult wealth, and so on. I then present more complex models that incorporate multiple interacting effects that allow me to discuss the relative importance of the various factors that combine to produce adult wealth ownership. Figure 5.1 highlights the portion of the full conceptual model (Figure 4.1) that is the focus of this chapter and Chapter Six.

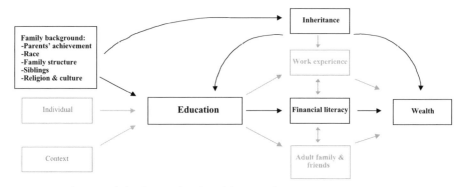

Figure 5.1. Family background and wealth ownership.

FAMILY BACKGROUND: INDEPENDENT EFFECTS

INDEPENDENT EFFECTS: PARENTS; ATTAINMENT

Previous empirical research on wealth ownership has tended to focus on the role that adult human capital plays in shaping asset accumulation. In the past, the study of wealth has largely been the
purview of economists who emphasize the effects of such individual
attributes and resources as education, current income, and work behavior (Danziger and Gottschalk 1993; Kennickell and Kwast 1997;
Wolff 1998). Typical of human capital arguments, the theoretical
basis for these analyses was that individual traits improve decision
making regarding saving, investment, and the acquisition of debt
(Wolff 1995a, 1998). There was little effort to extend the analyses beyond these traits perhaps at least partly because longitudinal
data that included both information on adult wealth and detailed
information on other personal and family attributes was very limited
or completely unavailable. While individual attributes and discrimination are important, newer evidence using data that is relatively
recently available documents the importance of factors beyond the
individual (Keister 2003; Keister and Moller 2000).

In particular, family background is likely to be an important determinant of adult wealth accumulation and mobility. Childhood family
financial resources, for example, increase adult wealth directly when
parents make *inter vivos transfers* (financial transfers from parents to

children made while the parents are still living) to their children and when they leave an *inheritance*. Similarly, nonmaterial resources such as parents' time and attention can increase adult wealth by improving human capital, other important skills, and social networks that may affect adult wealth. Family background may also be an intermediating factor that explains some of the findings that are well established in research on wealth. Because family background varies greatly by race, for example, racial differences in wealth accumulation may also be attributable to such influences as family size and family structure.

A long tradition of research on intergenerational processes in sociology – and in related social sciences to a lesser degree – documents the very important role that family background, particularly parents' attainment, plays in shaping the adult outcomes of their offspring. Parents with high educations, in particular, are likely to have children with relatively high incomes (Behrman and Taubman 1990; Behrman, Pollak, and Taubman 1995; Henretta 1984; Hill and Duncan 1987). Extending these arguments to understand adult wealth suggests that parents with higher educations are also likely to have children who accumulate more wealth as adults. Empirically, there are countless ways to explore the relationship between parents' attainment and children's well-being. One simple way is to compare the parental attainment of those offspring who are successful – in this case wealthy – adults.

Indeed, the wealthy do have parents who were well educated. Figure 5.2 compares wealthy respondents in the National Longitudinal Survey of Youth, 1979 cohort (NLS-Y), with other respondents and demonstrates a considerable difference in fathers' education. The figure compares the highest level of education achieved for fathers of the respondents in the NLS-Y 1979 cohort by the adult wealth of respondents. I break respondents into wealth categories based on their 2000 net assets (total assets less total liabilities, all in 2000 dollars). Details regarding data and variable definitions are in the Appendix. The figure shows that 25 percent of millionaires, for instance, had fathers with an advanced degree. For each of the other groups identified in this figure, a much smaller percentage had fathers who were as

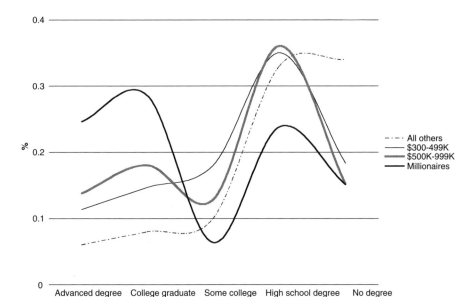

Figure 5.2. Family background: Father's education. *Source*: National Longitudinal Survey of Youth, 1979 Cohort. Wealth groups are defined by net worth in 2000.

well educated. Even those respondents who had between $500,000 and $999,999 in net worth, only 14 percent had a father with an advanced degree. Similarly, of those respondents who had more than $300,000 in net worth but less than $500,000, just 11 percent had fathers with advanced degrees.

Compared to the remainder of the sample, fathers' attainment is rather high for each of the high wealth groups. Of the remaining respondents, only 6 percent had a father with an advanced degree. Similar patterns are evident in the proportion of the fathers of the rich who completed college. The millionaires' fathers do best, with nearly 30 percent completing a college degree (but no more education). Somewhat fewer fathers of the other rich groups completed college (18 and 15 percent, respectively). Yet this is still an impressive college graduation rate, given that in the remainder of the sample, only 8 percent of fathers graduated from college.

Millionaires fall into two groups with respect to father's education: the highly educated and high school graduates. Figure 5.2

demonstrates that there is not a steady decline in the proportion of fathers who achieved each level of education (advanced degree down to no degree). Rather, the fathers fall into two relatively distinct groups. As I mentioned earlier, 25 to 29 percent of the fathers of millionaires graduated from college or received advanced degrees, and another 25 percent of the fathers had high school degrees but no additional education. Only 6 percent of the millionaires' fathers had begun college and not finished. What is interesting is that the fathers of the other respondents pictured here have very different education patterns. For the fathers of all the nonmillionaires, an increasingly large proportion falls into each of the education levels (advanced degree down to high school degree). Very few of the fathers of any of the rich respondents (any respondent owning more than $300,000 in net worth) had no degree. It is also important to note that the highest percentage of fathers receiving no degree are those whose kids were not rich as adults. That is, nearly 35 percent of those respondents who fall into the nonrich category (all others) had a father who had not even completed high school education.

Mothers of the rich respondents were also highly educated, but their educational attainment patterns were somewhat more typical of the overall population than was the case for the fathers of the wealthy. Figure 5.3 compares the highest level of education the mothers of NLS-Y respondents attained, comparing millionaires, two other groups of wealthy respondents, and all other respondents. Very few of the mothers of these respondents had advanced degrees. Millionaires' mothers were the most likely to have an advanced degree, but only 6 percent of these mothers had more than a college degree, and the difference between the millionaires' mothers and other mothers is not significant.

In contrast, millionaires' mothers were more likely than the mothers of other respondents to have college degrees. Nearly 30 percent of those respondents who were millionaires had a mother with a college degree, compared to less than 20 percent of the other mothers. Consistent with patterns in the U.S. population, the majority of the mothers had completed high school but had not gone beyond that level of education. The low levels of educational

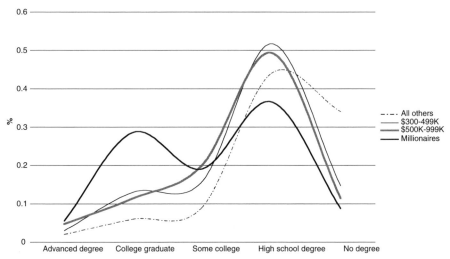

Figure 5.3. Family background: Mother's education. *Source*: National Longitudinal Survey of Youth, 1979 Cohort. Wealth groups are defined by net worth in 2000.

attainment for the mothers relative to those for the fathers (Figure 5.2) of the NLS-Y respondents is also consistent with generational differences that are evident in the United States. Specifically, given that educational attainment for women has increased dramatically in recent years, mothers of today's survey respondents tend to be less educated compared to fathers of the same respondents and to the respondents themselves. Clearly, while there are educational advantages for the millionaires, there is much less of a division of the mothers into two groups, as was evident for the fathers pictured in Figure 5.2.

INDEPENDENT EFFECTS: INHERITANCE

One mechanism through which parents' attainment, such as their educational attainment, probably affects the well-being of their children is inheritance. Successful parents are more likely to have high incomes, to save and accumulate assets, and ultimately to leave an inheritance for their kids than are parents who are less successful. The most apparent connection between inheritance and adult wealth is the direct increase in assets that comes when offspring receive the inheritance. Yet inheritance can also increase adult wealth because it can be invested, used as a down payment on a house, and used to reduce debt and in other ways that may increase saving and accumulation.

Because inheritance is such a crucial piece of the mobility puzzle, researchers have focused a considerable amount of attention on related questions. Several important themes emerge from research on intergenerational transfers. First, a large portion of wealth comes from inheritance (Menchik and Jiankoplos 1998; Wilhelm 2001). While it is difficult to identify exactly how much wealth is inherited, Blinder (1988) is typical in estimating that between 46 and 69 percent of household wealth can be attributed to intergenerational transfers, including both inheritance and inter vivos transfers. The literature documents that primogeniture, or equal sharing among offspring, is the typical pattern of intergenerational transfers in the United States (Menchik 1980). Menchik (1980) shows that this is true when intergenerational transfers are considered by sex, birth order, family size, estate size, and asset composition, and regardless of tax incentives. However, there is also compelling evidence that there are demographic differences in the amount of wealth that is passed from generation to generation. For instance, whites are much more likely than blacks to inherit. Indeed, current estimates suggest that between 10 and 20 percent of black–white differences in wealth ownership are attributable to inheritance (Menchik and Jianakoplos 1997). At the same time, a larger proportion of household wealth comes from inheritance for blacks than for whites and other races; similarly low income households and older people also receive a relatively high proportion of their wealth from inheritances (Wolff 2002).

Yet there is strong evidence that inheritance plays a minimal role in determining adult wealth overall. In particular, researchers are beginning to conclude that the vast majority of people will never inherit, that only a very small portion of the population ever inherits a sizable amount, and that most wealthy households did not inherit their wealth (Gale and Scholz 1994; Menchik and Jiankoplos 1998;

Table 5.1. *Inheritance and Wealth Accumulation (%)*

	1999	1997	1995	1993
Inherited any amount	9	8	7	7
Less than $50,000	8	6	6	7
More than $50,000	1	1	1	1

Note: Wealth groups are defined by net worth in 2000.
Source: National Longitudinal Survey of Youth, 1979 Cohort.

Wilhelm 2001). For example, Gale and Scholz (1994) estimated that less than 4 percent of all households ever received a bequest and that between 5 and 9 percent received inter vivos transfers. Similarly, Gokhale and Kotlikoff (2000) found that a very small portion of the population ever inherits. Moreover, inheritance does not affect the distribution of wealth much because inheritances and other transfers tend to be equalizing in terms of wealth inequality. Richer households inherit more but, as a proportion of their wealth, a small inheritance matters more to the poorer households (Wolff 2002).

Others have argued that certain generations are more likely than others to inherit. One popular argument is that baby boomers, in particular, might inherit great sums. Growth in Social Security and Medicare benefits in recent years has caused a relatively large transfer of financial resources from younger to old generations. At the same time, stock market booms have increased the value of savings for today's retirees (Avery and Rendall 1993). The implication of these patterns is that current adults can expect to inherit more than adults in the past. However, Gokhale and Kotlikoff (2000) used the 1998 Survey of Consumer Finances to show that 92 percent of respondents had never inherited anything. Even among those who had inherited, 6.5 percent had inherited less than $100,000, and only 1.6 percent had inherited more than $100,000.

Table 5.1 provides similar estimates from the NLS-Y. This table compares the percentage of today's young adults who had ever inherited in the years between 1993 and 1999. The proportion of respondents who had inherited increased slightly over the decade included in the table – rising from 7 to 9 percent – but the overall percentage of inheritors remains relatively low. Similarly, as the estimates included in the table demonstrate, few of these people inherited a sizable amount. Of all respondents, only 1 percent inherited more than $50,000 while between 6 and 8 percent inherited less than that amount. Of course, the respondents in the NLS-Y are somewhat younger than the respondents in the Survey of Consumer Finances and might continue to inherit, but Gokhale and Kotlikoff's (2000) estimates suggest that this pattern of low inheritance is likely to continue as the NLS-Y respondents age.

There are several reasons that inheritance is lower than we might expect. Looking at the baby boomers generation is instructive because of the arguments that suggest that this generation ought to inherit relatively large sums. As Gokhale and Kotlikoff (2000) note, each baby boomer has a relatively large number of siblings. Given that in the United States bequests are usually made equally among siblings, baby boomers are going to have to divide their inheritances among more people. The resources available to baby boomers as inheritance are also lower than we might expect because the degree to which the resources of the elderly are annuitized has increased in recent decades (Gokhale and Kotlikoff 2000). Annuitized resources, such as Social Security, stop when the recipient dies, and therefore cannot be passed to future generations. Finally, there is evidence that the elderly are increasingly depleting their savings. As people live longer, there are medical and living expenses that previous generations did not face. Moreover, the elderly are healthier than they were in the past and are increasingly using their savings to enjoy their final years.

INDEPENDENT EFFECTS: SIBLINGS

Other aspects of family background also affect adult wealth. As I argued in Chapter Four, it is likely that family size during childhood is an important component of the accumulation process that has attracted only limited attention in the past. Siblings reduce the material and nonmaterial resources available to each child in a family. The result is that each child probably attains less education than he or she might otherwise have attained. There is a well-established body of

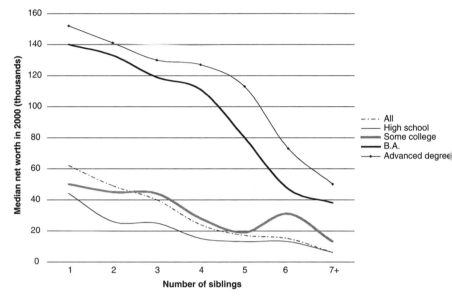

Figure 5.4. Siblings, education, and adult wealth. *Source*: National Longitudinal Survey of Youth, 1979 Cohort.

literature that documents the reductions in educational attainment each sibling faces, and to the extent that education increases adult wealth, siblings are also likely to reduce adult wealth accumulation. In fact, a negative relationship between sibship size and adult education is an extremely persistent finding in research on education (Blake 1989; Downey 1995b). Consistent with these arguments, descriptive statistics comparing adults by wealth level and childhood family size suggest that those from larger families do have less wealth as adults. Figure 5.4 provides a preliminary look at the relationship among siblings, education, and adult wealth attainment. The figure compares net worth in 2000 (in thousands) by highest education level of the respondent and number of siblings. The detailed definitions for the variables and estimates used in the figure are included in the Appendix.

This figure demonstrates a very clear negative relationship between number of siblings and adult wealth at all levels of education, and the negative relationship is most dramatic at higher levels of

Table 5.2. *Race of the Wealthy (%)*

	Millionaires	$500K–$999K	$300–$499K	All Others
White	94	94	94	79
Hispanic	4	4	5	7
Black	2	2	1	14

Note: Wealth groups are defined by net worth in 2000.
Source: National Longitudinal Survey of Youth, 1979 Cohort.

education. Median net worth for those with one sibling and an advanced degree is more than $150,000. At the other end of the spectrum, those with more than seven siblings and a high school diploma have a median net worth of merely $6,000. Research on wealth ownership commonly mentions the effect of childhood family behaviors and speculates that early patterns are formative and may be important indicators of adult wealth outcomes. The estimates in Figure 5.4 suggest that there is, in fact, an important relationship between childhood family size and adult wealth. If siblings dilute resources available for inheritance, formal education, and informal educational experiences, we would expect to see the pattern that is evident in Figure 5.4. I explore how robust these patterns are to the controls for other factors, but the basic relationship highlights the importance of family processes in the accumulation of wealth. Naturally, these estimates provide no evidence that the effect of siblings on adult wealth will remain when other factors are controlled. I explore this issue in the paragraphs that follow. Yet these descriptive estimates do demonstrate a very strong relationship between childhood family size and adult wealth accumulation.

INDEPENDENT ESTIMATES: RACE

Racial inequality in wealth ownership is one of the most well-documented forms of inequality in the United States, and racial differences in wealth accumulation and mobility are likely as extreme. The representation of blacks and Hispanics among the very wealthy is telling of the degree to which there is racial inequality in wealth ownership. Table 5.2 compares the percentage of four wealth groups that is accounted for by whites, Hispanics, and blacks in the 2000 NLS-Y. Of millionaires in that sample, for example, 94 percent are white, 4 percent are Hispanic, and 2 percent are black. Similar patterns are true for those who have $500,000 to $999,999 in total net worth and for those who have $300,0000 to $499,999 in total net worth. For all other respondents, 79 percent are white, 7 percent are Hispanic, and 14 percent are black. As I noted in reference to siblings, these initial estimates provide no evidence that racial differences in wealth are not a function of other intervening factors, but these estimates do demonstrate the degree to which there are racial gaps in asset ownership.

Combining Family Background Effects

While the basic descriptive relationships between family background characteristics and adult wealth are important, they tell us little about the relative importance of the various interrelated factors. For instance, the basic estimates leave the question of whether these relationships will still be evident when the various factors are considered together. In order to examine the relationship between various elements of family background and adult wealth, I also conducted a series of multivariate analyses. I first explore the relationship between family background and adult wealth by regressing overall adult wealth, measured as net assets, on individual and family traits. Table 5.3 reports the results of a series of regression equations estimated on the NLS-Y 1979 cohort using alternative model specifications. I include various alternative specifications to demonstrate the robustness of the central findings and to explore how the effects interact with each other. The regression results included in Table 5.3 and the remainder of tables in this chapter are partial models; the full models are included in the Appendix to conserve space. The Appendix also includes more detailed descriptions of and explanations for model specifications, variables, estimation procedures, and alternative model specifications.

While the Appendix provides model details, a brief explanation of the models presented in Table 5.3 will facilitate interpreting the

Table 5.3. *Intergenerational Transfers and Adult Assets,*
1985–2000

	Effect on Adult Assets
Intergenerational transfers	
Received a trust fund	334.76[***]
	(11.66)
Ever inherited	20.62[***]
	(6.60)
Estimated wealth in 1979	2.21[***]
	(0.45)

Note: These are PARTIAL MODELS; other test variables and control variables are included but not displayed. See Appendix for full
models. Cells are coefficient estimates with standard errors in parentheses.
[*] $p < .10$; [**] $p < .05$; [***] $p < .01$.
Source: National Longitudinal Survey of Youth, 1979 Cohort.

results. The outcome variable in these models is net assets in adulthood (total assets less total liabilities). I present models of net assets
in adulthood because in trying to understand wealth accumulation,
it is total wealth or net worth that is ultimately of interest. I begin
the analysis of adult wealth in 1985 when all respondents in these
data are at least 20 years old. I allow the dependent variable to vary
over time, between 1985 and 2000, as individual and family characteristics in adulthood change. I standardize net assets by adding a
constant. The dependent variable is also so highly skewed by a relatively small number of very wealthy respondents, consistent with
the U.S. population, that standard transformations do not reduce
the skew. Using various transformations (e.g., logging), alternative
specifications of the dependent variable (e.g., gross assets, total financial assets) and removing outliers do not affect the substance of
the results I present. In these models, I control for individual and
family traits such as race, age, gender, marital status, divorce history, children, adult family resources, immigrant status, and region
of residence. This means that these estimates can be interpreted
as the effect of the specified family trait on the dollar value (in
thousands of 2000 dollars) of adult wealth, all other factors held
constant.

These results can also be interpreted in terms of mobility. Table 5.3 includes a coefficient for the effect of family wealth in 1979, calculated using other available information about the respondent's family at the time. I describe this estimation procedure in more detail in the Appendix. I include the estimated effect of 1979 wealth to demonstrate that, as we would expect, those who start life with more wealth are likely to accumulate assets more quickly during adulthood. Including this estimate of wealth during childhood also allows interpretation of the other effects in terms of changes in wealth since childhood. That is, the measure of education (discussed later) can be interpreted in terms of its effect on how the respondents' adult wealth is different from their childhood wealth. That is, the effects I discuss below can be interpreted in terms of mobility since childhood.

MULTIVARIATE RESULTS: THE ROLE OF INHERITANCE

The effect of inheritance on adult wealth is extremely strong, even when a host of other factors are held constant. In other words, those who inherit do have more wealth on average than those who do not inherit. The coefficient estimates in Table 5.3 are those related to intergenerational transfers, and again, these are the effects that remain when all other influences are held constant. Specifically, Table 5.3 highlights the effects of ever receiving a trust fund and ever inheriting. The size of the coefficient estimate for receiving a trust fund is particularly large both in absolute terms and when it is compared to the effects of other factors (see Appendix and Tables 5.4 and 5.5). The effect of receiving an inheritance is also significantly different from zero, implying that it is a real effect rather than an artifact of the data. The implication of this is that people who receive a trust fund accumulate more assets as adults and are more upwardly mobile. The effect of ever receiving an inheritance is also quite strong, implying that those who inherit accumulate assets more quickly and are more upwardly mobile than those who do not inherit. These results provide strong support for the arguments I outlined in Chapter Four and that Figure 5.1 summarizes. In particular, the empirical results highlighted in Table 5.3 demonstrate that inheritance has a direct

Table 5.4. *Family Background and Adult Assets, 1985–2000*

	Childhood Family	Add Education
Parents' financial resources		
Family income (log)	1.02*	1.05*
	(0.51)	(0.50)
Father's education		
High school	17.26***	12.42***
	(4.54)	(4.55)
Some college	20.43***	10.25
	(6.73)	(6.77)
College degree	37.17***	21.18***
	(7.20)	(7.34)
Advanced degree	55.54***	32.38***
	(8.46)	(8.62)
Mother's education		
High school	14.00***	6.48***
	(4.47)	(4.5)
Some college	29.39***	16.15**
	(7.03)	(7.11)
College degree	56.67***	33.94***
	(8.40)	(8.53)
Advanced degree	24.69**	4.51
	(12.74)	(12.80)
Respondent's education		
High school	—	17.85***
		(4.86)
Some college	—	34.11***
		(5.72)
College degree	—	57.58***
		(6.64)
Advanced degree	—	74.57***
		(7.41)

Note: These are PARTIAL MODELS; other test variables and control variables are included but not displayed. See Appendix for full models. Cells are coefficient estimates with standard errors in parentheses.
* $p < .10$; ** $p < .05$; *** $p < .01$.
Source: National Longitudinal Survey of Youth, 1979 Cohort.

effect on adult wealth. That is, the results provide support for the argument that parents' wealth has a positive effect on childrens' wealth through direct transfers during life (*inter vivos transfers*) and after the parents' death (*inheritance*).

Table 5.5. *Family Structure and Adult Assets, 1985–2000*

	Childhood Family	Add Education
Family at age 14		
Number of siblings	−2.84***	−2.53***
	(0.45)	(0.85)
Stepparent family	−17.11***	−12.50**
	(6.39)	(6.38)
Single-parent family	−8.18	−8.14
	(5.85)	(5.84)
Father worked full-time	9.28**	8.45
	(4.73)	(4.72)
Mother worked full-time	−3.64	−2.31
	(3.65)	(3.65)
Black	−44.65***	−38.85***
	(5.73)	(5.99)
Hispanic	−32.36***	−31.88***
	(7.75)	(7.77)
Respondent's education		
High school	−	17.85***
		(4.86)
Some college	−	34.11***
		(5.72)
College degree	−	57.58***
		(6.64)
Advanced degree	−	74.57***
		(7.41)

Note: These are PARTIAL MODELS; other test variables and control variables are included but not displayed.
See Appendix for full models. Cells are coefficient estimates with standard errors in parentheses.
* $p < .10$; ** $p < .05$; *** $p < .01$.
Source: National Longitudinal Survey of Youth, 1979 Cohort.

Multivariate Results: The Role of Parents

What is perhaps more interesting is the effect of other factors that remain even after controlling for inheritance. Family background, in particular, has an effect on adult wealth and wealth mobility that is quite strong even after inheritance and inter vivos transfers are controlled. Parents' achievement, for example, has a very strong effect on adult wealth and wealth mobility, other factors held constant. Research on parents' educations suggests that more highly educated parents will have higher incomes and more prestigious occupations and will be more successful in their jobs (Warren and Hauser 1997). As a result, their children are likely to be more educated and more successful. The coefficient estimates included in Table 5.4 demonstrate that parents' success, their income and educations, does affect the children's wealth as adults. Parents' income and education both increase adult wealth. Family income during childhood is a strong positive predictor of adult wealth. Family income increases the resources available for saving and for education. Both translate into higher adult wealth for adult children.

Similarly, parents' education is associated with higher levels of adult wealth. All levels of education for fathers and mothers increase the adult child's wealth. For fathers, the relationship becomes increasingly pronounced as the level of education increases. That is, the effect of a father with a high school degree (compared to a father with no degree) is strong, but the effect of some college is even stronger. The effect of an advanced degree is the strongest. Again, these are the effects that remain when other influences are held constant. For mothers, the effect of education increases through having a college degree. There is a positive effect for adult wealth of having a mother with an advanced degree, but the effect of a college degree is most pronounced. This is at least in part because women with advanced degrees were rare in the generations represented here. I argued that parents' resources, evident in their income and education, improve education opportunities for their children, provide access to educational materials such as newspapers, and allow parents to teach their children about saving and investing. The results included in Table 5.4 provide strong support for this argument.

If family resources improve educational attainment, the respondent's own education should have a strong, positive effect on adult wealth. Respondent's education should also reduce the effects of test variables introduced in the first model included in Table 5.4. The second model in the same table investigates this. Specifically, in the second model, I introduce the measures of respondents' education and find support for my argument. Education has a strong, positive relationship with adult wealth, and it decreases the effect of parents' resources. Cox tests confirm that the additional measures of respondent's education reduces the effect of parents' education on adult wealth.

Multivariate Results: The Role of Siblings

I argued that siblings decrease adult wealth accumulation by reducing the resources available to each child in the family of origin. Table 5.5 includes results that support this argument. This table reports additional results from the regression analyses I discussed earlier, but this table highlights the effects of family structure when the respondent was a child. The first model in Table 5.5 includes the total number of siblings and all control variables to demonstrate how family size affects adult wealth. Consistent with the notion that having more siblings decreases well-being later in life, there is a strong negative relationship between sibship size and adult net worth. The basic model is also consistent in other respects with previous literature on wealth ownership. For example, blacks and Hispanics have considerably less wealth than whites, married couples have more wealth than singles, and income and age both increase wealth.

There are several mechanisms through which siblings shape adult wealth. Perhaps the most visible and direct effect is through education. Siblings affect wealth, at least in part, by reducing the resources available to each child in the family of origin. In larger families, parents have less time to devote to informal education and fewer resources to devote to formally educating each child. As a result, the educational attainment of each sibling will be, on average, lower than it might have been otherwise. If this argument is valid, the effect of family size in childhood on adult wealth will be reduced by educational attainment. In the second model included in Table 5.5, I add the effects of the respondent's educational attainment to explore the viability of this argument, and the result provides support for my argument. That is, adding respondent's educational attainment to the basic model reduces the effect of siblings. Education does not completely eliminate the effect of siblings on adult wealth, but the effect is lower. Cox tests provide support for the argument that the addition of measures of respondents' education reduces the effect of siblings on adult wealth.

In addition to affecting educational attainment, siblings reduce direct financial transfers from parents to children, which in turn is likely to reduce adult wealth. In models pictured in the Appendix, I introduce three measures of intergenerational transfers to test this. I include measures of receiving a trust account, ever inheriting, and estimated family wealth during childhood. These are the measures I highlighted in Table 5.3. The effect of these measures on adult wealth is very strong, as I noted earlier. In addition, adding these measures to the analysis decreases the effect of siblings, suggesting that the mechanism I proposed has some merit. What is perhaps most interesting is that the effect of siblings remains even when direct intergenerational transfers are controlled. This implies that direct transfers are important predictors of adult wealth, but other forces are also important.

While these models control for a host of influences on adult wealth, the effect of siblings remains after all controls are entered. This suggests that there are other ways in which siblings matter that are not included in the models. Some of the remaining effect of siblings is probably a result of individual financial behavior in adulthood and the trajectory or path along which people accumulate wealth. People learn about saving and investing from both formal sources, such as formal education, and from informal sources, including their parents. Those with more education tend to make financial decisions that yield higher wealth; likewise, those who learn about financial behavior from their parents are likely to make better financial decisions, to save earlier, and to accumulate wealth faster. Moreover, those who receive direct financial transfers of resources from their parents – both inter vivos transfers and inheritance – are likely to make financial decisions and to save in ways that will increase their wealth. Including additional measures of financial behavior, such as having a higher percentage of the portfolio invested in stocks and bonds, increases wealth. Similarly, those who make an early transition to financial wealth (invested in stocks and bonds early and before other assets) increase the value of their wealth considerably, while those who follow a more traditional path in their savings accumulate markedly less than other investors. I do not include these results here, but they are consistent with previous findings and provide at least a partial explanation of the direct effect of siblings on wealth that remains even after intergenerational transfers are controlled (Keister 2003).

In addition to financial behavior, social contacts are likely an important factor that is not controlled in these models. Social contacts, such as friends from college, can provide capital for entrepreneurial ventures, can be an important source of information about investments, and can give referrals to those who can provide these important things. Another omitted group of measures are indicators of the nonmaterial resources that siblings dilute. I argued that the time parents have to assist their children with homework, to create educational opportunities, to encourage them, and to intervene with problems are all reduced in larger families. I also argued that this is likely to affect adult wealth by reducing children's educational attainment. Practically, it is not possible to test this argument because data including parents' time spent with children and adult wealth ownership are not available. Ideally the NLS-Y would contain data on parents' nonmaterial resources such as the frequency with which respondents spent time with their parents, whether the parents knew their children's friends, and the parents' educational aspirations for their children. Unfortunately, this information is not available in the NLS-Y. While I do not demonstrate a causal relationship between nonmaterial resources and adult wealth, the relationship between the dilution of family resources, both material and nonmaterial, and educational attainment has been well documented elsewhere (Downey 1995b). Of course, it is not necessary to test all elements of a theoretical argument empirically to provide useful support for the arguments (see, e.g., Popper 1965; Cohen 1989). The empirical evidence I provide lends support for but does not falsify my arguments regarding parents' nonmaterial resources.

Family differences in the propensity to postpone consumption may also explain the remaining sibling effect. People who have a relatively high propensity to postpone consumption tend to accumulate greater wealth because they are more likely to save. Children learn saving behavior from their parents, and to the extent to which parents convey a message of postponed gratification either in their own saving behavior or in their other behaviors, children are likely to learn to save. In families where postponed consumption, including postponing childbirth, is not the norm, children are less likely to learn to defer consumption and less likely to learn to save. The result is not a spurious relationship between sibship size and adult wealth, but it reflects a family's propensity to save and to socialize children to behave similarly.

These analyses may be limited in other ways by spurious relations, a problem that is common in survey research and that has been debated in the literature on siblings (Downey et al. 1999; Guo and VanWey 1999). Specifically, because I am unable to control all factors that affect wealth accumulation, I cannot completely dismiss the potential for a spurious relationship. While I am able to control for a large number of individual, family, and regional effects on wealth accumulation, there are naturally some factors that I have not been able to measure directly. For example, it is possible that parents who plan carefully and save for their children's future also have fewer children. These parents may transfer resources to their children while they are alive – inter vivos transfers – which the children do not report as an inheritance but which improve the offspring's ability to save and invest. Such transfers may affect wealth but are not controlled in my models. Controlling for the receipt and size of inherited wealth is the single strongest control for this potentially spurious relationship. Moreover, even with inheritance controlled, the relationship between family size and wealth outcomes is relatively strong and consistent across wealth measures.

In order to explore the mechanisms underlying the relationship between siblings and adult wealth in more detail, I include an additional set of analyses in which financial transfers and financial behavior are the outcome variables. In Table 5.6, I model the effect of siblings and a series of other endogenous variables on the likelihood of receiving an inheritance, receiving a trust fund, owning a home, and owning stocks. One of my core arguments is that additional siblings

Table 5.6. *Family Background and Adult Wealth*

	Ever Inherited	Received a Trust Account	Own a Home	Own Stocks
Family at age 14				
Number of siblings	−0.05***	−0.08***	−0.03***	−0.04***
	(0.01)	(0.01)	(0.01)	(0.01)
Stepparent family	0.21***	0.05	−0.12***	−0.07
	(0.04)	(0.10)	(0.04)	(0.05)
Single-parent family	−0.14***	−0.19***	−0.12***	−0.04
	(0.04)	(0.07)	(0.04)	(0.05)
Father worked full time	0.05	0.10	0.20***	0.22***
	(0.03)	(0.07)	(0.03)	(0.04)
Mother worked full time	−0.01	0.22***	−0.02	−0.03
	(0.02)	(0.05)	(0.02)	(0.03)
Black	−0.69***	−0.51***	−0.98***	−0.26***
	(0.05)	(0.12)	(0.04)	(0.06)
Hispanic	−0.78***	−0.13	−0.46***	−0.38***
	(0.06)	(0.12)	(0.05)	(0.07)

Note: These are PARTIAL MODELS; other test variables and control variables are included but not displayed. See Appendix for full models. Cells are logistic coefficient estimates with standard errors in parentheses.
* $p < .10$; ** $p < .05$; *** $p < .01$.
Source: National Longitudinal Survey of Youth, 1979 Cohort.

reduce the resources that parents transfer directly to their children in the form of inter vivos transfers such as trusts and inheritances, and this in turn adversely affects adult wealth accumulation. The results reported in the first two columns of Table 5.6 provide strong support for the first part of my argument. At all levels of family income and parental education, additional siblings reduce the likelihood of receiving a trust or inheriting. I also explored the size of the trust and the amount of inheritance received by regressing the value of the inheritance on the same independent variables. These analyses (not reported here) also supported the argument that siblings have a direct, negative impact on inheritance. In both models, parents' financial resources and mothers' education are directly related to receiving a financial transfer. Fathers' income is positively related to receiving an inheritance, but with the exception of fathers with advanced degrees, fathers' education is a weak predictor of receiving a trust. In these models, I do not control for respondents' education because I argue that intergenerational transfers are logically prior to educational attainment; that is, respondents whose parents have resources will complete additional schooling (as opposed to education affecting transfers).

SIBLINGS AND PORTFOLIO BEHAVIOR

Differences in portfolio behavior might also explain differences in wealth ownership. Portfolio behavior, which is the combination of assets and debts that families own at a point in time, can affect overall wealth and wealth mobility. Those with greater adult wealth tend to own foundational assets such as a home and financial assets such as stocks and bonds. Thus, when explaining adult differences in total wealth owned by such factors as number of siblings, it is useful to consider differences in how adults own key assets.

Why focus on the home or stocks and bonds? The family home is the cornerstone of most Americans' portfolios and has traditionally been the most common asset owned by households in the United States, largely because it combines use value with an investment (Kennickell 2000). Homeownership has also historically been a relatively lucrative investment and has, therefore, been an important component of the portfolios of those who are financially secure (Keister 2000c). In recent years, stock ownership has become more accessible to a greater number of Americans as mutual funds have become more common, online investing has grown in popularity, and new financial instruments that invest in stocks have become accessible to more people (Norris 1996). At the same time, stock market booms during the 1990s and early twenty-first century have made investing in stocks a central component of a growing investment portfolio. Of course, these are generalizations, and the likelihood of owning either of these investments is likely to vary dramatically with resources, both in childhood and adulthood, and other demographic traits. It is these differences that provide insight into the role that portfolio behavior may play in determining differences in overall adult wealth.

Portfolio differences by family size in childhood is a useful example. Indeed, sibship size is negatively related to the adult ownership of both the home and stocks/bonds. The third and fourth models in Table 5.6 report results of logistic regression equations that reveal that people with more siblings are less likely to own either a home or stocks as adults. There are at least two reasons for this finding. First, people from smaller families are more likely to receive an inheritance and the inheritance they receive is likely to be greater than what they would have received if their family had been larger. Inherited wealth, even a small amount of inherited wealth, can enable educational attainment, reduce the need to acquire debt for educational and other expenses in young adulthood, and can provide a financial basis that both reduces the expenses associated with life transitions and is a source of capital for investment. Each of these outcomes, in turn, can significantly increase the recipient's ability to purchase a home and to invest in stocks.

Second, people from smaller families enjoy greater financial and nonmaterial wealth in childhood that can also be translated into more resources in adulthood. In models not reported, I omitted the exogenous controls for inheritance, and the sibling result was very strong. In Table 5.6, columns 3 and 4, I do not include the controls for the amount of wealth inherited in order to isolate the effect of siblings on the ownership of these assets. The effect of sibship size is also strong when inheritance is controlled (models not displayed). Thus the results reported in this table provide some evidence that the relationship between additional siblings and the ownership of a home or stocks operates through a reduction in the availability of other (noninheritance) resources that can be diluted by family size.

MULTIVARIATE RESULTS: THE ROLE OF RACE

There are also very clear racial differences in wealth ownership. Race itself is not necessarily a component of family background; it can be considered either an individual or a family trait. Regardless of how it is grouped, however, race affects wealth ownership. The results in Tables 5.4 through 5.6 demonstrate that blacks and Hispanics accumulate much less wealth than whites, inherit less, and are less likely to own homes or stocks. This is consistent with previous research and with my own conceptual model. I argued that education largely mediates the effect of race on wealth, and the models presented in Table 5.5 provide some support for this argument. Including respondents' educational attainment does reduce the effect of race on wealth, and Cox tests provide additional support for the apparent decrease in the effect of race between the first and second models in that table. One model in which the effect of race is somewhat different than might be expected is the model of receiving a trust account. Blacks are much less likely than whites to receive a trust, but the Hispanic effect is not significantly different from zero. In models not reported here, I explored the reasons for this difference and discovered that, in the absence of controls, Hispanics received significantly fewer trusts. Controlling for parents' education, however, eliminated the effect. This suggests that parents' attainment is particularly important for Hispanic respondents. The effect of being Hispanic on trusts is mediated by parents' attainment.

MULTIVARIATE RESULTS: THE ROLE OF FAMILY DISRUPTION

Education does decrease the effect of race on adult wealth, but it does not eliminate the effect, suggesting that race may also affect adult wealth through its effect on other family traits. There are clear racial differences in family structure (Keister 2004), and these differences in family background are a potentially important cause of disparities in wealth ownership. Particularly, fertility, overall family size, and marital disruption are greater among minorities than they are among whites (Horton and Thomas 1998; Ruggles 1994; Wilson 1987). Because family structure during childhood shapes both childhood and adult outcomes, racial differences in these components of childhood family are important clues to racial differences in adult well-being. I have argued that sibship size (number of siblings) decreases educational and occupational attainment. Similarly, parental marital disruptions may have a negative effect on adult outcomes (McLanahan

1985; Sandefur and Wells 1999). Family disruptions interrupt education and learning, distract parents, dilute resources, and ultimately decrease children's attainment (Hanson and McLanahan 1998).

Previous research demonstrates that parents' separation or divorce decreases children's well-being both during childhood and into adulthood (Baydar 1988; Cooksey 1997; Demo and Acock 1988; McLanahan and Sandefur 1994). Experiencing divorce or separation decreases performance in school, reduces educational attainment (Downey 1995a; Houseknecht and Spanier 1980), and ultimately decreases occupational attainment and mobility (Biblarz and Raftery 1993). Children whose parents divorce or separate are less healthy both physically (Horwitz, White, and Howell-White 1996) and mentally (Cherlin, Chase-Lansdale, and McRae 1998) than those from intact families. There are also economic costs of experiencing marital dissolution. Divorce increases poverty rates (Duncan and Hoffman 1985; McLanahan and Sandefur 1994; Nestel, Mercier, and Shaw 1983) and decreases per capita income (Cherlin 1981; Mott and Moore 1978; Peterson 1996), labor force participation (Cherlin 1979), and the ratio of income to needs (Corcoran 1995), particularly for women (Holden and Smock 1991; Stirling 1989).

Status attainment literature linking family structure to adult outcomes demonstrates extensively and consistently that being raised in a nonintact family reduces educational advancement, occupational attainment, and a host of other measures of adult well-being (Corcoran 1995). Experiencing parents' divorce or separation as a child is also associated with lower adult wealth. In the models included in Tables 5.5 and 5.6 and in the Appendix, I include a measure that indicates that the respondent lived in a stepparent family. Similar results are obtained if I indicate divorce in other ways, consistent with prior research (Keister 2004). Because divorce and separation reduce school performance, educational attainment, occupational mobility, and health, these experiences also reduce adult wealth.

Divorce and separation are also likely to decrease direct transfers of assets from parents to children. Financial resources will be spread across two households following the separation. If either parent does not remarry or remarries a person with few independent financial resources, the resources available to that parent will be diluted. Resources may also be strained by settling financial disputes between parents, which can further reduce the resources that are devoted to raising children or transferred directly to them as financial assets. In addition, parental divorce and separation are likely to take an emotional toll on children that may decrease adult attainment, including wealth accumulation. Finally, family disruption may reduce the time parents have available to nurture children, to create stimulating educational experiences, or to intervene when they have problems (Mechanic and Hansell 1989). Because black and Hispanic children are disproportionately affected by family disruption, they will disproportionately suffer the negative effects of these experiences on wealth.

Research on poverty suggests that the negative effect of a family crisis such as divorce or separation may be lessened when the child is part of a larger family network (Keister 2004). In intact families, extended family members living in the home are likely to dilute resources and reduce children's long-term attainment. Additional family members reduce the resources that can be devoted to each child and have a long-term negative effect on the child's wealth. However, when a marriage dissolves, extended family may provide emotional support and possibly contribute additional financial resources that lessen the negative long-term effect of the crisis. I do not test this idea directly here, but there is a tradition of qualitative research arguing that extended family can alleviate the effects of poverty for these reasons, and quantitative explorations of the effect have provided some support for this argument (Stack 1974). There is also some evidence from research on wealth ownership that extended family may mediate the effect of separation or divorce (Keister 2004). Of course, extended family in nonintact families might also dilute resources. Likewise, extended family members in intact households may have a positive effect, but the effect is less noticeable because the need for intervention is lower. Once again, these processes are likely to contribute to racial inequality in adult wealth as black and Hispanic children are more likely to spend time with extended family members in the home.

RACE AND PORTFOLIO BEHAVIOR

Race might also reduce adult wealth in more indirect ways, including through its effect on investment behavior or portfolio behavior. Similar to the effect of siblings on adult portfolio behavior, minority race is negatively related to the adult ownership of both the home and stocks/bonds. The models included in Table 5.6 demonstrate these differences. The results do show that both race and family background affect the likelihood of adult home and stock ownership. The third model in the table shows that blacks and Hispanics are much less likely than whites to own a home, and the fourth model shows that the same relationship is true for stock ownership. Experiencing a divorce or separation also reduces home ownership but does not affect stock ownership. Models not included here show that including the indicator of spending time in a stepparent family reduces the direct effect of race, but the results in Table 5.6 show that the direct racial effect obtains even after the inclusion of the family structure measures. The remaining direct effect of race might be accounted for by discrimination in lending and interest rates differences experienced by minorities. These differences are clearly important but are beyond the scope of this research. Future research should examine these relationships in greater depth than is possible here.

Conclusions

This chapter began to explore the relationship between family background and adult wealth accumulation and mobility. I first isolated several components of family background and examined how these relate to adult wealth. For instance, I showed that adults with relatively high wealth tend to have parents with higher education. My conceptual model proposed that parents with high levels of educational attainment are likely to have children who advance farther in education and thus have greater wealth. The estimates I presented in the first part of this chapter provided initial support for this argument. I have also argued that parents' success is likely to translate into higher wealth for the parents that can be transferred directly to children as inter vivos transfers or inheritance. My conceptual model proposed that some of the relationship between family background and adult wealth is thus likely to be a result of inheritance. In this chapter, I presented evidence that inheritance does shape wealth ownership and does increase mobility. However, I also showed that only a very small portion of Americans ever inherit and the effect of inheritance is at least partially mediated by educational attainment. More importantly, my regression results showed that once the effect of inheritance on adult wealth ownership and mobility is controlled, other factors remain very important.

I then turned to discussing the relative importance. I began the discussion of the multivariate models by discussing the effects of family size on adult wealth accumulation and mobility. I argued that siblings decrease total adult wealth by diluting resources available to each child in the family of origin. As a result, sibship size decreases both educational attainment and direct intergenerational transfers of financial resources. During childhood, additional siblings strain the material resources available for education costs, books and magazines, computer resources, music and dance lessons, and travel. Additional siblings may also dilute the nonmaterial resources parents devote to their children, including encouragement, educational experiences, and intervention. In addition, more children reduce parental savings, inter vivos transfers, and the wealth that is available to bequeath at the end of the parents' lives. Decreased educational attainment and intergenerational resource transfers, in turn, alter financial behavior and saving trajectories, or paths. As a result, those from larger families accumulate smaller portfolios throughout their lives.

I examined the relationship between family background and adult wealth accumulation patterns using the NLS-Y 1979 cohort and found considerable support for my arguments. There was a strong negative association between sibship size and overall adult wealth. Consistent with the mechanisms I proposed, the effect of siblings was reduced when I controlled parents' financial resources and education. Similarly, controlling for respondents' education and intergenerational financial transfers reduced the effect of siblings on wealth even further but did not eliminate the effect. I argued that siblings continued to affect wealth, because I was not able to measure the effects of respondent's social connections or parents' nonmaterial resources. I also investigated the proposed mechanisms further by exploring the direct effect of siblings on the likelihood of receiving direct financial transfers from parents, including a trust (an inter vivos transfer) and an inheritance. In both cases, the effect of siblings was very strong and negative. Finally, I explored the direct effect of siblings on the likelihood of adult financial behavior, including stock ownership and home ownership. Again the effect of sibship size was strong and negative, even in the presence of the proposed controls such as childhood family resources, parents' education, respondents' educational attainment, and intergenerational financial transfers.

I also explored the relationship between other elements of family structure during childhood and adult wealth, focusing on how race interacts with these relationships. Yet once these processes were controlled, the race indicators remained significant. This is likely because there are important processes that are impossible to control with these (or any existing data) that also contribute to racial differences in wealth ownership. Informal education regarding saving and investment, for example, might account for accumulation differences. Yet there is no reliable way to test this possibility with current data. I also found evidence that the mechanisms by which family background reduces the effect of race on wealth is via portfolio behavior and savings trajectories. Blacks and Hispanics are less likely than whites to own homes and stocks, two critical assets. Introducing family background into the equation, however, reduced the direct effect of race and provided additional explanatory power.

These findings provide additional support for the idea that family background matters. The findings support the idea that sibship size reduces attainment. Previous research on resource dilution has been largely limited to studies of educational attainment. While the negative relationship between sibship size and adult educational outcomes has been one of the most persistent findings in the education literature (Blake 1989; Downey 1995b), debate regarding the conditions under which the relationship holds and the reason for the effect has continued (Downey et al. 1999; Guo and VanWey 1999). Critics charge that a spurious relationship between unobserved family traits accounts for the relationship. Yet proponents of the resource dilution approach have successfully defended the argument that resource dilution does largely account for the negative relationship between sibship size and educational attainment. My results extend the discussion of resource dilution beyond the study of education and demonstrate that additional siblings do reduce the financial resources that parents transfer directly to their children in the form of inheritance. My results also suggest that sibship size affects other aspects of wealth accumulation, including the types of assets that people eventually acquire and the overall level of wealth they eventually attain.

These results also provide some evidence that the extreme and persistent racial divide in wealth ownership is at least partially traceable to family processes during childhood. It is important to note that in emphasizing the relationship between family background and wealth ownership, I do not intend to reduce the complex process of wealth accumulation or wealth inequality to a single set of inputs. Other research clearly documents that wealth ownership is associated with a number of factors, including individual and family processes such as marital behavior, investment patterns, and union separation and aggregate processes such as demographic trends, market fluctuations, and policy shifts (Keister 2000c; Keister and Moller 2000). The results that I discuss in this chapter, however, highlight an important part of the picture that has been neglected previously. Understanding that family background is related in critical ways to adult wealth accumulation, net of its indirect effects on other demographic behaviors, casts light on the importance of family processes that shape the way people behave and, in this case, the way they accumulate assets. Likewise, understanding that family structure can facilitate this process suggests that providing incentives to change some behaviors could enhance efforts to increase equality.

Perhaps most important, these findings underscore the importance of family processes in the accumulation of wealth. Recent research has documented extreme inequalities in wealth ownership, but the processes by which these inequalities develop and are perpetuated have received relatively little attention. Inherited wealth certainly accounts for much of the wealth that is acquired particularly by the extremely wealthy, but inheritance does not explain even the majority of the variation across families in wealth holding. Researchers have pointed to the importance of family processes, but data limitations have prevented systematic analysis of the relationship between processes in the family of origin and adult wealth outcomes. The results I presented here provide support for the argument that family traits, particularly family size in childhood, can either facilitate or impede wealth accumulation both early in life and throughout the life course. This suggests that efforts to reduce inequality in wealth ownership may be most effective if they seek to reduce the effect of depravation early in life.

CHAPTER SIX

FAMILY BACKGROUND:
CULTURE AND RELIGION

Family culture during childhood may also affect adult wealth accumulation and mobility. I argued in Chapter Four that families – their practices, interaction patterns, and styles with which the family members behave – vary in qualitative ways that may affect the life trajectories and adult well-being of children. Yet evaluating the effects of family culture can be difficult because culture is difficult to measure. Religious beliefs and practices, however, are an important exception. Religion is a relatively tangible indicator of culture that can be measured and studied empirically. Religion can also be an important attribute characterizing a family, and it is clear that religion affects such outcomes as fertility, marriage, and work behavior (Alwin 1986; Ellison, Bartkowsi, and Segal 1996; Lehrer 1996a, 1996b; Sherkat and Ellison 1999). In Chapter Four, I extended these ideas to propose that religious upbringing will affect adult wealth *indirectly* through its effect on education and the outcomes that education affects, such as marriage and fertility. I also argued that religion affects wealth *directly* because it shapes the strategies of actions and sets of competencies on which people draw while making important decisions. In this chapter, I explore these proposals empirically. Figure 5.1 highlighted the portion of the full conceptual model (Figure 4.1) that I began to explore in Chapter Five and that is the focus of this chapter.

Why Religion?

An important question regarding the relationship between religion and wealth is whether writing about such issues is good for anyone. I understand the degree to which this issue can create apprehension, particularly my focus on the remarkable success many Jewish families have at accumulating wealth. At the same time, I feel strongly that a scientific examination of the role of religion in shaping people's well-being is not bad. Religion is such a pervasive part of American life. If it does affect the way people approach decision making, it really cannot be ignored when discussing the paths people take as they move through life.

In the introduction to their book *Jews in the Protestant Establishment*, Richard Zweigenhaft and G. William Domhoff noted that they wrote "in the belief that only more discussion and information, not silence, will continue the decline in prejudices toward many minority groups that has occurred over the years since the second World War" (Zweigenhaft and Domhoff 1982). I share their sense that discussion and information have to be central to understanding inequality, and discussing success is just as important as discussing lack of success. Zweigenhaft and Domhoff also quoted sociologist E. Digby Baltzell who claimed that "the story of the Jews is one of the great untold stories of the twentieth century in America." Again, I agree. Telling even part of the story about how religion and wealth are related will contribute to reducing discrimination, not feeding it. It is also likely that telling even a small part of the story of the American Jews as part of a larger story about the role that religion plays in shaping people's lives will make clear what lessons may benefit other minority groups. It is in this spirit that I use this chapter to explore the role that religion – particularly religious upbringing – plays in shaping adult wealth accumulation and mobility.

Religion and Ethnicity

Although most people have a clear sense of their own religious identity – that is, they have a clear sense of the religious organization to which they belong and how that group relates to other religious groups – defining religious affiliation, and grouping people into clear religious groups, is no easy task. There are always finer distinctions that can be made, and there are numerous ways to sort groups. In the estimates I present in this chapter, I explicitly identify those who were affiliated during childhood with the following: Baptist, Episcopalian, Lutheran, Methodist, Presbyterian, Other Protestant, Roman Catholic, Jewish. Because their number was so small, I include only the following in a group called "other": Buddhist, Christian Science, Hindu, Jehovah's Witness, Mormon, Muslim, and all other religious affiliations. Also because of small sample issues, I do not identify the sect to which Jewish respondents belonged. That is, I do not distinguish Reform, Conservative, and Orthodox Jews. I experimented with a wide variety of classifications for religious affiliation, and I found little difference across different definitions. The estimates of childhood religious affiliation I use in this chapter all rely on reports that respondents made in the 2000 wave of the National Longitudinal Survey of Youth, 1979 Cohort (NLS-Y). Respondents also reported their childhood religious affiliation in 1979 and 1982, and I experimented with using those reports. There was virtually no difference in the substance of the results as a function of the reporting year I used.

Of course, it would be useful to be able to distinguish between more specific categories within larger groupings such as "Jewish" and "other." In particular, there is evidence that financial behavior does vary among Jewish denominations. Waxman (2001) found a difference of about $10,000 a year in income between Reform and Conservative Jews, and a similar difference between Conservative and Orthodox Jews. That means that Reform Jewish families have, on average, $20,000 a year higher income than the Orthodox. Waxman also proposes that many of the factors that I discuss with respect to the conservative Protestant account for the lower incomes among the Orthodox.

Unfortunately, sample size makes it very difficult to make more precise distinctions than those I make in this chapter, and the results are substantively indistinguishable from those I report. In order to provide the type of estimates I include here, particularly the multivariate models included at the end of the chapter, it is necessary to use a single data source that contains adequate detail regarding childhood religion, other important controls (e.g., details on family background, information about transitions to adulthood, and information about adult behaviors and characteristics), and adult wealth. It is also necessary to use data that contains information on wealth at more than one point in time. The NLS-Y offers all of these, and the NLS-Y sample includes a large number of respondents. The survey began by interviewing nearly 13,000 young adults, has followed these respondents for 20 years, and has retained nearly 10,000 respondents. Given the data detail that the NLS provides for such a large sample, the data are excellent for answering questions about religious affiliation and adult wealth.

Related to the definition of religions is the issue of ethnicity. For many American Jews, Judaism is also an ethnicity (Sklare 1971; Waxman 1983; Waxman 2001). Waxman (2001) is particularly interested in the degree to which Jewish identity has waned since World War II. He finds evidence that, among Jewish baby boomers, there has been a rather significant decline in identification as Jewish. He explores patterns of residential segregation and mobility, socioeconomic behavior, language, and mate selection, and argues that there has been a dramatic waning of a sense of Jewishness in this cohort in recent decades. Yet even if there has been a decline in Jewish ethnic identity, there is still little doubt that Jewishness is an ethnicity, particularly when compared to other dominant religious groupings in the United States such as Protestantism and Catholicism. Unlike other religious groups in the United States, Jews are more likely to live with other Jews, to attend Jewish schools, to have friends who are also Jewish, and to marry other Jews. There are two implications of this difference for the results I present in this chapter. First, the repertoires of skills that are characteristic of religious groups, and that I argue shape wealth accumulation, are likely to be relatively more salient for Jews than for those who were raised in other religions. This suggests that relations between religious affiliation and wealth outcomes may be stronger for Jews than for others. Second, there are likely to be higher correlations between childhood

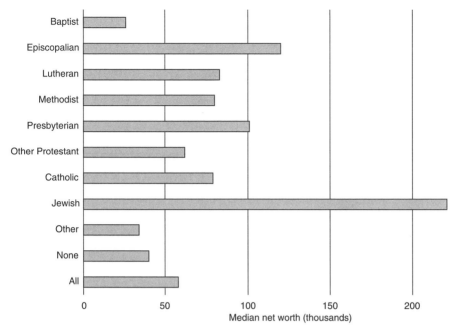

Figure 6.1. Childhood religion and adult net worth. *Source:* National Longitudinal Survey of Youth, 1979 Cohort. $N = 4,963$. Wealth estimates are for the year 2000.

and adult religious affiliation for Jews. This implies that it will be more difficult to ascertain the differential effects of childhood and adult religion for Jews. I explore each of these issues in more detail below.

Childhood Religion and Adult Net Worth

If there is an effect of childhood religion on adult net worth, there should be noticeable differences in adult wealth given family religious background. Unadjusted estimates from the NLS-Y suggest that there are indeed very large differences in adult wealth by childhood religion. Figure 6.1 shows median adult net worth in thousands of 2000 dollars by religious affiliation in childhood. Median 2000 net worth for all families in the sample was about $58,000. For those raised Baptist, however, the median was much lower at about $26,000. Mainline Protestants and Roman Catholics, who comprise the bulk of the sample, had net worth that was slightly higher than the overall median. Those raised as Lutherans and Roman Catholics all had approximately $80,000 in net worth in 2000. Those raised as Episcopalians and Presbyterians had slightly higher wealth in 2000. Specifically, for both of these groups, the median was greater than $100,000. The most dramatic difference, though, is between those who were raised Jewish and all other families. The median wealth for the Jewish group is more than $200,000. It is important to remember that these estimates do not control for any differences in childhood or adult conditions such as family SES or family structure. There are also no controls for demographic traits such as race and age. However, these unadjusted estimates indicate such dramatic differences in adult wealth by childhood religion that it is worth trying to ascertain the exact nature of these differences as well as the factors that contribute to what is clearly remarkably different accumulation stories.

Childhood Religion and Getting Rich

A logical place to begin exploring the detailed patterns of wealth accumulation by religious upbringing is to look at the position that people hold in the wealth distribution given their backgrounds. Table 6.1 provides details regarding wealth position in 2000 by childhood religion. I include estimates for those who were raised Baptist, the largest conservative Protestant group represented in the data. I also include several mainline Protestant, Roman Catholic, and Jewish denominations. I do not include more detailed classifications because of space considerations and also because additional detail provides no new information. That is, the same story emerges when I use data from various years (different reporting years), for more detailed classifications, and when I group denominations differently.

The estimates in Table 6.1 demonstrate that there are very important differences in the percentage of people who are rich as adults given their religious upbringing. About 3 percent of the full sample are millionaires in 2000. However, only 1 percent of those who were Baptists during childhood are this wealthy. Similarly only

Table 6.1. *Religion and Wealth: Adult Wealth Ownership by Childhood Religious Affiliation*

| Childhood Religion | % Sample Total | % with Net Worth | | | | | Median Net Worth (Thousands) |
		> $1 Million	$500K–$999,999	$300K–$499,999	< $300K	Zero or Negative	
All	100	3	4	6	87	15	$58
Protestant	55						
Baptist	24	1	2	4	93	21	26
Episcopalian	2	12	11	7	70	7	120
Lutheran	8	2	6	6	86	11	83
Methodist	7	4	3	5	88	11	80
Presbyterian	3	4	9	9	78	11	101
Other Protestant	11	1	2	5	92	17	62
Catholic	32	2	6	8	84	10	79
Jewish	2	18	15	12	55	3	221
Other	6	2	3	4	91	19	34
None	5	3	2	5	90	18	40

2 percent of those raised Roman Catholic or Lutheran have become millionaires. For the Roman Catholics and Lutherans, getting rich more typically means having a slightly smaller fortune. For both groups, 6 to 9 percent have net worth in the next two wealth groups pictured (greater than $300,000 but less than $1 million). A slightly larger group of those raised Methodist or Presbyterian are millionaires, perhaps because of the residual effects of the wealth of prior generations. That is, given that mainline Protestants are the wealthy of prior generations, it is likely that when Methodists and Presbyterians inherit, they inherit greater amounts. The most striking difference again is in the percentage of those raised Jewish who are millionaires. A full 18 percent of Jewish youth owned more than $1 million in net worth in 2000.

CHILDHOOD RELIGION AND ASSET POVERTY

On the flip side, there are also important differences in the percentage of people who are asset poor as adults given their religious upbringing. There are many ways to define asset poverty, but a simple and very effective measure is having zero or negative net worth. Zero net worth means no savings net or debts, and negative net worth means that debts exceed the value of accumulated assets. This is an important indicator because it demonstrates that differences in vulnerability to the potential problems of not owning wealth are not evenly distributed across the population. Zero or negative net worth also indicates that saving and the accumulation of debt (which is necessary for net worth to be negative, of course) are not evenly distributed. I noted in Chapter One that 15 to 20 percent of the U.S. population has zero or negative net worth in most years, and the estimates in Table 6.1 demonstrate that representation in this lowest portion of the wealth distribution varies with childhood religion. In particular, Table 6.1 shows that for this sample in 2000, 15 percent of the respondents had no wealth. For those who were raised Baptist, 21 percent were asset poor. The group with the fewest asset-poor members was the Jewish group. In the middle of this continuum were the mainline Protestants and Roman Catholics. About 10 percent of each of these respondents were asset poor. One difference was the Episcopalians; only 7 percent of this group had no wealth.

Several patterns emerge from these estimates. First, conservative Protestants, such as Baptists, tend to be more likely than others to have no wealth and less likely to be very wealthy. In contrast, very few of the Jewish respondents had no wealth and a disproportionate percentage were very wealthy. Roman Catholics are very similar to mainline Protestants, consistent with other evidence that suggests these groups are diverging demographically in recent decades. However, it appears that Roman Catholics and Lutherans who have become rich have not become as rich as other mainline Protestants.

These patterns are evidence when within-group differences are compared in the same figure. Figure 6.2 provides a summary of the patterns that distinguish respondents by religious background. That is, this figure shows the percentage of respondents who have no wealth or have $500,000 to $999,999 in net worth in 2000, and the percentage of those who had $1 million or more in 2000, broken down by childhood religious affiliation. I argued that children raised as conservative

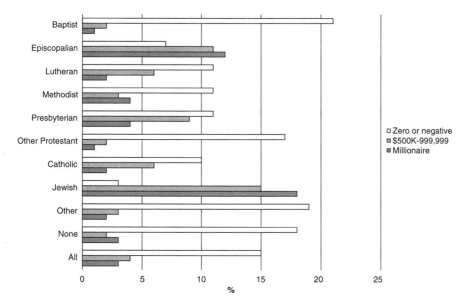

Figure 6.2. Childhood religion and adult net worth: Percentage in wealth groups. *Source:* National Longitudinal Survey of Youth, 1979 Cohort. $N = 4,963$. All wealth estimates are for the year 2000.

Protestants are likely to have less wealth as adults for several reasons, including higher fertility rates and lower levels of educational attainment. High fertility decreases adult wealth by reducing inheritance, making saving difficult, and reducing adult achievement. Decreased educational attainment, too, has both direct and indirect effects on wealth. Among other effects, education equips a person with skills and social contacts that increase the likelihood of investing and saving as well as improving investment quality. While the mechanisms by which conservative Protestants accumulate less wealth are not clear in this figure, it demonstrates wealth ownership patterns consistent with these arguments. Respondents raised as Baptists, the first group pictured in the figure, are significantly more likely than the overall sample to accumulate no wealth, and they are significantly less likely to become rich. In fact, those raised Baptist are the least likely group in the unadjusted estimates to either be millionaires or fall into the next highest wealth group.

In contrast, those raised as mainline Protestants, Roman Catholics, and particularly Jews are less likely to be asset poor and more likely to be rich than the average respondent. This is also consistent with the arguments I proposed in Chapter Four. Among other patterns, these groups achieve higher levels of education, tend to have lower fertility rates, and have higher incomes than average. Again, the estimates included in Figure 6.2 do not demonstrate that these patterns affect adult wealth (the estimates are definitely consistent with my arguments). As I have mentioned, it is a rather new phenomenon for mainline Protestants and Roman Catholics to be so similar demographically, but the evidence in Figure 6.2 suggests that on wealth ownership these groups are very similar. I will explore the mechanisms underlying these patterns in more detail in the remainder of this chapter.

CHILDHOOD RELIGION AND ADULT PORTFOLIO BEHAVIOR

One reason that total adult wealth varies across groups is that the components of total wealth vary. That is, families may own different types of assets – whether through saving, investment, or inheritance – which affects how much wealth they own overall. An important component of the portfolios of most Americans is the home. The home is a real (or tangible) asset that has use value as well as value as an investment. The home also generally provides long-term growth in assets that can be tapped in times of financial crisis. Of course, there are also tax advantages to homeownership, and government programs that make homeownership accessible to even poor families attempt to spread the benefits of investing in the primary residence across the entire population. Consistent with population estimates, nearly 70 percent of respondents in the NLS-Y were homeowners in 2000.

Table 6.2 shows that homeownership is spread rather evenly across the population, although there are some notable differences by religious background. This table includes estimates of the percentage of respondents who owned five assets, including the home, in 2000. For those who were raised as mainline Protestants and Roman Catholics,

Table 6.2. *Religion and Wealth: Adult Portfolio and Childhood Religious Affiliation*

	% Sample Total	Home	Stocks and Bonds	Checking and Savings	Trust Account	Business
			Percentage Owning			
All	100	68	26	77	5	11
Protestant	55					
Baptist	24	60	16	66	3	8
Episcopalian	2	68	38	86	10	6
Lutheran	8	78	30	90	5	16
Methodist	7	75	31	82	6	12
Presbyterian	3	80	35	85	4	7
Other Protestant	11	67	25	78	4	10
Catholic	32	70	30	81	5	10
Jewish	2	83	62	88	15	18
Other	6	63	24	70	6	13
None	5	64	26	72	6	11

these estimates suggest that Lutherans and Presbyterians are most likely to be homeowners. By contrast, only 60 percent of those raised Baptist were homeowners. Again, those who were raised Jewish tend to have higher rates of homeownership than other families. As Table 6.2 shows, more than 80 percent of those raised Jewish were homeowners in 2000. As I will demonstrate in a series of multivariate analyses later, however, the increased homeownership rate for Jewish families is reversed when I include controls for other processes that affect wealth accumulation.

Financial assets are also an important part of a wealth portfolio, and stocks and bonds are the financial instruments that a typical family is likely to own. While stocks and bonds can take a variety of forms, such as individual equities and mutual funds, I combine all stock and bond ownership in a single category in Table 6.2, because basic patterns tend to be the same for different types of stocks, bonds, and mutual funds. This table indicates that about 26 percent of all respondents own some type of stocks or bonds. Of those raised as Baptists, only 16 percent owned any stocks or bonds in 2000, while more than 60 percent of those raised Jewish owned these financial assets. Between these two extremes were the mainline Protestant and Roman

Catholics. In each of these groups, approximately one-third of respondents owned stocks and bonds. Those raised as Episcopalians
were most likely to be owners, but these groups were otherwise relatively consistent in the ownership of these financial assets. These
differences accounted for much of the overall differences in overall
wealth we saw earlier in this chapter, and these differences are likely
to exacerbate the between-group differences in wealth ownership as
the NLS-Y sample ages. Financial assets have historically increased
in value over long periods, and owners of financial assets such as
stocks tend to get rich must faster than those who do not own these
assets. As stock values increase, in particular, those who own stocks
tend to see very large increases in the value of their overall portfolios
(Keister 1997). As a result, those who do not own stocks fall farther
behind.

A much more commonly held financial asset is a checking or
savings account. While cash savings accounts such as these are less
critical to getting rich, ownership of these financial instruments does
provide insight into the saving patterns that are important for understanding group differences in wealth accumulation. Table 6.2 shows
that nearly 80 percent of the NLS-Y sample owned either a checking
or savings account in 2000. Again, this ownership rate is consistent
with estimates for the U.S. population. What is telling, however, is
that only 66 percent of those raised as Baptists owned cash savings
accounts. There are many reasons that people provide for not owning
a cash account, including distrust of banks and government financial
insurers and convenience (Kennickell, Starr-McCluer, and Sunden
1997). Information on reasons for owning particular financial instruments is not included in the NLS-Y, and information on religion
is not included in the Survey of Consumer Finances (which does
include information about why respondents do not have checking
and savings accounts). Cash savings accounts are relatively easy to
open and can be opened with very little money. Low ownership rates
for Baptists suggests a distrust of formal institutions, a distrust that
may extend to other types of savings and investments. This distrust
could have negative long-term effects on overall savings and wealth
because it is extremely difficult to save significant amounts of money

outside formal savings institutions. While there is no way to provide conclusive evidence for such arguments using these data, the
ownership patterns evident in Table 6.2 are consistent with these
suggestions.

To what extent can differences in adult wealth for these groups
be explained by differences in intergenerational transfers of wealth?
Receiving a trust account is an important indicator of the effect of
direct intergenerational transfers of financial resources. A trust account is an account established by one person, usually a parent or
older relative, for another person, usually a younger person. Receiving a trust account has obvious advantages in wealth accumulation,
and understanding how the receipt of intergenerational transfers such
as these varies can provide some answer to how people get rich. To
begin to answer this question, Table 6.2 also includes the percentage of NLS-Y respondents who ever receive a trust account. The
table shows that 5 percent of all respondents had received a trust
account. It is interesting to note that 3 percent of those who were
raised as Baptists inherited. Although this is lower than the overall
average, it is not significantly lower, suggesting that it is not intergenerational transfers alone that account for differences in adult wealth
by religious upbringing. Likewise, 10 percent of Episcopalians received trust accounts. This is twice the average for the entire sample,
but Episcopalians are not that much wealthier than other mainline
Protestants. Again, this suggests that other processes are important
in understanding adult wealth. One finding in this table is consistent
with other findings. That is, 15 percent of those raised Jewish receive
trust accounts. This finding suggests that, at least for Jewish families,
intergenerational processes are definitely important.

Yet the receipt of trust accounts is definitely balanced by the investment behaviors of the respondents themselves. The final column
in Table 6.2 shows the percentage of respondents who owned any
business assets in 2000. This includes both businesses owned entirely
by the respondent and investments in businesses owned primarily by
others. The variable as I use it here does confound entrepreneurial behavior with a specific type of investment behavior, but the patterns
are same when I disaggregate the variable. For the entire sample,

Table 6.3. *Childhood Religious Affiliation and Family Traits*

	% Sample Total	Siblings	Dad with Advanced Degree (%)	Mom with Advanced Degree (%)	Dad Full-Time worker (%)	Mom Full-Time Worker (%)
All	100	3.1	7	2	78	40
Protestant	55					
Baptist	24	3.5	2	1	70	41
Episcopalian	2	2.3	29	10	86	41
Lutheran	8	3.0	5	2	86	49
Methodist	7	2.7	8	3	78	39
Presbyterian	3	2.3	15	8	85	37
Other Protestant	11	3.2	7	1	77	37
Catholic	32	3.4	6	2	81	37
Jewish	2	1.7	42	7	87	20
Other	6	3.2	10	5	77	37
None	5	3.1	7	3	75	41

Note: All wealth estimates are for the year 2000.
Source: National Longitudinal Survey of Youth, 1979 Cohort ($N = 4,963$).

the mean percentage of respondents who owned a business was 11 percent. However, 18 percent of those raised Jewish owned business assets. By contrast, of those raised as Baptists, only 8 percent owned any business assets as adults. What is perhaps more interesting is that only 6 percent of Episcopalians and 7 percent of Presbyterians owned business assets. These patterns suggest that portfolio behavior clearly varies across these groups in ways that affect their overall wealth. These patterns also suggest that portfolio behavior is likely to tell only part of the story.

CHILDHOOD RELIGION AND CHILDHOOD FAMILY

In addition to portfolio behavior, family behaviors and processes in both childhood and adulthood are likely to account for at least part of the differences in wealth ownership by religious upbringing. We have already seen that childhood family structure and parents' education and work behavior affect children's adult wealth. But how do these background traits vary by family religion? Table 6.3 compares family traits by religion during childhood and demonstrates that there are, indeed, important patterns. The second column in the table shows the mean sibship size by family religion. While the variance in family size is relatively small, as it is in the U.S. population, there are important differences by religious affiliation. The average number of siblings for all respondents was 3.1, and mainline Protestants, too, tend to have had about three siblings. One exception is Episcopalians who came from slightly smaller families. The respondents who are more unusual are those raised Roman Catholic, Baptist, or Jewish. The Roman Catholics came from families slightly larger than average families. However, this slightly higher fertility is part of a larger pattern of decreasing fertility. In more recent years, Catholic fertility rates are approaching those of mainline Protestants (Sherkat and Ellison 1999). In fact, for the NLS-Y respondents themselves, fertility rates for Catholics and mainline Protestants are essentially identical. The table also demonstrates that Baptist families were also relatively large. In the case of Baptists, however, there has been much less change in family size in recent years. Finally, the table demonstrates that sibship size for those respondents raised in Jewish families was extremely low, reflecting consistently low Jewish fertility rates. Although there is evidence that fertility rates vary across Jewish denominations (Waxman 2001), sample size issues make it difficult to explore this using NLS-Y data. Waxman (2001) also demonstrates that family size for Jewish American families has declined since World War II, and this decline in family size is likely to increase the differences in wealth ownership and mobility that are already clear between Jewish and Protestant families.

Parents' achievement also varies with religion in ways that are likely to account for religious differences in wealth ownership. Table 6.3 shows the percentage of respondents' fathers and mothers who completed advanced degrees. I might have included other measures of parents' educational attainment, such as college degrees or high school graduation, but trends in the completion of advanced degrees are consistent with trends in the completion of other degrees. The table shows that, for all respondents, 7 percent of fathers had advanced degrees and 2 percent of mothers had advanced degrees. When we disaggregate the sample, it is clear that parental education differs dramatically by religious upbringing. Again, we see that mainline Protestants and Catholics are near the mean for the overall sample. Two important exceptions are the Episcopalians and Presbyterians. Episcopalians are particularly unique: nearly 30 percent of the fathers and 10 percent of the mothers of these respondents had advanced degrees. For the Presbyterians, 15 percent of the fathers and 8 percent of the mothers had completed some form of higher education. The most extreme difference, however, is fathers' attainment for respondents raised Jewish. More than 40 percent of those respondents had fathers with advanced degrees. Consistent with what we know from other research on Jewish families, however, mothers of the Jewish respondents were not as extreme as the fathers. Specifically, 7 percent of the Jewish respondents' mothers had advanced degrees, compared to 2 percent for all respondents.

Parents' work behavior is another childhood family trait that helps explain differences in adult wealth by religious upbringing. For the generation to which the NLS-Y respondents' parents belonged, a working father was generally a sign that the family was doing well financially. In contrast, a working mother was often, although not always, a sign of financial difficulty. Table 6.3 shows that there were important differences by religion in whether mothers and fathers worked full-time (measured when the respondent was aged 14 years), and these differences may help account for religious differences in wealth accumulation and mobility. For the entire sample, 78 percent of respondents' fathers worked full-time. Consistent with research on parents' work behavior, a relatively low percentage, only 70 percent, of Baptist respondents had a father who worked full-time. In contrast, for the mainline Protestant and Catholic respondents, at least 78 percent and usually a higher percentage of the fathers worked. For Jewish respondents, nearly 90 percent of the fathers worked.

Mothers' work behavior reveals a somewhat different story. For the entire sample, 40 percent of mothers worked when the respondent was 14 years old. For Baptists, 41 percent of mothers worked. Unlike other indicators, Baptists are not extreme on this measure for two reasons. First, traditional values in Baptist families discourage women from working. Second, low family income tends to push more women into work, and there is a higher incidence of poverty

Table 6.4. *Religion and Adult Attainment: Childhood Religious Affiliation and Adult Outcomes*

	% Sample Total	Education (Years)	Urban Resident (%)	Median Family Income (Thousands)
All	100	13.4	67%	50
Protestant	55			
Baptist	24	12.4	60	40
Episcopalian	2	15.0	73	62
Lutheran	8	13.7	64	55
Methodist	7	14.0	59	54
Presbyterian	3	14.3	68	54
Other Protestant	11	13.4	68	50
Catholic	32	13.4	73	55
Jewish	2	16.0	85	74
Other	6	13.4	60	43
None	5	13.0	66	50

Note: Income estimates are for the year 2000.
Source: National Longitudinal Survey of Youth, 1979 Cohort ($N = 4,963$).

among Baptists. These two trends likely offset each other and produce a relatively normal pattern of female work. For Jewish families, there is a relatively low incidence of mothers working. Consistent with previous research, only 20 percent of the mothers of Jewish respondents worked. The implications of these patterns for children's wealth accumulation, however, is likely to be consistent with other influences. For Baptists, high poverty and traditional values are likely to decrease attainment and reduce children's wealth. For Jewish families, high income, highly educated mothers, and working fathers are likely to increase attainment and lead to high levels of wealth accumulation and mobility. Multivariate analyses (discussed later) explore this in more depth.

CHILDHOOD RELIGION AND ADULT BEHAVIORS

Religion also affects wealth indirectly by shaping other adult outcomes. Differences in educational attainment by religious upbringing are particularly important to the conceptual arguments I made in Chapter Four, and Table 6.4 shows that patterns of education do vary as I argued they might. For the entire sample, average years of education completed by the 2000 survey was slightly more than 13. Baptists averaged slightly fewer years, while mainline Protestants and Catholics had attained 13.5 to 14 years of education. One outlier among the mainline Protestants was the Episcopalians who had attained 15 years of education on average. This slightly higher level of education for Episcopalians is consistent with the evidence I presented, which shows that these respondents had highly educated parents and were more likely than the average to receive a trust fund. While the Episcopalians do not emerge as unique in the multivariate analyses, these slightly different demographic patterns may suggest that future generations will see more distinct patterns of wealth accumulation for Episcopalians. Educational attainment for those raised Jewish is also quite high compared to the overall sample; Jewish respondents were extremely well educated, averaging 16 years of schooling. These patterns are consistent with other evidence of religious differences in education attainment (Lehrer 1999). There is some evidence that there are denominational differences in educational attainment within the Jewish community (Waxman 2001), but again, the NLS-Y data do not include large enough samples of Jewish families to disaggregate the sample further.

Patterns of residence can shape adult wealth ownership, particularly residence in urban areas where patterns of homeownership and real estate values can inflate or diminish the size of a portfolio. There are also likely to be differences in urban residence by religious affiliation during childhood. Table 6.4 shows that this is the case, indeed. Among all respondents in the full NLS-Y sample, 67 percent were urban residents. There is nothing particularly unique about the residential patterns of those raised mainline Protestant or Catholic. However there are notable differences for the Baptists and Jewish respondents. Slightly fewer of those who were raised Baptist lived in urban areas, and significantly more of the respondents who were raised in Jewish families lived in urban areas. While there is some concentration of Jewish respondents in New York City, there are representatives from various parts of the country. I also explain in the Appendix that I found no unique effect for residence in the multivariate models. It is difficult to determine from data of this sort whether the relationship between religion and residence is causal and, if so, to determine the direction of the causal relationship. That is, do people who are raised Baptist tend to live away from urban areas, or do more people living outside urban areas become Baptist? I disaggregate the sample in Table 6.4 by childhood religion and adult residence, because the order in which the events occur (childhood is first) suggests causality. However, as I will show later in this chapter, the correlation between childhood and adult religion is very high, and it is thus difficult to ascertain whether there is any real causal relationship. Moreover, there is little reason conceptually that there would be a causal relationship between childhood religion and adult residence, with the exception of family ties. That is, people tend to live near their families, and these ties may create pockets of people with the same religious affiliations.

In contrast to residence, family income is a very important component of the conceptual model I proposed, and Table 6.4 shows that income is certainly a critical intervening factor between religion and wealth. Median 2000 family income for all respondents was $50,000. Consistent with what we know about Baptists from other research, those raised in Baptist families had considerably lower median income at $40,000. Those raised as mainline Protestants and Catholics largely earned incomes at about the overall average. One exception was Episcopalians who, once again, were somewhat unique. The median income for respondents raised in Episcopalian families was $62,000, significantly higher than the overall mean, but not as high as the median for those raised in Jewish families. Again, this is consistent with the high levels of educational attainment for Episcopalians in this sample and might suggest interesting patterns of future wealth accumulation and mobility for this group. Those raised in Jewish families did earn substantially higher than average incomes. In fact, the median family income for Jewish respondents was $24,000 above the overall median. Clearly there is an effect of income differentials by religious background that is relevant to understanding differences in wealth ownership.

Table 6.5. *Adult Religion and Wealth*

Adult Religion	% with Net Worth					
	> $1 Million	$500K–$999,999	$300K–$499,999	> $300K	Zero or Negative	Median Assets (Thousands)
All	3	4	6	87	15	$58
Protestant						
Baptist	1	1	3	94	20	26
Episcopalian	7	8	14	71	8	115
Lutheran	2	5	7	86	9	90
Methodist	4	5	6	85	11	88
Presbyterian	6	9	9	77	11	121
Other Protestant	2	3	5	90	18	45
Catholic	2	7	9	82	11	90
Jewish	20	14	13	53	4	239
Other	3	4	5	87	18	40
None	2	3	5	90	11	44

Note: All wealth estimates are for the year 2000.
Source: National Longitudinal Survey of Youth, 1979 Cohort ($N = 4,963$).

ADULT RELIGION

My focus so far has been on *childhood* religion, and I began the chapter by documenting a series of relationships between childhood religious affiliation and adult wealth. Table 6.5 shows that there are similar relationships between *adult* religious affiliation and adult wealth. Comparing Tables 6.1 and 6.5, it is clear that adult wealth ownership is nearly identical when the sample is disaggregated by childhood religion and when it is disaggregated by adult religion. Only 1 percent of those who are Baptist as an adult are millionaires, compared with 3 percent of the total sample and 20 percent of adult Jews. About 4 percent of the full sample falls into the second highest wealth category (net worth of $500,000 to $999,999 in 2000). Only 2 percent of adult Baptists are wealthy enough to fall into that category, while 15 percent of those who consider themselves Jewish as adults are that wealthy. The median net worth for all respondents was $58,000, but it was only $26,000 for adult Baptists. In contrast, adult Jews owned more than $200,000 in net worth on average in 2000. In both of the top wealth categories, adults who are mainline Protestants

Table 6.6. *Childhood and Adult Religion:*
Correlations

Childhood Religion	Correlation with Same Adult Religion
Baptist	0.76
Episcopalian	0.65
Lutheran	0.71
Methodist	0.61
Presbyterian	0.58
Other Protestant	0.56
Catholic	0.77
Jewish	0.87
Other	0.54
None	0.36

Note: Reports are for the year 2000.
Source: National Longitudinal Survey of Youth, 1979
Cohort ($N = 4,963$).

and Catholics have net worth holdings that place them close to or slightly above the overall median. There are similar – but opposite – patterns at the other end of the wealth spectrum. Table 6.5 also includes the percentage of families who had zero or negative wealth in 2000. Fifteen percent of all respondents had zero or negative wealth, while 20 percent of Baptist respondents and only 4 percent of Jewish respondents were this asset poor.

The relationships between adult and childhood religious affiliation and adult wealth ownership are nearly identical at least partly because the correlation between childhood and adult religion is high. In fact the correlation between childhood religion and adult religion is high for all religious groups, particularly for those raised in Jewish and Baptist families. Table 6.6 shows that the correlation is at least 0.5 for all groups. For Baptists, Lutherans, and Catholics, the correlation is between 0.7 and 0.8. Because Judaism is an ethnicity as well as a religion, it is not surprising that the correlation between being Jewish as a child and as an adult is nearly 0.9. For both Baptists and Jews, high rates of intermarriage combine with high correlations between childhood and adult religious affiliation to exacerbate trends across generations. That is, if there is an effect of religion on the strategies of action people use to approach important decisions, and if members of particular groups marry others inclined toward the same strategies, these strategies are likely to be reinforced. I do not parse out these effects here, but they are important subjects for future research. While these high correlations explain the similarity between the estimates in Tables 6.1 and 6.5, they also make it difficult to parse out the separate effects of childhood and adult religious experiences on outcomes such as wealth. For this reason, I do not present multivariate estimates linking adult religious affiliation to wealth. As I discuss in the Appendix, the results are virtually identical to the results I present linking childhood religion and adult wealth.

Multivariate Results: Childhood Religion and Adult Wealth

Multivariate analyses corroborate the patterns that emerged in the descriptive statistics relating religion and wealth. That is, they provide additional support for the argument that people raised in conservative Protestant families tend to accumulate less wealth and to be less upwardly mobile than those raised in other families, while people raised in Jewish families accumulate more wealth and are more upwardly mobile.

In Chapter Five, I presented results from multivariate analyses exploring the effects of family background and other traits on adult wealth. Those models also included indicators of childhood religious background. I did not discuss the results related to religion in Chapter Five, but the same models I discussed there do provide clear evidence that there is a strong effect of religious upbringing on adult wealth, net of other individual and family traits. Table 6.7 reports generalized least squares estimates of net worth with the indicators of inheritance omitted from the equation. The effect of the religious factors was much stronger before I added the controls. I do not include the "gross" results because the fully specified models reflect the true underlying process more accurately.

Table 6.7. *Childhood Religion and Adult Assets, 1985–2000*

	Childhood Religion	Add Education
Family religion in childhood		
Jewish	138.52***	124.08***
	(17.80)	(17.80)
Baptist	−8.79**	−12.33**
	(4.83)	(4.87)
Other conservative Protestant	−6.65**	−12.09**
	(2.88)	(5.91)
Respondent's education		
High school	–	17.85***
		(4.86)
Some college	–	34.11***
		(5.72)
College degree	–	57.58***
		(6.64)
Advanced degree	–	74.57***
		(7.41)

Note: These are PARTIAL MODELS; other test variables and control variables are included but not displayed. See Appendix for full models. Cells are coefficient estimates with standard errors in parentheses.

$*p < .10; **p < .05; ***p < .01.$

Source: National Longitudinal Survey of Youth, 1979 Cohort.

The Appendix provides detailed descriptions of these models and the measures of religion that I include in them. The complete models for Tables 6.7 and 6.8 are also included in the Appendix. Briefly, in the multivariate models I report, I included indicators of whether the respondent was raised Baptist, in another conservative Protestant denomination, or Jewish. The omitted category is all other religious affiliations. I based my classification of Protestants largely on categories used by Lehrer (1999) and Lehrer and Chiswick (1993). I did not include indicators that the respondent was raised mainline Protestant or Roman Catholic because these measures were not significantly different from zero in similar models and exploratory analyses. I did not include measures for underrepresented religious groups such as Muslims or for Jewish denominations, because sample sizes for these groups were too small. What is perhaps most important is that the

Table 6.8. *Childhood Religion and Adult Assets, 1985–2000*

Childhood Religion	Ever Inherited	Received a Trust Account	Own a Home	Own Stocks
Jewish	0.53***	0.34**	−0.41***	0.22**
	(0.10)	(0.16)	(0.11)	(0.11)
Baptist	−0.27***	−0.07	−0.02***	−0.31***
	(0.03)	(0.08)	(0.01)	(0.04)
Other conservative Protestant	−0.08***	−0.18**	−0.10***	−0.10**
	(0.03)	(0.07)	(0.03)	(0.04)

Note: These are PARTIAL MODELS; other test variables and control variables are included but not displayed. See Appendix for full models. Cells are logistic coefficient estimates with standard errors in parentheses.
* $p < .10$; ** $p < .05$; *** $p < .01$.
Source: National Longitudinal Survey of Youth, 1979 Cohort.

regression models were extremely robust to various categorizations of religious groups and subgroups, numerous alternative definitions of wealth and wealth mobility, and various model estimation methods. Across innumerable combinations of variable definitions and model specifications, the patterns I report here were clear. I do not report separate multivariate analyses using measures of adult religious affiliation in place of the measures of childhood religious affiliation because the high correlations between childhood and adult religion (reported earlier) make the results essentially indecipherable.

The first model shown in Table 6.7 includes measures of childhood religion but does not control for education in order to demonstrate the base effect of religion. I also did not include inheritance measures in this model to demonstrate the relationship between religion in childhood without considering the role that assets acquired from prior generations have on adult wealth. As my conceptual model predicts, the relationship between being raised in a Jewish family and adult net worth is significantly greater than zero. In fact, the coefficient estimate for Jewish religious affiliation in childhood is more than 7 times greater than its standard error. The second model pictured in Table 6.7 also controls for the respondent's educational attainment. The effect of education on wealth accumulation is quite strong and increases with the level of education achieved. Adding education controls to the model does somewhat decrease the effect of the religion indicators (confirmed with Cox tests), but the strong positive effect of being raised in a Jewish family remains. In models included in the Appendix, I also added other adult traits and inheritance indicators, and the relative size, direction, and significance of the religion indicators remained.

The estimates shown in Table 6.7 provide evidence that (1) being raised Jewish increases adult wealth accumulation and mobility, even controlling for financial resources, family background, and other important individual and family predictors of wealth; (2) being raised Jewish increases adult wealth and mobility at least partly because of its effect on educational attainment; and (3) there is a direct effect of being raised Jewish on adult wealth and wealth mobility that remains after controlling for a host of other predictors of wealth.

The results presented in Table 6.7 also provide support for my proposal that being raised in a conservative Protestant family decreases adult wealth and wealth mobility. The first model in the table shows that there is a strong, significant, and negative effect of the two indicators of being raised in a conservative Protestant church, before controlling for education. The second model demonstrates that the effect remains after controlling for education. Again, in models shown in the Appendix, I also include an additional set of indicators of adult traits and inheritance, and these do not change the results I present in Table 6.7. Together these analyses provide support for claims that (1) being raised conservative Protestant decreases adult wealth accumulation and mobility, even controlling for financial resources, family background, and other important individual and family predictors of wealth; (2) being raised conservative Protestant decreases adult wealth and mobility at least partly because of its effect on educational attainment; and (3) there is a direct effect of being raised conservative Protestant on adult wealth and wealth mobility that remains after controlling for a host of other predictors of wealth.

To what extent does inheritance account for these patterns? The results in Table 6.7 and related models in the Appendix show that inheritance is positively associated with net worth. But to what extent are there religious differences in inheritance? Table 6.8 includes coefficient estimates from logistic regression models predicting (1) the likelihood that the respondent ever received an inheritance and (2) the likelihood that the respondent ever received a trust account, both as a function of childhood religious affiliation and all control variables. Again, the full models are included in the Appendix.

Consistent with my conceptual model, those who were raised in Jewish families were significantly more likely to ever receive an inheritance. Likewise, affiliation with a conservative Protestant faith in childhood was negatively associated with receiving an inheritance. Similarly, there is a positive relationship between being raised Jewish and receiving a trust account. The negative relationship between being raised in non-Baptist conservative Protestant churches is still present in models of receiving a trust, but the effect of being raised Baptist is not present in this model. The relationship between being raised Baptist and receiving a trust account was present in preliminary models, but adding parents' educational attainment to the models eliminated the significant effect. This underscores the fact that measures of intergenerational transfers are strongly related to measures of parents' achievement, and it is difficult to disentangle the effects of these influences.

Multivariate Results: Religion and Wealth Portfolios

What other factors might account for the relationship between religion and wealth ownership? Asset allocation, or portfolio behavior, is certainly an important contributing factor. *Asset allocation* refers to decisions about how to save money that a family is able to save or invest. The most simple distinctions in asset allocation are between real assets and financial assets, and decisions within each of these categories vary in the degree to which they are risky with riskier assets typically creating higher returns. Table 6.8 also includes logistic regression coefficient estimates for models predicting (1) the likelihood of homeownership and (2) the likelihood of owning stocks and bonds. Purchasing a home is traditionally one of the first major investments Americans make, and homeownership, though it can be lucrative, is a relatively low risk investment. These results suggest that both those raised Jewish and those raised conservative Protestant are less likely than other families to purchase a home.

Lower homeownership rates for conservative Protestants likely contribute to the relatively small portfolios that people raised in these faiths amass, but how does lower homeownership affect the portfolios of Jews? That is, if homeownership is such an important part of a strong wealth portfolio, and controlling for other factors, if the propensity of Jewish families to own homes is low why do these families still amass more wealth than the average family? Part of the answer is that when Jewish families do own homes, they tend to be in urban areas (Table 6.4) and thus more valuable (Table 6.2).

However, an even more important explanation is the propensity of Jews to invest in financial assets. In contrast to the effects of child-hood religion on adult homeownership, the findings presented in Table 6.8 show that those raised Jewish are much *more* likely than others to own stocks or bonds, while conservative Protestants are *less* likely to be owners of stocks or bonds. Moreover, the paths people take during their financial lives can also impact adult wealth in critical ways. For instance, saving early in life can disproportion-ately affect adult wealth because of compounding. Naturally, early saving in high-return financial instruments can have an even more noticeable impact. An important part of the financial repertoire that children learn, and that can be associated with the family's religious preferences, is a propensity to begin saving early or to save in particu-lar ways. There is evidence that those raised as Jewish begin to invest in financial assets early in life and continue to invest in these assets more heavily than average throughout the life, even controlling for other individual and family factors that shape wealth ownership. In contrast, very few of those raised as conservative Protestants follow this final path, and mainline Protestants and Catholics are also less likely than Jews to accumulate assets in this way (Keister 2003a). It is this pattern of financial wealth ownership, and the ability of financial assets to increase the value of total wealth, that accounts for the increase in overall wealth for Jews, even in the presence of lower homeownership rates. These results also imply that the repertoire of skills and decision-making abilities learned in childhood may very well set a course of action that ultimately translates into high wealth.

OTHER ASPECTS OF FAMILY CULTURE

Family culture during childhood does appear to affect the skills children use to approach important life decisions. If we grant that religion is an important aspect or indicator of family culture, the results noted earlier suggest that culture does shape adult wealth accumulation and mobility. Of course there are other aspects of family culture that are also likely to be important influences on the repertoire of skills that children use in decision making in both childhood and adulthood. Measuring these, however, is extremely difficult and will need to be the task of future research.

Financial literacy is one of the keys to doing well as an adult, and it is likely that people at least begin to learn their financial skills during childhood from the adults they see dealing with money. Part of my argument about religion is that elements of family culture, which are embodied in religious beliefs and practices, shape financial literacy and the skills with which people approach financial decision making. I do not provide direct empirical estimates of variance in financial literacy because it is such a diffuse concept and because the data sets that contain wealth information do not contain information on financial literacy. The popular book *Rich Dad, Poor Dad* (Kiyosaki and Lechter 2000) is based on a similar notion that the wealthy teach their children lessons that others do not. The book is a guidebook for improving your own financial literacy; it is not an empirical study. Yet it does outline the lessons that children learn to varying degrees in the family of origin. Skills such as paying yourself first, tolerating a certain amount of risk to enjoy the rewards that high-risk financial instruments provide, and saving early in life all contribute to wealth and may be learned at home.

There is some empirical evidence that for financial information and advice, people rely on those they know, particularly family and friends (Chang 2002). It is also likely that some of the effect of education on adult wealth reflects financial skills that are learned in formal education, either in courses or by being exposed to others with a different set of skills for managing money. Again, however, these are not mechanisms that I can explore empirically with the data I use here. Future research may be able to uncover the exact nature of the relationship among religion, other elements of family culture, financial literacy, and adult wealth.

Conclusion

In this chapter, I argued that religion is an important determinant of wealth accumulation and mobility, and I identified important patterns in the relationship between religion and wealth that isolate the mechanisms underlying these relationships. I argued in Chapter Four that religious affiliation in childhood can shape action indirectly by altering fertility and marriage behavior, educational attainment, work behavior, and other behaviors and processes that influence wealth ownership. However, I also argued that religion is an important element of culture. As such, religion directly affects wealth accumulation by defining the goals people identify as important, by creating a repertoire of skills and knowledge that people draw on when making decisions, and by determining the nature of people's social contacts. When they are exposed to religious ceremonies, rituals, and values, people develop a set of competencies and habits that they draw on while making decisions about consumption, saving, and investment. Affiliation with a religious group also creates social capital that may improve understanding of saving and investing and may actually provide investment opportunities.

I identified distinct patterns in the relationship between religious affiliation and wealth ownership. Those who were raised Jewish owned considerably more wealth than others. I showed that those who were raised Jewish are more likely to receive an inheritance, and I demonstrated that Jews own more high-risk, high-return financial assets than others and that Jews are relatively less likely to own a house. Both findings are consistent with the argument that, for historic reasons, Jews have a preference for human capital and other types of capital that are transportable rather than fixed. I also found evidence of a distinct negative relationship between affiliation with a conservative Protestant church and wealth ownership. In direct contrast to Jews, conservative Protestants owned less overall wealth and fewer financial assets. Through most of the chapter, I focused on those who were raised as Baptist, but the results are the same for other conservative Protestant denominations.

By focusing on the relationship between religion and wealth, I do not intend to reduce the complex process of wealth accumulation or wealth inequality to a single set of inputs. In the full conceptual model I propose in Chapter Four and in other portions of this book, I show that wealth accumulation and mobility are the result of various interacting processes, including family structure, marital behavior, and union separation, and aggregate processes, such as demographic trends, market fluctuations, and policy shifts. The results that I present in this chapter, however, highlight an important part of the picture. Understanding that religion is related in critical ways to wealth accumulation, net of its indirect effects on other demographic behaviors, casts light on the importance of family processes that shape the way people behave and, in this case, the way they accumulate assets.

CHAPTER SEVEN

WORK AND OCCUPATIONS

Individual behaviors and processes naturally affect wealth accumulation and mobility apart from the effects of family and family background that have been the subject of the past two chapters. However, the nature of the relationship between individual actions and wealth accumulation can be complex. In this chapter, I focus on the portions of the conceptual model (Figure 4.1) that relate to individuals and their work experiences. Figure 7.1 highlights the portion of the full conceptual model that is the focus of this chapter. The highlighted portions of the model include adult work experiences and job characteristics. I have also highlighted the portion of the model that includes individual traits such as ability, ambition, and early-life behaviors. The focus of the chapter is work and occupational effects on wealth, but I do discuss some individual inputs in the chapter's final section. My objective is to demonstrate how my conceptual model works. Moreover, there is not enough room in a single chapter to explore each of these factors in depth, even though the analyses I present later in the chapter include indicators of as many of these factors as possible.

THE IMPORTANCE OF WORK AND JOBS

Rather than discussing all individual traits that shape wealth accumulation and mobility, I concentrate on elements of work behavior that affect adult wealth. I ask whether there are occupational differences in wealth ownership and what factors account for patterns that emerge. I explore the role that recent increases in nonstandard

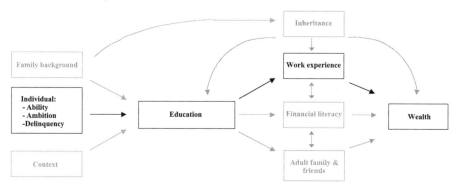

Figure 7.1. Individuals and wealth.

work, such as temporary work, plays in shaping adult wealth owner-ship. I then ask what role entrepreneurship plays in creating wealth. The role of entrepreneurship, or self-employment, is particularly im-portant because it is among the most direct ways to determine the de-gree to which it is possible to get rich in the United States. I show that entrepreneurs do own more wealth, but this does not necessarily im-ply that they are upwardly mobile or that upward mobility in wealth ownership is possible. That is, while the potential advantages of en-trepreneurship are undeniable, it is not clear whether the benefits of self-employment are accessible to most people. Many workers would like to become self-employed, and there is evidence that workers are willing to overlook the high stakes of leaving a stable position to attempt a business start-up (Aldrich 1999). At any single time, only about 10 percent of the U.S. labor force is considered self-employed. However, a much larger number of workers have experimented with self-employment or express an interest in becoming self-employed. In fact, between 30 and 40 percent of workers have been self-employed at some point during their careers, and nearly 60 percent intend to start a business eventually (Steinmetz and Wright 1989).

To really understand getting rich, it is necessary to also know whether those who become entrepreneurs are simply richer to be-gin with. Adjudicating between these two scenarios is central to understanding wealth mobility. If entrepreneurs are wealthy because they started with more financial resources, we can conclude that a significant number of the wealthy are rich because they had financial advantages when they started. If, however, entrepreneurs did not start with more resources, and if, other factors held constant, self-employment leads to more wealth, the conclusion would be that at least a significant portion of the self-employed wealthy created their wealth. Answering this question is an important objective of this chapter.

In this chapter, I continue to use data from the National Longitudinal Survey of Youth, 1979 Cohort (NLS-Y). However, I also use a unique new data set, the Panel Study of Entrepreneurial Dynamics (see Appendix for detailed description of the data) to understand the complex relationship between entrepreneurship and wealth ownership. The results are rather surprising and certainly instructive.

Occupations

Researchers have shown in many contexts that a person's occupation determines a great deal about their salary or wages and other benefits such as pension plans, health care, and life insurance. Because each of these also shapes saving and asset accumulation, it should not be surprising that adult wealth varies in important ways with occupation. Figure 7.2 illustrates how total adult assets vary across a set of broadly defined occupational categories. These estimates are from the NLS-Y and are for the year 2000. The estimates in this figure are rather simple but also quite insightful. I grouped respondents into seven occupation categories on the basis of much more detailed information about their jobs and job classifications. Although I could have defined the categories in a host of different ways, I found that the general patterns were similar across different definitions. The figure shows that there are tremendous differences in median net worth (total assets less total debts) for these groups. It is particularly noteworthy that laborers have, on average, almost no accumulated net worth. The median for the lowest group shown here is $19,000. Clerks and craftspeople have saved slightly more than laborers, and both groups have median wealth approximately equal to the overall median for the population. At the other extreme are professionals

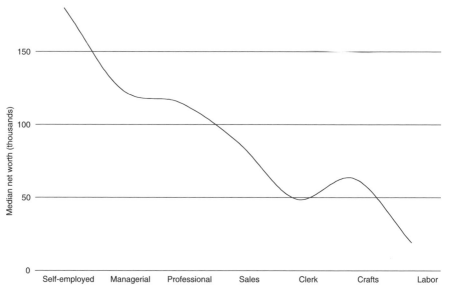

Figure 7.2. Work and wealth. *Source*: National Longitudinal Survey of Youth, 1979 Cohort. $N = 4,963$. All wealth estimates are for the year 2000.

and those in managerial positions. Median net worth for these groups was $125,000 and $115,000, respectively, well above the total sample median of $58,000.

Perhaps most striking in Figure 7.2 are the self-employed individuals. The median net worth for this group is $180,000, clearly the highest in the sample. Yet only 1 percent of the sample is self-employed. The broad category that I have labeled "self-employed" includes all people who were not employees of a separate entity but who, in some way, earned money to support themselves. This is clearly a unique group, and the large size of their wealth holdings is consistent with the idea that entrepreneurship leads to high levels of wealth accumulation. Of course, this does not rule out the possibility that this group was rich from the start, and I will explore that possibility in more detail later in this chapter. But establishing that entrepreneurs have accumulated a relatively large amount of wealth is an important first step. The findings in this table were robust to various definitions of self-employment, and they are consistent with patterns that emerge in other research on entrepreneurs.

Similar trends are evident when the wealthy are isolated. Table 7.1 illustrates the percentage of people who had high net worth by occupation. This figure also reports estimates from the 2000 NLS-Y and shows that there were no extremely wealthy labors and very few very wealthy craftspeople, clerks, or salespeople. In fact 99 percent of the laborers, 97 percent of the craftspeople, and 94 percent of the clerks had net worth in the lowest category (less than $300,000), and up to 20 percent of these people had zero or negative net worth. What is perhaps more surprising, again, is the degree to which the self-employed respondents are represented in the highest wealth groups. More than 13 percent of the self-employed were millionaires, and 16 percent had net worth greater than $500,000 but less than $1 million. This supports the common perception that self-employment can be a way to get rich. It is also noteworthy, however, that 11 percent of the self-employed respondents had zero or negative net worth. This suggests that self-employment is not a guaranteed ticket to wealth, and it raises questions about who the self-employed are.

The self-employed do appear to have unique wealth accumulation patterns, even though their patterns of human capital accumulation and the help they receive from other generations are rather average. Table 7.2 uses the NLS-Y to compare the education levels and wealth portfolio behavior of the entrepreneurs to that of people in other occupations. The table also shows that the mean education for the entire sample is 13 years, and it is 14 years for the self-employed. Similarly, managers have 14 years of education on average. The group that is unique on educational attainment is the professionals who, partly by definition, have more education than the other groups. However, the self-employed are considerably more likely than the typical respondents to own a home, stocks and bonds, and a checking or savings account. In the entire sample, 68 percent of respondents were homeowners, 26 percent owned some form of stocks and bonds, and 77 percent owned a checking or savings account. In contrast, of the self-employed respondents, more than 80 percent were homeowners, nearly one-half owned stocks or bonds, and 87 percent had a checking or savings account. Self-employed respondents do

Table 7.1. *Occupation and Wealth*

	%Sample Total	>$1 Million	$500K–$999,999	$300K–$499,999	<$300K	Zero or Negative	Median Net Worth (Thousands)
			% With Net Worth				
All	100	3	4	6	87	15	$58
Self-employed	1	13	16	10	61	11	180
Managerial	12	7	9	10	74	7	124
Professional	17	4	7	8	81	10	115
Sales	3	3	9	10	77	12	88
Clerk	12	1	2	3	94	15	49
Crafts	8	0	1	2	97	10	63
Labor	1	0	0	1	99	22	19

Note: All wealth estimates are for the year 2000. Those in occupations not specified are not included. Self-employed individuals can be in any occupation.

Source: National Longitudinal Survey of Youth, 1979 Cohort ($N = 4,963$).

Table 7.2. *Occupation, Education, and Asset Ownership*

| | % Sample Total | Education (Mean Years) | Percentage Owning | | | | |
			Home	Stocks and Bonds	Checking and Savings	Trust Account	Business
All	100	13	68	26	77	5	11
Self-employed	1	14	83	49	87	8	89
Managerial	12	14	79	40	88	7	13
Professional	17	16	77	39	89	6	11
Sales	3	13	75	37	86	4	10
Clerk	12	13	65	20	80	4	9
Crafts	8	12	75	18	75	5	12
Labor	1	12	58	13	65	2	8

Note: Wealth ownership estimates are for the year 2000. Those in occupations not specified are not included. Self-employed individuals can be in any occupation.

Source: National Longitudinal Survey of Youth, 1979 Cohort ($N = 4,963$).

report much higher rates of business ownership than the average respondent, but again, this difference is largely definitional. Perhaps most interesting and most important is that 8 percent of the self-employed, compared with 5 percent of the total sample, had ever received a trust account. Moreover, the difference is not statistically significant, suggesting that at least in the descriptive statistics, the entrepreneurs were no more likely than the average respondent to have access to gifted funds.

There is also a tradition in sociology of looking at intergenerational mobility using father's occupation as the starting point (Blau and Duncan 1967; Sewell and Hauser 1975). The normal endpoint would be the child's occupation, but as Table 7.3 shows, some interesting patterns appear when the child's wealth is the outcome. That is, Table 7.3 asks again how respondents' wealth varies by occupation, but in this table, occupation refers to the respondent's father's occupation. Again, these estimates are from the NLS-Y and use wealth information for the year 2000. The row labeled "all" includes all respondents, but I omitted some relatively small occupational categories from the table. As a result, the column labeled "percent of sample total" does not sum to 100. Because it is unclear from the information in this survey whether the father was self-employed, I

Table 7.3. *Father's Occupation and Child's Adult Wealth*

| | % Sample Total | Education (Mean Years) | % With Net Worth | | | | | Median Net Worth (Thousands) |
			> $1 Million	$500K–$999,999	$300K–$499,999	< $300K	Zero or Negative	
All	100	13	3	4	6	87	15	$58
Managerial	13	14	7	6	9	78	11	109
Professional	10	15	6	8	9	77	9	116
Sales	4	14	4	7	9	80	9	89
Clerk	5	13	2	6	6	86	11	74
Crafts	20	12	1	4	5	90	14	60
Labor	25	12	1	3	5	91	17	44

Note: All wealth estimates are for the year 2000. Those in occupations not specified are not included.
Source: National Longitudinal Survey of Youth, 1979 Cohort (N = 4,963).

do not include entrepreneurs in the occupational groups. However, in the analyses later in this chapter, I explore how having families and friends who are entrepreneurs affects movement into entrepreneurship. The estimates in this table show that the majority of respondents had fathers who were laborers or craftsmen and that these people were not particularly upwardly mobile. That is, 25 percent of respondents had fathers who were laborers, and only 1 percent of those became millionaires by the time they were adults. Likewise, 20 percent of respondents had fathers who were craftsmen, and again, only 1 percent of those became millionaires by the time they were adults.

These relationships between occupations and wealth provide initial insight into the role that work and job traits play in the wealth accumulation process. For instance, in order to understand who gets rich, it is useful to know that the self-employed are much richer on average than others. If there is mobility, and if self-employment is one way to get rich, it is necessary to know that the self-employed are, indeed, richer than others. The descriptive statistics relating occupation to wealth show that the self-employed are, indeed, wealthier than people in other occupations. It is also useful to know that laborers and those in craft-oriented occupations tend to be asset poor on average. In contrast to self-employment, these occupations are clearly not associated with high wealth. In contrast, respondents in the less wealthy occupations appear to accumulate more debt than assets, on average. They also tend to be less likely than the average respondent in the NLS-Y to be a homeowner, to own stock, and even to own a checking or savings account. Of course, these occupations require less education than professional and managerial occupations. Labor and craft positions also pay relatively low wages and generally provide benefits with lower value than the other occupations included in the tables. The degree to which the occupation itself versus other traits of the job account for wealth differences is the subject of the remainder of this chapter.

That is, while these patterns provide some information about the role that work plays in wealth accumulation, the descriptive statistics raise at least three additional questions about the relationship between work and wealth. The first question is whether there is

something else unique about the type of work that people perform
in their occupations that is responsible for the differences. In particular, recent increases in nonstandard employment practices, such
as temporary work, might affect how work and wealth are related. I
explore this question in the next section. The second, and related,
question is whether entrepreneurs simply start with more capital that
allows them to become self-employed or whether their wealth gains
reflect wealth accumulation net of starting values. I explore this question in the following section. Finally, the third question is whether
occupational status and work practices affect wealth independently
or whether these patterns reflect income differences across the jobs.
That is, is there something about some occupations or the type of
work that people perform that affects their portfolio behavior or the
value of a person's assets or debts? Or does the relationship between
occupation and wealth, for example, largely reflect occupational differences in income and benefits? I explore this question in multivariate analyses presented later in this chapter.

Nonstandard Work

Recent changes in the way Americans work suggest that an important and growing segment of the labor force may, in fact, be accumulating assets in ways that are unique and potentially important to understanding trends in wealth accumulation. In particular,
the proliferation of nonstandard employment practices is well documented (Houseman 1997; Kalleberg 2000; Tilly 1996), but there is a
continuing controversy about how these arrangements affect workers (Appelbaum 1992; Blank 1998; Callaghan and Hartman 1991).
During the 1970s, both workers and the firms that employed
them began to demand greater flexibility in work arrangements
(Houseman 2001b; Kalleberg 2000). Firms began to demand a more
adaptable labor force in order to deal with increasing global competition and changes in technology (Cappelli 1999; Lee 1996). During the 1970s and 1980s, increasing numbers of married women
and older people in the labor force increased demand for jobs
that were part-time, temporary, or otherwise not traditional, permanent employment relations. As I noted in Chapter Four, there is

evidence that approximately one-fourth of U.S. workers have some type of nonstandard job, and more than 30 percent of female workers hold nonstandard positions (Cassirer Forthcoming; Kalleberg 2000).

Workers who accept nonstandard positions may have relatively more flexibility in scheduling their work, the freedom to discontinue one job without giving up all of their income, and opportunities to evaluate potential employers before agreeing to a permanent position (Kalleberg 2000). Yet there are also important drawbacks associated with nonstandard work arrangements that are relevant to understanding the way these workers accumulate wealth. Wages for nonstandard workers are relatively poor, and job stability is lower in nonstandard than in permanent, full-time positions (Houseman and Polivka 2000; Segal and Sullivan 1997). Workers in nonstandard jobs are less likely than full-time workers to have health insurance through their employers or from any source (Cassirer Forthcoming; Houseman 2001a). Those in nonstandard jobs are much less likely to have pensions and generally do not qualify for unemployment benefits (Houseman 2001a; Kalleberg et al. 1997).

An important benefit of owning assets is that assets can be used to finance spending during retirement. During retirement, assets provide a reserve that can be drawn on as a source of regular income or to fund emergencies, and in recent decades, retirees have increasingly turned to their assets to finance expenditures. If nonstandard workers accumulate fewer assets, they are likely to be left behind in retirement. This disadvantage will be exacerbated for today's workers if social security benefits are limited in the future. Nonstandard workers are also seldom protected by unions (Kalleberg, Reskin, and Hudson 2000). Moreover, because they do not meet minimal hours of service requirements, nonstandard workers are typically not covered by the Family Medical Leave Act or the Occupational Safety and Health Act (Carnevale, Jennings, and Eisenmann 1998; Houseman 2001a). While these drawbacks of nonstandard work may not directly affect asset accumulation, they may force nonstandard workers out of the labor force more often than other workers, which will result in lower lifetime income and savings.

More directly, because nonstandard workers receive lower incomes and usually do not qualify for pension benefits, they are likely to accumulate both pension assets and other assets differently than traditional workers. They may accumulate relatively more assets in somewhat more flexible financial instruments such as housing, stocks, or Individual Retirement Accounts, or they may miss out on individual retirement saving altogether. If nonstandard employment reduces asset accumulation on average, it does not necessarily follow that all nonstandard workers will be affected equally. In reality, asset accumulation is likely to vary with the type of employment as well as such factors as worker traits, work history, and employer traits.

Although a complete exploration of the role that nonstandard work plays in wealth accumulation is beyond the scope of this book, trends in wealth ownership for this may be an important component of the relationship between work and wealth. Table 7.4 compares the asset accumulation patterns of an important segment of the nonstandard worker population, temporary workers, to the rest of the NLS-Y sample. I chose to focus on temporary workers because they are one of the largest groups of nonstandard workers and because the NLS-Y includes sufficient numbers of these workers. Wealth estimates in this table are for the year 2000, and "temporary work" refers to the number of weeks the respondent spent in temporary work between 1984 and 2000. The table shows that workers who spent no time in temporary work had a median net worth of $68,000, a full $10,000 greater than the sample median. However, the median net worth declines with the number of weeks spent in temporary work. For those who spent a year or less in temporary work, median net worth is $45,000. For those who spent one to two years in temporary work, the median is $43,000, and it is $40,000 for those who were temporary workers for more than two years. The differences within the temporary-worker categories are only marginally statistically different from each other. However, the difference in net worth between temporary workers and those workers who spent no time in temporary work is a statistically significant difference.

Temporary workers are also underrepresented among the wealthy and underrepresented among the asset poor. Table 7.4 shows that

Table 7.4. *Nonstandard Work and Wealth*

			% With Net Worth				
	% Sample Total	< $1 Million	$500K–$999,999	$300K–$499,999	< $300K	Zero or Negative	Median Net Worth (Thousands)
All	100	3	4	6	87	15	$58
Time in temporary jobs							
None	64	5	6	7	82	12	68
One year or less	25	1	4	5	90	18	45
One to two years	8	1	3	3	93	18	43
Two or more years	3	1	2	2	95	19	40

Note: "Temporary work" refers to the number of weeks spent in temporary work between 1984 and 2000. "One to two years" includes those who spent 52 through 103 weeks in temporary work. Wealth estimates are for the year 2000.

Source: National Longitudinal Survey of Youth, 1979 Cohort ($N = 4,963$).

5 percent of workers who spent no time in temporary positions between the mid-1980s and the year 2000 are millionaires, 6 percent have assets between $500,000 and $1 million, and another 7 percent have between $300,000 and $500,000 in wealth. In each of these categories, workers who did not spend time in temporary work are better represented than the average NLS-Y respondent. In contrast, those who spent time as temporary workers are underrepresented in each of the wealth categories compared to both the full sample and to those who were never temporary workers. By contrast, temporary are over-represented in the group of people who have zero or negative net worth. In the full sample, 15 percent of respondents reported that their assets had no value or that they had more debt than assets. Only 12 percent of those who never worked as temporary workers were this asset poor, but at least 18 percent of each group of temporary workers had zero or negative net worth.

The implications of these patterns are that a large and growing segment of the population is saving and accumulating relatively slowly. To the extent to which workers increasingly rely on personal savings to finance retirement, these workers will be at a disadvantage in retirement. In terms of wealth accumulation and mobility more generally, this group of workers may be important if they accumulate assets differently even when other factors are held constant. Again, it is possible that the effect of nonstandard work, particularly temporary employment, on wealth is mediated largely by income differences. Alternatively, it is possible that this effect is largely, or exclusively, an effect of age, gender, or marital status. That is, if married women and older workers are more likely to take temporary positions to increase flexibility in their jobs, the effect of nonstandard work is likely to disappear in the presence of controls for these other effects. I explore this in more detail at the end of this chapter.

Entrepreneurship

The descriptive statistics in the beginning of this chapter demonstrated that entrepreneurs are wealthier than the average American, suggesting that self-employment may be one way that people get rich.

However, entrepreneurs may be rich because they got rich through self employment, or they may be rich because they had more wealth to start. Determining which of these answers is true is fundamental to understanding wealth mobility. That is, if the self-employed simply started with more wealth, it suggests that an important segment of the very wealthy are rich because they started life with a particular advantage. In contrast, if the self-employed did not start with more wealth, but rather they got rich because they became self-employed, it suggests that this group of wealthy were upwardly mobile. Clearly the second scenario is much more optimistic for the possibility of wealth mobility. It implies that it is possible to get rich regardless of where one starts and that self-employment is one path to wealth regardless of one's financial background. An important caveat, of course, is that even if self-employment is a path to wealth, there may be other structural constraints that limit and prohibit certain people or certain groups of people from becoming mobile. Yet a well-specified empirical test would answer at least some of the concern about additional factors that might intercede.

To determine whether entrepreneurs start with more wealth or accumulate more wealth through self-employment, it is necessary to answer two questions. First, it is necessary to know whether having financial capital affects starting a business, all other factors held constant. A positive answer to this question would provide evidence that it is factors such as human capital or social contacts that contribute to business start-ups. Answering this question is the objective of the remainder of this section of the chapter. Second, it is necessary to determine whether entrepreneurs accumulate more wealth and are more upwardly mobile than those who are not self-employed, when other factors that shape wealth are held constant. In other words, it requires returning to the multivariate modeling strategy that I used in previous chapters to isolate and explore whether certain factors (e.g., family background factors in Chapters Five and Six) affect wealth accumulation and mobility. A positive answer to this question implies that there is something unique about entrepreneurs that is central to understanding wealth mobility. After answering questions about what leads to business start-ups, I return to the second question.

Understanding the factors that shape business start-ups requires consulting a different type of data source. So far in this chapter, I have used the NLS-Y because this sample represents the U.S. population well (see Appendix for comparisons of NLS-Y to other data) and because it contains extremely detailed and complete data on the behaviors and processes that affect wealth accumulation. However, business start-ups are better understood using data that focus on the entrepreneurial process. Fortunately, a unique new data set exists that does this. The Panel Study of Entrepreneurial Dynamics (PSED) includes a large sample of nascent entrepreneurs, that is, people who are in the process of starting a business. The PSED also includes detailed financial, demographic, and background information about the respondents that is useful in understanding what factors affect the process of business start-ups. Oversamples of women and minorities improve coverage of these groups. This is clearly a somewhat unique sample, but it is representative of the U.S. population on critical dimensions (Kalleberg and Reynolds 2000; Ruef, Aldrich, and Carter 2003). The Appendix also includes a comparison of the relative strengths and weaknesses of the data that have been used to study entrepreneurship. Compared to other sources of information on business start-ups, the PSED is particularly compelling because it includes observations of transitions to self-employment over time, together with detailed information about respondents and their backgrounds.

There are several reasons that entrepreneurs and entrepreneurship are worthy of special attention. At an aggregate level, entrepreneurship encourages innovation, fosters job creation, enhances firm competitiveness, increases economic growth (Bednarzik 2000), improves aggregate social welfare (Baumol 1993), and leads to the formation of organizations that distribute life chances and determine social standing (Haveman and Cohen 1994). Entrepreneurship is associated with high social status (Breiger 1981; Duncan 1961; Warner 1960). Occupations related to entrepreneurship typically score among the highest occupational prestige ratings, and as a result, entrepreneurs often enjoy significant local and national power. More directly relevant here is the fact that entrepreneurship

Table 7.5. *Who is an Entrepreneur?*

	Mean		Mean
Household net worth		Work experience	
Median	$87,000	Full-time work (years)	19.3
Mean	$209,805		(11.6)
Standard deviation	($499,173)		
$100,000 or more	42	Managerial	9.4
$0–100,000 (%)	51	(years)	(9.0)
Negative (%)	7		
Household income	$55,410	Either parent self-	50
	($42,681)	employed (%)	
Education (%)		Family members	25
Advanced degree	16	self-employed (%)	
College degree	18		
Some college	43	Friend	25
High school degree	23	self-employed (%)	
Age (years)	42.1	Either parent foreign	11
	(13.9)	born (%)	
Race (%)		Foreign born (%)	6
White	75		
Black	11	Married (%)	54
Hispanic	7		
Other	7	Male (%)	48

Note: Numbers in parentheses are standard deviations. This is collaborative research with Phillip Kim and Howard Aldrich.
Source: Panel Study of Entrepreneurial Dynamics.

can also shape the nature of social and economic stratification in an economy (Stinchcombe 1965, 1986). New business start-ups may be a vehicle for immigrant assimilation (Fischer and Massey 2000; Nee and Sanders 1985; Quadrini 1999).

Although the benefits of entrepreneurship are clear, researchers are only beginning to understand who becomes an entrepreneur and the processes that lead to new business start-ups. Table 7.5 uses PSED data to describe the typical nascent entrepreneur. As the table indicates, the entrepreneurs in this sample have a median net worth of $87,000. This is lower than the median net worth for self-employed people in the NLS-Y (whose median is $180,000, included in Table 7.1), because the PSED sample comprises people who are just beginning to make the transition to self-employment. Those in the NLS-Y have already spent at least a year, and in some cases much longer, working for themselves. The median net worth for the PSED sample is also higher than the median for the entire NLS-Y sample (whose median is $58,000, included in Table 7.1).

The mean household net worth for the PSED sample was much higher than the median net worth, suggesting that the distribution of wealth for the nascent entrepreneurs is highly skewed, as it is for the U.S. population. The mean net worth for the PSED sample was slightly more than $200,000. For comparison, the mean net worth for the NLS-Y sample was $198,000. The mean net worth for the Survey of Consumer Finances (SCF) was much higher because the SCF included an oversample of high-income households (see Table A.3 in the Appendix). At the other end of the spectrum, only 7 percent of the PSED sample had zero or negative net worth, compared with 15 percent of the entire NLS-Y sample and 11 percent of the self-employed NLS-Y respondents. Together, these patterns suggest that prior wealth might, in fact, affect the transition to entrepreneurship. Of course, other factors also affect business start-up, and it is not possible to draw conclusions about the role of wealth in this process on the basis of this information alone.

In particular, human capital, work experience, and social contacts may contribute to business start-ups. Table 7.5 also indicates that 16 percent of the PSED respondents had completed advanced degrees, and 18 percent were college graduates. The nascent entrepreneurs had spent on average nearly 20 years working full-time before beginning to start a business, and they had spent nearly half of their full-time work years in managerial positions. Half of the nascent entrepreneurs had a parent who was self-employed, one-quarter had other relatives who were self-employed, and another one-quarter had friends who were self-employed at the time of the survey. Given that only 1 percent of the NLS-Y sample is self-employed, this suggests that the PSED sample has more contact with other self-employed people than average. There is evidence that those who are currently self-employed are more likely to be involved in other new business ventures than those who are work-

Table 7.6. *The Effect of Wealth on Becoming an Entrepreneur*

Financial resources		Experience and contacts	
Household net worth (ln)	0.08	Years work experience (ln)	0.39[*]
	(0.09)		(0.30)
Negative net worth	0.30	Years managerial experience (ln)	0.02
	(0.42)		(0.11)
Household income (ln)	0.02	Helped start other businesses	−0.74[***]
	(0.08)		(0.09)
Education		Currently self employed	1.54[***]
Vocational/technical	0.04		(1.00)
	(0.43)	Parents self employed	0.20
Some college	0.38[*]		(0.23)
	(0.34)	Relatives self employed	0.82[*]
College graduate	0.68[**]		(1.00)
	(0.56)	Friends self employed	−0.02
Advanced degree	0.39		(0.47)
	(0.46)		
N	995		
−2 log likelihood	−200.72[***]		

Note: This is collaborative research with Phillip Kim and Howard Aldrich. These are PARTIAL MODELS; other test variables and control variables are included but not displayed. See Appendix for full models. Cells are coefficient estimates with standard errors in parentheses. Household income was recoded as a continuous variable from a categorical variable. [*] $p < .10$; [**] $p < .05$; [***] $p < .01$.
Source: Panel Study of Entrepreneurial Dynamics.

ing for others (Renzulli, Aldrich, and Moody 2000), suggesting that social contacts might be an important factor contributing to business start-ups.

In order to understand the relative role of these factors, I include results from logistic regression equations predicting becoming an entrepreneur in Table 7.6. This is collaborative research with Phillip Kim and Howard Aldrich. The dependent variable in this equation is a dichotomous indicator that the respondent was a nascent entrepreneur. That is, the explanatory variables predict the likelihood that the respondent was trying to start a business independently, with others, or as part of a new venture for an employer. We only included individuals as nascents if they expected to be owners or part owners in the firm, reported being active in trying to start the new business in the past twelve months, and were still in the start-up phase. The Appendix includes additional details about the data and analyses.

The results pictured in Table 7.6 demonstrate that financial resources have no effect on business start-up in the PSED data. The
equation pictured in the table includes three measures of financial
resources: the logged value of household net worth, a dichotomous
indicator that household net worth was negative, and the logged
value of household income. We included household measures of financial resources because it is likely that entrepreneurs have access
to all jointly owned resources, including spouses' resources; these
also provide a more conservative test of the hypothesis that financial resources increase entrepreneurship. Yet none of these indicators
of household financial resources is a significant predictor of becoming an entrepreneur. In most cases, a variable that is not a significant predictor of the dependent variable in a regression model is
not particularly interesting. In this case, however, the absence of
a significant effect provides evidence that, once other factors are
controlled, access to financial resources is not an important indicator that a person will make a transition to self-employment. This
finding is explored in more depth in Kim, Aldrich, and Keister
(2004).

The finding that financial resources do not affect business
start-ups clarifies a question that had produced mixed results in
previous research on entrepreneurship (Dunn and Holtz-Eakin
2000; Hurst and Lusardi Forthcoming; Reynolds and White 1997).
Previously, researchers proposed that significant financial resources
are necessary to encourage entrepreneurship and that liquidity
constraints prevent transitions to self-employment (Bates 1997;
Blanchflower and Oswald 1998; Evans and Jovanovic 1989; Fischer
and Massey 2000). It seems logical that terminating a relatively secure employment relationship would be too risky for most people
in the absence of sufficient savings. Others have argued that entrepreneurs rely on borrowed start-up funds and that accumulated
savings are necessary for prospective entrepreneurs to gain access
to credit (Bates 1997). Thus high net worth should be positively
related to business start-up (Evans and Jovanovic 1989; Fischer and
Massey 2000). There is evidence that inherited wealth increases the

likelihood of self-employment (Banerjee and Newman 1993; Holtz-Eakin, Joulfaian, and Rosen 1994).

Consistent with the evidence presented in Table 7.6, others have argued that personal savings may not be necessary for a business start-up. Although bank loans and outside investors may sound appealing, they may not be necessary for a business start-up, reducing the need for personal collateral to secure these loans. Bank loans can have high interest rates for the first-time business person, and identifying potential investors involves high search costs. Moreover, many businesses do not require substantial initial investments (U.S. Census Bureau 1992), and even when entrepreneurs do use personal savings, there is evidence that significant personal wealth is not necessary for new business start-up (Aldrich, Renzulli, and Langton 1998). There is also evidence that entrepreneurs are effective at using available nonfinancial resources to reduce the need for start-up capital. Personal credit cards, loans from relatives, withheld personal salary, and leasing equipment all reduce the need for capital from formal, institutional sources and make it possible for entrepreneurs with little personal savings to start businesses (Bhide 1992; Freear, Sohl, and Wetzel 1995; Harrison and Mason 1997; Winborg and Landstrom 2000). Similarly, the prospect for earning additional income from a start-up may motivate those with relatively *low* income to pursue a start-up. Those with lower incomes may decide that the potential for higher income from the new business is great enough, that potential future income from the current employer is low enough, and that the risk of forgoing current employment is worth taking (Blanchflower and Oswald 1998). Similarly, those with high current income may not be willing to risk a secure salary in the hopes of succeeding at an entrepreneurial venture.

If new entrepreneurs do not use personal financial resources to start their new businesses, how do they fund their new business ventures? Table 7.7 shows the percentage of PSED respondents who used nine sources of capital in the initial phase of their business start-ups. More than 30 percent of the PSED sample used personal credit cards to pay for initial costs, and more than 20 percent borrowed

Table 7.7. *Nascent Entrepreneurs:*
Funding Sources

Funding Source	(%)
Credit cards	31
Spouse	21
Friends/family	15
Bank loan	13
SBA loan	4
Second mortgage	3
Venture capital	3
Personal finance company	3
Current employer	3

Note: This is collaborative research with Phillip Kim and Howard Aldrich.
Source: Panel Study of Entrepreneurial Dynamics.

funds from their spouse. Loans from other family members and friends was the third most common source of funds, with 15 percent of the new entrepreneurs using this method of fund-raising. Consistent with arguments that new entrepreneurs do not need to rely on personal savings or formal means of capital acquisition, the results in Table 7.7 show that the less popular sources of funds were home equity loans, bank loans, and Small Business Association (SBA) loans. Only 3 percent of the sample used venture capital, a loan from a personal finance company, or funds from the current employer. If financial resources do not affect transitions to self-employment, what does? The results in Table 7.6 show that human and social capital are important. Education and work experience are both positively and significantly associated with becoming an entrepreneur. Similarly, having relatives who are self-employed affects business start-up. Formal education provides skills and creates access to social networks that might facilitate entrepreneurship (Bates 1997; Fairlie and Meyer 1996; Robinson and Sexton 1994), particularly in certain industries such as knowledge-based service industries and real estate, insurance, and high-tech industries. Likewise, the indicator of current self-employment is significant. It implies that once a person has started one business and has acquired skills useful to entrepreneurship, or entrepreneurial capital, starting additional businesses is more likely (Aldrich et al. 1998). Other work experience can also provide useful skills and social contacts (Shane 2003; Young and Francis 1991). There is evidence from previous research that those whose parents were self-employed and who have self-employed relatives are more likely to be self-employed themselves (Aldrich et al. 1998; Altonji and Dunn 1991; Dunn and Holtz-Eakin 2000; Lentz and Laband 1990). The findings reported in Table 7.6 are consistent with arguments about other relatives. However, there is no effect in this analysis of self-employed parents affecting the transition to business ownership.

These findings imply that it is not simply the rich who are able to become self-employed. Access to financial resources – either household wealth or income – was not significantly associated with becoming a nascent entrepreneur. Of course, it may be that the success of a business venture is related to access to financial resources, but it is not yet possible to explore this possibility with PSED data. The PSED is useful because it focuses on the right population for studying entrepreneurship, but the data are limited because they do not follow the new entrepreneurs into the start-up phase. Follow-up studies are planned, but they are not complete yet. Moreover, these data were collected during a period of low unemployment, substantial returns from equity markets, and relatively liberal availability of credit financing and venture capital. In other historic periods, the entrepreneurial process might unfold differently. Despite these important caveats, our results are robust to multiple specifications of the models, definitions of key variables, definitions of the relevant sample, and corrections of the regression models (Kim et al. 2004).

THE NEW RICH: UPWARDLY MOBILE ENTREPRENEURS

Another way to explore who the upwardly mobile entrepreneurs are is to isolate the self-employed NLS-Y respondents and compare their traits to the traits of the entire NLS-Y sample. Tables 7.8 through 7.10 do this. Table 7.8 compares those who are self-employed, have at

Table 7.8. *Who are the Upwardly Mobile Entrepreneurs?*
Parents' Traits

	Entrepreneurs	Entire Sample
Parents' education (%)		
Father had advanced degree	20.0	6.8
Mother had advanced degree	5.4	2.3
Father's occupation		
Craft	12.3	20.2
Clerk	5.4	3.5
Laborer	20.0	25.6
Manager	20.0	13.1
Professional	20.0	10.8
Sales	9.0	4.6
Mother's occupation		
Craft	1.8	1.2
Clerk	18.8	17.3
Laborer	12.3	23.4
Manager	5.4	2.8
Professional	9.0	7.6
Sales	0	3.5
Parent's work behavior (%)		
Father worked full-time	83.4	77.1
Mother worked full-time	40.0	39.8
Parents (%)		
Father born in U.S.	89.1	91.8
Mother born in U.S.	90.9	92.9

Note: Upwardly mobile entrepreneurs are millionaires who have not inherited a majority of their wealth and who are self-reported entrepreneurs.
Source: National Longitudinal Survey of Youth, 1979 Cohort.

least $1 million in net worth, and did not inherit the majority of their
wealth to the entire NLS-Y sample. This approach to understanding
mobility is somewhat crude, but it does provide a unique glimpse into
this important, upwardly mobile portion of the population.

The table shows that significantly more of the upwardly mobile
entrepreneurs had a father with an advanced degree than the typical NLS-Y respondent. Likewise, the entrepreneurs' fathers were
more likely to be professionals or managers and less likely to be
laborers or craftspeople. The mothers of the entrepreneurs were
not particularly different from the typical respondent's mother on

Table 7.9. *Who are the Upwardly Mobile Entrepreneurs?*
Family Background

	Entrepreneurs	Entire Sample
Race (%)		
White	85.5	80.4
Black	1.8	12.3
Hispanic	12.7	7.3
Born in United States (%)	90.9	95.3
Family structure (%)		
Two-parent household	87.7	74.7
Single parent household	3.6	12.5
Stepparent household	3.6	8.2
Other composition	5.4	4.4
Siblings (mean number)	2.7	2.9

Note: Upwardly mobile entrepreneurs are millionaires who have not inherited a majority of their wealth and who are self-reported entrepreneurs.
Source: National Longitudinal Survey of Youth, 1979 Cohort.

educational or work behavior measures, but significantly fewer of the mothers were laborers. There were also no real differences between the entrepreneurs included in Table 7.8 and those in the full sample in terms of their parents' immigrant status. However, Table 7.9 shows that there are some important differences in other traits. A much smaller percentage of the upwardly mobile entrepreneurs are black than in the entire sample. About 12 percent of all NLS-Y respondents are black, consistent with the U.S. population, but only 1.8 percent of the upwardly mobile entrepreneurs are black. Similarly, the upwardly mobile entrepreneurs are more likely to be from two-parent households and much less likely to be from single-parent or stepparent households. These results are consistent with the findings presented in Chapter Five, with the exception of family size. In Chapter Five, I found that having more siblings decreases adult wealth accumulation and mobility, but the estimates in Table 7.9 show that this relationship does not hold for the group of upwardly mobile entrepreneurs. That is, the entrepreneurs have virtually the same number of siblings as the typical NLS-Y respondent. Yet this finding is consistent with the arguments I made in Chapter Five.

Table 7.10. *Who are the Upwardly Mobile Entrepreneurs?*

	Entrepreneurs	Entire Sample
Education (%)		
No degree	5.5	8.3
High school	27.3	37.2
Attended some college	21.8	18.4
College degree	25.5	12.2
Advanced degree	20.0	8.3
Marital status (%)		
Single	23.8	28.8
Ever married	49.1	41.4
Ever divorced	9.1	17.7
Residing with opposite sex partner	3.0	4.6
Age at first marriage (mean)	24.3	23.4
Children		
At least one child (%)	76.4	79.7
Number of children (mean)	1.0	1.1
Age at first birth (mean)	20.6	18.7
Living in an urban area (%)	77.2	73.9

Note: New rich entrepreneurs are millionaires who have not inherited the majority of their wealth and who are self-reported entrepreneurs.

In that chapter, I argued that the effect of siblings on adult wealth accumulation is largely evident through their effect on educational attainment. Indeed, Table 7.10 shows that the upwardly mobile entrepreneurs do have considerably more education than the overall sample, and multivariate models (not included here) indicated that the effect of family size was absorbed by the inclusion of education in the model.

Upwardly mobile entrepreneurs are also somewhat unique in their marriage and fertility behaviors. A significantly higher percentage of the entrepreneurs included in Table 7.10 had ever been married, and significantly fewer remained single. Given the importance of marriage to overall wealth and to the process of becoming an entrepreneur, this difference is certainly important. Compared with the typical NLS-Y respondent, the entrepreneurs also delayed having children by nearly more than two years, yet there was no difference in the average number of children for the entrepreneurs.

Table 7.11. *Work and Wealth, 1985–2000*

	Education	Add Adult Work
Respondent's education		
High school	17.85***	2.56
	(4.86)	(5.36)
Some college	34.11***	10.53*
	(5.72)	(6.26)
College degree	57.58***	28.46***
	(6.64)	(7.20)
Advanced degree	74.57***	40.51***
	(7.41)	(8.00)
Adult resources		
Entrepreneurial income	–	56.22***
		(7.65)
Temporary work (weeks)	–	−8.01*
		(3.80)
Family income	–	0.00***
		(0.00)

Note: These are PARTIAL MODELS; other test variables and control variables are included but not displayed. See Appendix for full models. Cells are coefficient estimates with standard errors in parentheses. * $p < .10$; ** $p < .05$; *** $p < .01$.

Source: National Longitudinal Survey of Youth, 1979 Cohort.

MULTIVARIATE RESULTS

While it is useful to examine descriptive statistics and to isolate survey samples in unique ways, as I have noted in previous chapters, multivariate analyses are critical to understanding the relative importance of various predictors of wealth accumulation and mobility. In Chapters Five and Six, I discussed results from multivariate analyses, focusing on the role of family background traits in shaping adult wealth accumulation and mobility. The models I discussed in those chapters also included measures of adult resources that are relevant to understanding the relationship between work and wealth accumulation. Table 7.11 includes results of generalized least squares estimates of adult net worth. These are the same models that I discussed in previous chapters, but I focus on a different set of variables here.

In particular, the variables I showcase in this table are education, adult income, and income from entrepreneurial work. Again, these are partial models; the complete models are included in the Appendix. As I noted previously, the effect of educational attainment on adult wealth accumulation and mobility is very strong. The results in the first column of Table 7.11 demonstrate that high school graduates accumulate more wealth and are more upwardly mobile than those who have less than a high school education. These results hold when all other family background characteristics and individual traits are held constant (for coefficients for other variables, see Appendix). The results in Table 7.11 also demonstrate that the effect of education beyond high school on adult wealth ownership is even stronger. Indeed, the effect increases steadily through the completion of an advanced degree. Each level of education is also highly statistically significant, suggesting that these are results that are very unlikely to occur just by chance.

In preliminary models, I also controlled for a person's adult occupation directly in several ways. The descriptive statistics included in the tables in the beginning of this chapter suggested that there are important differences in adult wealth accumulation between occupational categories, such as laborers, craftspeople, and professionals. In exploratory multivariate analyses, I investigated the role of occupation in shaping wealth when other factors are controlled. Specifically, I investigated how current occupation, various past occupations, changes in occupation, and various combinations of occupations that a person might have had affect adult wealth accumulation and mobility. In separate models, I explored measuring each of these concepts using general occupational groupings and very precise indicators of occupation. I also created occupational clusters – based on wages and benefits – and grouped people into these clusters.

In all of these models, the occupation indicators were signification predictors of adult wealth accumulation and mobility in the directions suggested by the descriptives statistics (e.g., laborers had less wealth than other occupations, whereas professionals had more). However, once educational attainment and adult income were controlled, the effect of most occupational indicators did not remain. I do not include these preliminary models; rather, I include the models that contain variables that do affect adult wealth. This suggests that occupation does affect adult wealth, but it does so through education and income rather than in some other direct way.

Although most adult occupations are related to adult wealth accumulation and mobility only through education and income, entrepreneurship is an important exception. In fact, entrepreneurship has a very strong effect on adult wealth accumulation and mobility even when all other factors are controlled. The results in the second column of Table 7.11 show that receiving entrepreneurial income is a significant and very strong predictor of adult wealth. The measure included in the model and displayed in the table is the amount of entrepreneurial income received in the year prior to the year in which the dependent variable is measured, between 1985 and 2000. Although I only show the results of the model including the dependent variable measured as a continuous indicator, the strong, positive effect is robust across multiple specifications of both the dependent and independent variables.

Entrepreneurial income has a strong, positive effect on other measures of adult wealth, including gross assets, gross financial assets, gross real assets, and various logged forms of these wealth measures. As I have done throughout this book, I report models using thousands of dollars of net worth as the dependent variable, because logging the dependent variable does not reduce the highly skewed nature of the variable as there is a large group of respondents at zero. Logging entrepreneurial income does not change the results. I report results using nonlogged entrepreneurial income because it is easier to interpret. Similarly, including such measures as years of entrepreneurship, transition to entrepreneurship, and other indicators of self-employment does not change the results in substantive ways.

Including entrepreneurship in the model does decrease the effect of education on adult wealth. That is, in Table 7.11, the second column shows that once entrepreneurship is controlled, having a high school education is no longer significantly related to adult wealth and having some college is only moderately significant. However, both completing college and completing an advanced degree continue to be strong, significant predictors of adult wealth accumulation and mobility. This is consistent with the models in Table 7.6

Table 7.12. *Childhood Religion and Adult Assets,*
1985–2000

	Own a Home	Own Stocks
Adult resources		
Entrepreneurial income	0.33***	0.03
	(0.05)	(0.06)
Temporary work (weeks)	−0.07**	0.01
	(0.03)	(0.01)
Family income	0.01***	0.01***
	(0.00)	(0.00)

Note: These are PARTIAL MODELS; other test variables and control variables are included but not displayed. See Appendix for full models. Cells are logistic coefficient estimates with standard errors in parentheses. * $p < .10$; ** $p < .05$; *** $p < .01$.
Source: National Longitudinal Survey of Youth, 1979 Cohort.

that showed that educational attainment increases the likelihood of becoming an entrepreneur. This finding is also consistent with the conceptual model I developed in Chapter Four and that Figure 7.1 outlines. That is, those with higher educations are likely to have more varied work opportunities, including opportunities in self-employment. As I outline in the diagram of the conceptual model, various family background and individual traits shape educational attainment, education shapes adult work including entrepreneurship, and work in turn affects adult wealth. Of course, as the results in Table 7.6 demonstrated, although education does have a positive relationship with self-employment, it is not critical for movement into entrepreneurship.

Yet, entrepreneurs do not appear to have higher wealth on all measures when other factors are controlled. In particular, Table 7.12 shows that entrepreneurs are more likely to be homeowners than nonentrepreneurs, but that entrepreneurs are no less likely than others to own stocks and bonds. Again, these models control for all other variables included in the full models, and details are included in the Appendix. In the descriptive statistics shown in Table 7.2, higher proportions of self-employed respondents than other respondents owned stocks and bonds, as well as housing assets. However, the multivariate analyses showed that this apparent effect operated through the effect of entrepreneurship on income and that there was not a direct effect of self-employment on stock ownership.

It is tempting to conclude that perhaps entrepreneurs use home as collateral in starting their business. Although this is certainly true sometimes, the multivariate results shown in Table 7.6 suggest that it is not home wealth or other types of financial resources that affect entrepreneurship, with all other factors held constant. Similarly, the estimates in Table 7.7. show that only 3 percent of the respondents in the entrepreneurship study used a second mortgage to finance their entrepreneurial venture. Of course, these findings are from different data sources and therefore need to be interpreted carefully. However, the results do provide some evidence that entrepreneurs accumulate wealth at least partially through the accumulation of real assets.

In contrast, people who spend time in temporary work tend to accumulate less wealth as adults and to be less upwardly mobile than those who have not spent time in temporary positions. The results in Table 7.11 show that the number of weeks a person spent in temporary work is negatively related to total adult wealth. That is, the more the time respondents spent in temporary work, the less wealth they accumulate and the less upwardly mobile they are. The results in Table 7.12 suggest that at least part of the reason that temporary workers accumulate less wealth is that the more the time respondents spent in temporary jobs, the less likely they are to become homeowners. There was no effect of temporary work on the accumulation of financial assets such as stocks as bonds (results pictured in Table 7.12) and other financial assets (not pictured).

These results suggest that a new type of dual economy may be developing in the United States. In the primary sector, workers have strong ties to their employers or are self-employed, earn relatively high wages, and accumulate assets more rapidly than other workers. Those who are not in the primary sector, such as temporary workers, are not well connected to a particular employer, earn lower wages, and also appear to accumulate fewer assets. Before drawing this conclusion, however, additional research is necessary. First, the effect of temporary workers is marginal in the models presented in both Tables 7.11 and 7.12. Second, it is possible that other types of non-standard workers have very different accumulation patterns than temporary workers. Specialized, highly educated, or technically expert contract workers, for example, are likely to differ in important ways from the typical temporary worker represented in the NLS-Y data. I explored the effect of temporary work on asset accumulation to illustrate the working of the conceptual model I proposed. However, in order to thoroughly understand the effect of nonstandard work on wealth, it would be useful to draw on additional data and, perhaps, to use additional modeling techniques, such as simulation modeling, to more fully exploit available data on nonstandard work. Further investigation of the relationship between nonstandard work and wealth accumulation is beyond the scope of this book, but related questions would make important research topics for future studies.

OTHER FACTORS

This chapter highlighted the importance of work experience on wealth accumulation and mobility. I looked at occupational differences in wealth accumulation, and in order to document the way my conceptual model works, I focused on the role that entrepreneurship and nonstandard work play in this process. An exhaustive discussion of all work and occupation-related issues that affect wealth is beyond the scope of this book. Yet there are certainly many other aspects of work and work experiences that shape wealth accumulation and mobility.

Career trajectories, for example, vary in important ways that may shape wealth. Time and opportunity structures shape career development and work experiences (Rosenfeld 1992). The job-relevant experiences that individuals have when they first enter the labor force and their contacts interact with other structural constraints to generate the career (Rosenfeld 1992). The nature of careers varies across individuals, by generation, and across time within generations. Job mobility varies with occupation, education at the individual level, and market characteristics (Hachen 1992) and with firm traits such as organizational diversity (Fujiwara-Greve and Greve 2000) at a more aggregate level. Underlying each of these sources of variation are differences by race, ethnicity, and gender that alone would be worthy of a volume (McCall 2001). Naturally, variation at each of these levels would affect an individual's work experience in ways that would certainly translate into changes in adult wealth.

Similarly, the notion that technological advances have fundamentally changed the way people work, interact with each other, and organize their lives has become pervasive in both academic and popular writing. Entry into technology-dominated careers differs in noticeable ways from entry into traditional professional careers. There is a sense in current writing that technology-based careers are more merit based and egalitarian in their selection of workers. This implies that the traditional gender, race, education, and family background influences on career decisions may be fundamentally altered in high-tech careers. A related issue is persistence in a technology-dominated career. It is possible that high-tech careers propel people to immediate and, perhaps, lasting success. If this is true, wealth accumulation will be different for people in high-tech careers. I do not investigate these questions here, but future research may profitably address them.

Military occupations are another important example of a class of occupations that is likely to shape wealth ownership in important ways. Both enlisted personnel and officers in all branches of the military receive unique forms of compensation and face a unique set of incentives regarding saving. Compensation for military personnel usually includes a housing allowance. The individual may live in base housing or may use the housing allowance to live off-base. At least in past decades, military personnel also moved from station to station much more frequently than the typical worker would change jobs, much less move to a different city. The frequent changes of station make it difficult for the military family to have two adult income earners, which is likely to reduce the household income relative to other families. Similarly, although compensation for housing expenses is certainly a benefit, when combined with frequent changes of station, it creates a disincentive to purchase a home. Of course, homeownership is not impossible in the military, but it is less common than in the general population. Finally, until 1986, military personnel pensions did not take advantage of high returns associated with pensions at least partially invested in the stock market. The military did implement the Thrift Savings Plan (TSP) a few years ago. The TSP is a government-sponsored retirement savings and investment plan that allows military personnel to take advantage of the benefits of investing retirement savings in stock-associated financial instruments. The result of differences in income and historic differences in opportunities to save suggest that military personnel, particularly those who spend significant numbers of years in the military, may accumulate fewer assets than comparable workers in civilian occupations. Recently, there have been some increases in the length of military tours, and these changes may make it more feasible for spouses to contribute to earnings and may improve incentives for homeownership. In either case, there is little previous evidence to support these arguments, and future research may usefully explore this question.

There are also individual-level behaviors and processes that would affect wealth accumulation that I have not specifically addressed in this chapter. Individual motivations and abilities, for example, are likely to shape educational attainment and job opportunities in ways that affect adult wealth accumulation and mobility. There is evidence that indicators of intelligence such as the Armed Forces Qualification Test (AFQT) scores predict educational attainment and, to a lesser extent, income (Armor 2003). It is possible that intelligence, too, affects wealth.

Similarly, delinquency during adolescence would also affect education and work outcomes and, ultimately, wealth ownership. Although still subject to some debate, research on delinquency has begun to demonstrate that delinquency during adolescence can impact later-life outcomes in important, and usually negative, ways (Tanner, Davies, and O'Grady 1999). Research on education has shown that delinquency has a negative impact on school grades and retention (Davies and Guppy 1997; Mensch and Kandel 1988). Related status attainment research has provided clear support for the idea that educational success determines occupational achievements and income in adulthood (Warren and Hauser 1997). There is also evidence of a more direct effect of youth delinquency on occupational and later financial outcomes (Tanner et al. 1999), net of deficits associated with educational shortfalls. Although there continues to be some disagreement in the delinquency literature regarding the relationship between youth delinquency and adult outcomes (Monk-Turner 1989), evidence in favor of a negative association is mounting. If this speculation is accurate, it is also likely that delinquency affects adult wealth. Again, however questions of this sort are beyond the scope of this book. Again, this and the other topics I introduced in this section are issues that future research might explore in more depth.

CONCLUSION

In this chapter, I identified patterns in wealth accumulation and mobility by occupation and job characteristics. I first explored the relationship between occupation and wealth, and I showed that self-employed people are much wealthier than most others, that professionals and those in managerial positions have above average wealth, and that craftspeople and laborers have relatively low wealth. These conclusions were the result of descriptive statistics that did not control for other factors that shape wealth. When I conducted multivariate analyses, specific occupations did not affect wealth beyond occupational differences in income. However, two important job traits did continue to shape wealth ownership: self-employment and nonstandard work.

Entrepreneurs had higher wealth, and they were more likely than others to be homeowners. There was no effect of entrepreneurship on stock ownership once income was controlled. In most of this chapter, I used data from the National Longitudinal Survey of Youth 1979 cohort (NLS-Y) in my empirical analyses. In discussing entrepreneurs, I also used the Panel Study of Entrepreneurial Dynamics (PSED) to explore who becomes an entrepreneur. I argued that self-employment is critical to understanding wealth mobility because it may be one way that people get rich. On the other hand, it may be that entrepreneurs are self-employed because they had the resources to access this unique occupation. I used the PSED to show that there was no relationship between prior financial resources and making a transition to self-employment. Combined with the finding that entrepreneurs are wealthier than other workers, this finding implies that entrepreneurship is an occupation that is relatively accessible and may be an important avenue to getting rich.

I also used an important example of workers at the other end of the wealth spectrum: temporary workers. I showed that temporary workers have less wealth than other workers and argued that this finding needs further study because it is only marginally significant. The more hours people spent in temporary work, the lower their adult wealth. Of course, temporary work is only one example of the many types of nonstandard work that are becoming more common and that are likely to affect wealth in important ways. I did not explore patterns of wealth accumulation for contract workers and other types of nonstandard workers, but future research may usefully extend the conceptual model I propose to investigate those questions.

CHAPTER EIGHT

Adult Family, Context, and Wealth

Marriage behavior, fertility behavior, the timing of life events, and context all are, of course, important predictors of adult wealth. These factors have received perhaps the most attention from researchers in the past both because they are the most direct predictors of wealth ownership and also because they are among the more easily measured traits of individuals and families. As previous chapters have shown, other background traits and individual behaviors are also important predictors, but it would be a mistake to underestimate the importance of adult factors. In this chapter, I explore the portions of the conceptual model (Figure 4.1) that include adult traits such as marriage, divorce, fertility, and the timing of life events. I also discuss the role that portfolio behavior plays in wealth ownership. That is, I ask how different investment strategies shape wealth ownership and mobility. Near the end of the chapter, I also briefly address the importance of context, including such factors as stock market booms and busts, generational effects, and the importance of geography.

Figure 8.1 emphasizes the segment of the full conceptual model that is the focus of this chapter. Again, I need to note that my objective is to demonstrate the functioning of the conceptual model and to highlight as many of the important factors that contribute to wealth ownership as possible. In this chapter, I explore several adult behaviors and processes that are critical components of the wealth accumulation and mobility picture. However, because of space constraints, I am not able to discuss all relevant processes in great depth. As I have done in previous chapters, I present descriptive estimates throughout the beginning of the chapter that demonstrate

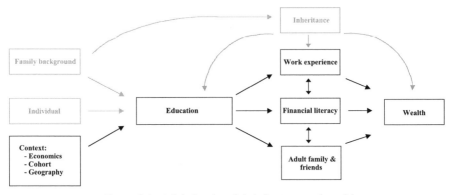

Figure 8.1. Adult family, adult behaviors, and wealth.

the relationship between key adult traits and wealth accumulation. I use these to discuss the basic relationships that emerge from analyses of the National Longitudinal Survey (NLS-Y) data. I then introduce relevant segments of the multivariate regression models that I have been describing throughout the book in order to discuss adult family influences net of other effects.

Marriage

The majority of people will get married at some point in their lives, and marriage is one of the most effective ways to increase assets. Marriage behavior affects wealth in important ways that are well documented but seldom discussed in detail. This is unfortunate because there are relationships between marriage, divorce, widowhood, and wealth that are fundamental to understand the accumulation of assets and wealth mobility. Married couples typically join assets, income is considerably higher for married couples, and expenses tend to be lower for married couples. As a result, the wealth of married couples is usually much higher than that of households headed by single individuals.

Table 8.1 shows that married couples do have considerably more wealth on average than other households. The table includes estimates of median net worth from the NLS-Y for all respondents as well as separate estimates for households headed by married couples

Table 8.1. *Marriage and Wealth*

		% With Net Worth					
	% Sample Total	> $1 Million	$500K–$999,999	$300K–$499,999	< $300K	Zero or Negative	Median Net Worth (Thousands)
All	100	3	4	6	87	15	$58
Married couples	63	3	6	8	83	9	97
Single females							
Never married	6	0	2	4	94	31	8
Separated	3	0	2	2	96	38	1
Divorced	9	1	1	3	95	23	14
Widowed	1	4	10	4	82	26	22
Single males							
Never married	9	1	2	2	95	28	9
Separated	2	0	0	2	98	26	6
Divorced	6	1	2	2	95	21	16

Note: All wealth estimates are for the year 2000. There are not enough widowed men in the sample to produce reliable estimates.
Source: National Longitudinal Survey of Youth, 1979 Cohort ($N = 4,963$).

and single people. I measure marital status in 1998 and wealth ownership in 2000 in order to allow for time for changes in marital status to affect asset ownership. As the table shows, married couples have median net worth of nearly $100,000, nearly twice the median for all respondents. Preliminary investigations showed little effect of a recent change in marital status beyond the effect of current marital status that Table 8.1 demonstrates. These are basic estimates that do not control for other important inputs such as household income, race, family background, or family size. However, the estimates in this table do document an important, and quite extreme, difference in wealth by marital status. I explore this relationship in greater detail throughout this chapter.

Among the households headed by single people, those of widows are rather unique. There were not enough widowers in the NLS-Y sample to include separate estimates for these households, and it is important to note that the NLS-Y respondents are still quite young on average. Thus these estimates are certain to change as the sample ages. The patterns that emerge here for widowed females, however, are consistent with patterns that are evident in other research on the wealth consequences of widowhood (Weir, Willis, and Sevak 2000). Table 8.1 shows that the median net worth for widows was approximately $22,000, compared to $58,000 for the full sample. Widows have more wealth on average than other households headed by single people, probably as a legacy of their marriage, but their wealth is considerably lower than the wealth of currently married couples.

The financial well-being of widows and widowers is an important concern for policy makers, although academics have not paid the issue much attention. There is some evidence that the death of a spouse can increase the overall risk of poverty (Burkhauser 1994; Grad 1996; Hurd 1989). There is also evidence that an important part of the reason that poverty is greater among widows is that they draw on savings to fund current consumption. Evidence from the Household Retirement Survey (HRS), which was formerly the study of Asset and Health Dynamics Among the Oldest Old (AHEAD), suggests that women who were widowed a relatively long time ago comprise the bulk of asset-poor widows (Weir et al. 2000). This same research shows that newly widowed women are in much better shape financially and provides evidence that early widowhood is likely to increase the lifelong risk of poverty. This evidence also suggests that the wealth of the widows in the NLS is likely to continue to decline over time given the young age of the sample.

Divorce also accounts for many of the differences in the finances of single households. In recent years, marital dissolution in the United States has increased dramatically, and there is considerable documentation of both trends in divorce and its consequences. In 1965, only 3 percent of U.S. households were divorced. However, by 1998 almost 10 percent were divorced (Cherlin, Chase-Lansdale, and McRae 1998). Researchers have demonstrated that separation and divorce affect educational attainment (Houseknecht and Spanier 1980), health (Horwitz, White, and Howell-White 1996), mental health (Cherlin et al. 1998), and children's well-being (Cooksey 1997; Demo and Acock 1988). There is also evidence that divorce and separation are highly detrimental to economic well-being. In particular, marital dissolution increases poverty rates (Duncan and Hoffman 1985; Nestel, Mercier, and Shaw 1983) and decreases per capita income (Cherlin 1981; Mott and Moore 1978; Peterson 1996), labor force participation (Cherlin 1979), and the income-to-needs ratio (Corcoran and Duncan 1979; Weitzman 1985), particularly for women (Holden and Smock 1991; Stirling 1989).

Divorce and separation are also likely to affect wealth ownership although the effect of divorce on wealth ownership has attracted limited attention (Zagorsky 2004). Married couples can live much more cheaply than two single individuals, and specialization in the division of labor needed to accomplish household chores can increase time available for other tasks as well. Divorce halts this advantage. Divorced couples split their assets, and the process of divorce might force the couple to tap into savings to pay legal fees. Indeed, divorcing may be even worse financially than not marrying initially – all other factors considered – because of the legal costs and because one-half of the couple will bear the cost of setting up a new household. This cost is compounded when children are involved because the household expenses are likely to be greater than for households of those that never married.

The estimates in Table 8.1 show that in the 2000 NLS-Y, median net worth for divorced females was about $14,000, and for divorced males it was about $16,000. The table also shows that wealth is even lower for separated respondents, particularly women. Although these values are not significantly different from each other, both are significantly lower (statistically) than the value for the full sample. They are also clearly lower than the value for married respondents, but not as low as for people who never married, and who are likely to be younger as well. The multivariate analyses distinguish these effects.

It is notable that there is no significant difference between divorced men and divorced women in the estimates in Table 8.1. There is evidence from other research that women bear a disproportionate economic burden from divorce (Airsman and Sharda 1993; Cherlin 1981; Holden and Smock 1991). Most of these findings reflect the fact that in the absence of male income, female-headed households incur a precipitous drop in salary and wages, which leads to a decline in the standard of living (Cherlin 1981; Weitzman 1985). On average, women do still earn less and are less likely to be the family's primary breadwinner or to be in high-status occupations. Women are also less likely than men to be entrepreneurs (Renzulli, Aldrich, and Moody 2000). Older women (55 years and older), in particular, who divorce and who have not been in the labor force for many years face limited job prospects and therefore limited possibilities for replacing the income of a primary breadwinner (Loew 1995).

Yet, there is little evidence that there are gender differences in household wealth following divorce. Estimates from the NLS-Y suggest that wealth does decline following divorce. In fact, wealth begins to decline four years before divorce and ultimately decreases to nearly four times less than it was at the peak of the couple's wealth (Zagorsky 2004). Previous research suggests that women are likely to suffer more than men after divorce; yet the results in Table 8.1 show that there is little difference by gender in this finding. This pattern may reflect the fact that assets are typically split equally between husband and wife at the time of divorce. Both parties are likely to fare worse than married couples, but neither gender is likely to fare worse than the other. My own preliminary estimates using the NLS-Y showed that the cumulative effect of limited income over time following divorce does little to increase the gender gap in wealth. However, this is a pattern that may become more clear as the NLS-Y sample ages. In the multivariate analyses covered later in this chapter, I explore the extent to which the wealth difference is a function of other gender differences, including income and occupational differentials.

There is also little gender difference in the wealth of never-married people. An increasing number of people are also deciding to stay single in the United States, and this may also affect household wealth estimates. While 15 percent were never married in 1965, by 1998 almost 24 percent had never married (Zagorsky 2004). The estimates in Table 8.1 show that median net worth for never-married women was about $8,000 and for never-married men it was about $9,000 in 2000. Again, these values are not different from each other, but they are significantly lower than the wealth owned by married couples. Naturally, much of this difference is an age effect, and later in this chapter, I explore the degree to which the effect of marital status persists after controlling for income, age, and other factors that shape asset accumulation.

The patterns that are evident in median net worth by marital status are also clear in the percentage of household with wealth in each of the segments of the distribution included in Table 8.1. There are no single women who are millionaires, and only 1 percent of single men are millionaires. There are also very few divorced or separated people in the highest wealth groups. Likewise, there are few never-married, divorced, or separated people in the other high-wealth groups. A large number of widows, however, are in the high-wealth groups even though their median wealth was considerably lower than the median wealth of married couples. This pattern reflects the considerable amount of variation in the wealth of those who have lost a spouse. That is, some of the widows in this sample did inherit considerable wealth, increasing the percentage of widows in the upper segments of the wealth distribution. On average, however, widows do appear to own less wealth.

At the other end of the wealth distribution, there are those who own no wealth or whose debt exceeds their assets. Across the entire sample, 15 percent of respondents had zero or negative wealth, and the estimates in Table 8.1 show that significantly fewer married couples are in this lowest wealth segment. However, disproportionate numbers of single households, both male and female, have zero or negative wealth. Again, there are no significant differences by gender in being in the lowest wealth group. Yet, there are a significantly greater number of widows in this category. This demonstrates that there are also significantly more widows than average who have no wealth. There is some evidence that the number of widows in the bottom of the distribution will grow as the NLS-Y sample ages, but it is not yet possible to know how this pattern will change over time. Although these patterns are extreme and worth noting, these estimates are basic estimates and do not control for other factors that shape wealth ownership. Multivariate analyses will indicate the degree to

Table 8.2. *Marriage and Portfolios*

			Percentage Owning			
	% Sample Total	Home	Stocks and Bonds	Checking and Savings	Trust Account	Business
All	100	68	26	77	5	11
Married couples	63	85	32	86	5	13
Single females						
Never married	6	38	19	65	4	4
Separated	3	33	13	45	0	6
Divorced	9	47	15	65	3	4
Widowed	1	65	13	48	4	9
Single males						
Never married	9	30	18	63	4	8
Separated	2	34	8	52	3	14
Divorced	6	41	15	62	5	9

Note: All wealth estimates are for the year 2000. There are not enough widowed men in the sample to produce reliable estimates.
Source: National Longitudinal Survey of Youth, 1979 Cohort ($n = 4,963$).

which these patterns reflect age, income, and other differences as opposed to being true differences by marital status.

An important reason for differences in wealth ownership by marital status is differences in the way households save. Table 8.2 demonstrates differences in portfolio behavior – that is, the ownership of particular assets and debts – by marital status. The estimates in this table suggest that married couples are unique in their ownership of each asset included in the table. For example, married couples are much more likely than the typical NLS-Y respondent to be homeowners. Of all respondents, 68 percent own the primary residence, but 85 percent of married couples are homeowners. Married couples are somewhat more likely than the typical respondent, but significantly more likely than single respondents, to own stocks and bonds and cash accounts such as checking and savings accounts. Part of this difference reflects the fact that married couples account for more than 60 percent of the sample, and these patterns may also reflect higher wealth that comes with joining assets, income, saving for children's futures, and age. However, it is possible that there are also likely to be other effects of marriage on wealth ownership. For instance, the patterns may reflect an ability to take greater risks – such as investing in stocks, bonds, and business assets – when there are more resources to invest. In the paragraphs that follow, I will explore the degree to which these other factors reduce the effect of marital status on wealth.

Widows are somewhat unique in the assets they own. They are much more likely than other divorced or never-married women and men to own their own home. This likely reflects homeownership rates from when the spouse was still alive. Yet homeownership for widows is much lower than for couples who are still married. Similarly, widows are much less likely than married couples to own stocks and bonds, cash accounts, and business assets. These patterns certainly reflect age and may suggest that widows are deliberately depleting their savings with age, but the patterns might also be a reflection of decreased income and thus be involuntarily low. The low rates of ownership of cash accounts is indicative that there may be an involuntary component to these patterns. Only 48 percent of widows in the sample had savings or checking accounts, compared to 77 percent of all respondents and 86 percent of married couples in the sample. The multivariate analyses will be able to distinguish the degree to which the effects are a function of other inputs, but the magnitude of the effect is worthy of a preliminary note.

In contrast, there are only limited gender differences in asset ownership evident in the estimates in Table 8.2. Never-married men and women are virtually indistinguishable in their asset ownership, with one exception. Never-married women are slightly more likely than never-married men to be homeowners, but the 8 percent difference (38 percent of women and 30 percent of men) is only marginally statistically significant. Divorced women are also slightly more likely than divorced men to be homeowners, reflecting the tendency of mothers to retain primary custody of children and to continue living in the family home after divorce. On all other dimensions, however, there is little evidence of a gender difference in the asset ownership of single households.

The story that does appear in Table 8.2, as it did in Table 8.1, is that marriage is the primary dividing line for wealth ownership. The differences in wealth ownership between the married couples and each of the single female and single male categories are tremendous, whereas the differences across gender groups are minimal. Widows and widowers are also unique in certain ways, and as the NLS-Y sample ages, increasing number of both men and women who have lost a spouse will allow examination of how gender and widowhood interact to shape saving and wealth accumulation. I explore these differences in more detail using multivariate analyses.

CHILDREN

Just as family size during childhood (discussed in Chapter Five) affects wealth ownership and mobility, so also does family size in adulthood. That is, wealth varies with the number of children you have. This might not seem particularly surprising, but in fact the nature of the relationship between the number of children in a family and the family's wealth is more nuanced than we might expect. Naturally, children use resources and might, therefore, deplete savings. The U.S. Department of Agriculture (USDA) has estimated that the cost of raising a child from birth through age 18 is approaching $200,000 (U.S. Department of Agriculture 2001). This cost includes expenses such as childcare, groceries, clothing, gifts, recreation, health and life insurance, and medical care. It includes educational expenses before college, the cost of buying a bigger car, and an estimate of the cost associated with buying a larger house. The USDA estimates are fairly thorough, but they do not include estimated lost wages or salary from one parent leaving work or working less. The estimates also do not include additional expenditures, such as buying a computer, that are almost requirements today. Still the point is clear: children cost money.

Yet children also provide an incentive to save for future expenses. Given that the USDA estimates mentioned in the previous paragraph do not include the expense of college, many parents are motivated to find additional ways to save for their children's college education. Parents may save for less substantial expenses, such as major holidays or family vacations, in ways they might not otherwise.

Table 8.3. *Children and Wealth*

| | % Sample Total | %With Net Worth | | | | | Mediannet Worth (Thousands) |
		> $1 Million	$500K–$999,999	$300K–$499,999	<$300K	Zero or Negative	
All	100	3	4	6	87	15	$58
Children							
None	22	3	4	6	87	15	48
One to three	68	3	4	6	87	15	66
Four or more	10	1	2	4	91	25	25

Note: All wealth estimates are for the year 2000.
Source: National Longitudinal Survey of Youth, 1979 Cohort ($N = 4,963$).

Buying a larger house or car to meet children's space, shelter, and transportation needs may also increase the family's wealth. Similarly, because some life insurance policies accrue investment value, some parents who buy additional life insurance for themselves or their children may increase their wealth. Yet many parents also accumulate additional debt that they might not have taken on otherwise, and this debt may reduce their overall wealth (Sullivan, Warren, and Westbrook 2000). Taken together, these points suggest that the relationship between children and wealth is less obvious than we might suppose.

Table 8.3 summarizes the relationship between family size and wealth ownership. The table shows that people who have never had children account for 22 percent of the population, and their median wealth is slightly lower than the median for the overall sample. That is, the childless households had about $48,000 in net worth on average, while the full sample had $58,000 in net worth in 2000. In contrast, those with relatively small families (one to three children) had slightly more wealth than the overall sample. However, there is no difference among these groups in their representation in the various segments of the wealth distribution. For instance, 3 percent of the full sample, 3 percent of those with no children, and 3 percent of those with one to three children are millionaires. Likewise, the percentage of families in the full sample, those with no children, and those with one to three children are identical in each of the other segments included in the table. This suggests that there are minor differences in the distribution of wealth ownership for these groups, but that the overall patterns of wealth ownership are quite similar. Naturally, some of the difference in overall wealth for these groups is an age difference. The groups with more children are also older on average and have had more time to save. Yet these patterns are also consistent with the argument that parents have incentives to save, and the low wealth of those with particularly large families (four or more children) suggests that this is more than an age effect.

In fact, the groups that suffers the most are those families with four or more children. Table 8.3 shows that these families have less wealth across the board, including low overall net worth. The median net worth for those with four or more children is $25,000, less than half that for the overall sample and nearly half that of those with no children. Very few of such large families are millionaires, and they are also underrepresented in the other high-wealth groups. The only wealth segments in which those with large families are over-represented are the lower segments of the distribution. These groups accounts for only 10 percent of the sample, but they account for one-quarter of those with zero or negative wealth. This demonstrates that high debt burdens and low overall saving are keeping the wealth of this group of families low relative to those with fewer children.

Of course there are some important caveats that come with these estimates. In particular, these are basic estimates that do not control for all the other important factors that shape wealth. They do not control for family background traits that I have argued are so critical to understanding wealth. They also do not control for family income, other family resources, marital status, respondent's age, work behavior, education, race, or portfolio behavior. They are simply raw estimates. Of course, they do provide important clues about the nature of the relationship between family size and adult wealth, but multivariate analyses will clarify the degree to which these relationships remain when other inputs are controlled.

A related issue is the degree to which these patterns are spurious. That is, is there some factor that causes people to have many

Table 8.4. *Children and Portfolios*

	% Sample Total	Home	Percentage Owning			
			Stocks and Bonds	Checking and Savings	Trust Account	Business
All	100	68	26	77	5	11
Children						
None	22	55	29	80	6	11
One to three	68	73	27	78	4	11
Four or more	10	62	15	61	3	9

Note: All wealth estimates are for the year 2000.
Source: National Longitudinal Survey of Youth, 1979 Cohort ($N = 4,963$).

children and that also causes them not to save (or worse, to accumulate large amounts of debt)? Again, the multivariate analyses include controls for various other inputs and will remove some concern about spuriousness. Of course, it is not possible to control for all possible influences, but the multivariate models are extremely comprehensive. Moreover, in both the descriptive statistics and the multivariate models, I approximate time order as realistically as possible. That is, I measure the number of children with a lag in order to show how the number of children in the household in the prior period affects wealth in the current period. Yet I found no evidence of changes in family size and no evidence of a cumulative effect of having children. Rather, family size seems to account for the bulk of the differences that are evident in family wealth in this sample. Before discussing the multivariate models, however, there are some possible mechanisms that may underlie the relationship between family size and wealth that I will discuss, including the family's portfolio behavior, the timing of fertility, and the family's investment behavior.

Portfolio behavior is an important mechanism relating family size to family wealth. That is, family size affects the assets that a family can and does own, and the particular combination of assets owned is likely to affect overall wealth. In Table 8.4, I explore the relationship between family size and portfolio behavior. This table shows that patterns of homeownership are similar to patterns of overall wealth by family size, but the table also shows that homeownership patterns may account for some of the trends that were evident in Table 8.3. Across the full sample, 68 percent of respondents were homeowners in 2000. The homeownership rate is significantly lower for those with no children, and significantly higher for those with one to three children. Only 55 percent of those with no children owned homes, while 73 percent of those with small families were homeowners. It would be tempting to attribute this difference to age, and some of the pattern may be accounted for by the respondent's age. However, those with four or more children had lower homeownership rates than the typical NLS-Y respondent, suggesting that family size is relevant and that homeownership is an important cause of the low overall wealth of those with large families. This pattern is particularly significant because the value of the family home accounts for a large financial cushion of many middle American families, as I have shown previously.

Families with large numbers of children are even less likely than the average family to own financial assets such as stocks and bonds or cash accounts. Table 8.4 shows 26 percent of the overall sample owned stocks and bonds, and slightly more of those with no children or small families owned these assets. By contrast, only fifteen percent of those with four or more children owned stocks or bonds. This difference is likely explained by differences in resources available to devote to high-risk investments.

Perhaps more interesting are differences in the ownership of relatively common financial instruments. Table 8.4 also shows there are important differences by family size in the ownership of checking and savings accounts. That is, 77 percent of the total sample, 80 percent of those with no children, and 78 percent of those with small families own some sort of checking or savings account. In contrast, only 61 percent of those with four or more children have a checking or savings account. These estimates are consistent with estimates from other data (Aizcorbe, Kennickell, and Moore 2001), and they hold even though in recent years, the percentage of families who owned any type of cash account increased slightly. Estimates from the Survey of Consumer Finances (SCF) show that between 1998 and 2001, the percentage of families with any type of cash account rose about one-half of a percentage point (Aizcorbe, Kennickell, and Moore 2001).

Given the relatively wide availability and convenience of owning a cash account, it often surprises people that anyone would not own one. Moreover, some argue that discrimination by banks, for example, against poor and minority families prevents these families from opening cash accounts even though they might want to (Caskey 1994; Oliver and Shapiro 1995). For these reasons, the SCF also asked families who did not own checking accounts why they were not owners. Of those with no checking account in 2001, the largest group, 28.6 percent, said that the family does not write enough checks to make it worth having a checking account, and 22.6 percent said they do not like to deal with banks (Aizcorbe, Kennickell, and Moore 2001). The same study showed that only fourteen percent of those with no checking account said that they did not have enough money, 6.5 percent said that the minimum balance was too high, and 5.3 percent said the they did not want or need such an account. While this does not provide conclusive evidence about why families do not have cash accounts, it suggests that at least part of the explanation is that they are choosing not to have these accounts. The implications for those with large families, who as Table 8.4 shows are less likely than average to own these accounts, is that they are not saving in even the most accessible financial instrument. Again, this pattern is part of the explanation for the lower overall wealth of those with large families.

TIMING OF LIFE EVENTS

The timing of life events such as fertility may also affect wealth accumulation and mobility. There has been considerable debate about whether patterns such as teenage childbearing have detrimental long-term effects (Furstenberg 2003). Yet in one area, timing of fertility is likely to have an important negative effect on adult outcomes: wealth ownership. Because wealth accumulation is a process, behaviors that interfere with or enhance the process matter differently depending on their timing. Starting to accumulate assets early in life, for example, can affect long-term accumulation patterns dramatically, particularly when those assets (e.g., stocks or mutual funds) grow and compound dramatically over long periods. Yet even saving early by buying a home when relatively young can create a sizable port-folio and some degree of financial security later in life. Life events that prevent or change saving make this rosy scenario impossible. Likewise, life events that lead to changes in saving – such as buying a bigger house to accommodate more children – can diminish wealth accumulation and mobility.

There is also evidence that teenage childbearing has an effect on women's wages, suggesting an indirect relationship between teenage fertility and adult wealth. Women who have children early in life may not complete as much education as they might have otherwise, and they spend less time building their careers. They may be consid-ered less productive or may actually be less productive because they take time off to have and rear children (Taniguchi 1999). For these reasons, researchers have found that those who bear children early are likely to have lower wages (Taniguchi 1999). Low wages, in turn, imply lower saving rates and lower levels of wealth accumulation. Of course, other life decisions and timing of other life events are also certainly relevant to understand patterns of wealth accumulation and mobility. I focus on teenage fertility and the timing of this behavior because it is an easily measurable behavior, there is evidence that it matters for other adult outcomes, it is a fairly common pattern, and it illustrates my point well.

Table 8.5 shows that early fertility is associated with considerably lower adult wealth. Of those who ever had children by the time the 2000 survey was conducted, those who had their children after age 18 had median net worth of $68,000, which was significantly higher than the overall average of $58,000. In contrast, those who had children before age 18 had net worth of only $8,000. Similar patterns are evident across the wealth distribution. None of the respondents who had children as teenagers were in the two highest segments of the wealth distribution, and only 1 percent of the teenage parents were in the third highest segment. This means that nearly all of the respondents who were teenage parents had net worth in the lowest

Table 8.5. *Children and Wealth*

	% Sample Total	% With Net Worth					Median Net Worth (Thousands)
		> $1 Million	$500K–$999,999	$300K–$499,999	< $300K	Zero or Negative	
All	100	3	4	6	87	15	$58
Had kids before 18	8	0	0	1	99	35	8
Had kids after 18	92	3	6	8	83	15	68

Note: All wealth estimates are for the year 2000.
Source: National Longitudinal Survey of Youth, 1979 Cohort ($N = 4,963$).

wealth segment. In fact, 35 percent of the teenage parents had zero or negative net worth in 2000 even though all of the respondents were at least 35 years old at the time of this survey. In contrast, only 15 percent of those who had children after age 18 had zero or negative net worth in 2000. While it is possible that other factors intercede between early fertility and wealth, it is also likely that this is a somewhat conservative estimate because the cohort represented in the NLS grew up during relatively favorable educational and work environments. The respondents of this cohort were born between 1957 and 1964, and if they did have children as teenagers, they would have been more likely than previous generations to be able to continue in school and to establish careers. This suggests that the wealth effect for earlier cohorts would have been more pronounced. Of course, it also implies that the wealth impact for teenage parents in later generations would be weaker. This is a question that future research may want to explore in more depth.

INVESTMENT BEHAVIOR

The rich are clearly unique in the assets they own. Table 8.6 shows that there are unmistakable differences in the ownership of nearly all assets by total wealth. The home is among the first assets that most families own, and ownership rates for the primary residence are

Table 8.6. *Portfolios of the Rich*

	% Sample Total	Home	Stocks and Bonds	Checking and Savings	Trust Account	Business
			Percentage Owning			
All	100	68	26	77	5	11
Net worth (2000)						
>$1 million	2	94	78	99	20	28
$500K–$999,999	4	93	65	98	14	22
$300K–$499,999	6	97	58	97	10	14
$0–$300,000	77	68	21	76	3	8
Negative	10	35	14	57	3	22

Note: All wealth estimates are for the year 2000.
Source: National Longitudinal Survey of Youth, 1979 Cohort ($N = 4,963$).

among the highest of all assets. In fact, as Table 8.6 demonstrates, nearly 70 percent of families owned their primary residence in 2000. Yet there are clear differences even in homeownership rates at different points of the wealth distribution. Among the very wealthiest households, those with more than $1 million in net worth, 94 percent were homeowners. Similarly, for the slightly less wealthy of the rich (those with net worth greater than $300,000 but not quite $1 million), homeownership rates are equally high or higher. It is interesting to note that among those with between $300,000 and $499,999 in net worth, 97 percent were homeowners, even more than for those in the higher wealth groups. This pattern largely reflects region of residence. More of the very wealthy live in large urban areas, such as New York City, where homeownership rates are lower. In contrast, a larger number of the slightly less wealthy households live in areas where homeownership is more accessible. The key point, however, is that nearly all of the very wealthy own their homes. In the middle of the distribution, homeownership rates reflect the overall average perfectly, and homeownership rates for households at the bottom of the distribution are markedly lower than for other households.

As we would expect, the wealthy are much more likely to own financial assets as well. Table 8.6 also includes estimates of ownership rates for stocks and bonds by total net worth. I use stocks and bonds to demonstrate ownership patterns, but the overall patterns are largely the same for other financial assets. When all families are included, 26 percent of respondents owned stocks and bonds, but the ownership rates are much higher for the wealthy. Of those with more than $1 million in net worth, 78 percent owned stocks and bonds, and the rates drop to 65 percent and 58 percent respectively for the next two segments of the distribution. Among those with positive net worth less than $300,000, just more than 20 percent owned stocks and bonds. Again, the most dramatic difference is for those with negative net worth: only 14 percent of these respondents owned these financial assets. Ownership rates are certainly low for those with negative wealth, and this suggests that there are important differences in the saving and investment behavior that relate to overall net worth. What is perhaps more interesting, however, is to ask who owns stocks and bonds but also has negative wealth. We might expect that those with more debt than assets do not have the resources to invest in financial assets. In reality, however, there are quite a few respondents who have accumulated large amounts of debt – usually debt on businesses, student loans, or other investment-related debt – who are also investing in potentially high return assets. These people are clearly different from those whose negative net worth reflects consumption debt.

Another interesting asset to explore is cash accounts. As I showed above, there are important differences in ownership of checking and savings accounts by family type that I argued are suggestive of how people accumulate assets and who gets rich. Consistent with these arguments, there are also differences in the ownership of cash accounts by total wealth. Table 8.6 shows that ownership rates for cash accounts are high: nearly 80 percent of all respondents own either a savings or a checking account. For those in the very wealthiest segments of the wealth distribution, 97 to 99 percent owned a checking or savings account. Again, the overall average is pulled down by those in the bottom of the distribution, in this case by those who have negative net worth. Fewer than 60 percent of those with negative wealth owned a checking or savings account in 2000. Consistent with analyses of the Survey of Consumer Finances (Aizcorbe, Kennickell, and Moore 2001), additional estimates from the NLS-Y (not included here) show that the percentage of families without a cash account has declined since the early 1990s. Also consistent with the SCF, more than half of the NLS-Y respondents who did not have a cash account in 2000 had one in the past, suggesting some volatility in ownership of this asset. By contrast, the wealthy respondents tended to own cash accounts consistently. The typical respondent who did not own a cash account also had income in the lowest segment of the income distribution, was young (under 40), and was nonwhite.

Indeed, the rich are unique in their asset ownership, and the estimates in Table 8.6 identify some of the basic differences between the rich and everyone else. However, these descriptive statistics do not demonstrate whether the rich invest differently and thus have more money or whether they have more money and thus invest differently. Later in this chapter, when I investigate the effects of adult traits and behaviors on assets net of other effects, I discuss this issue in more detail, and I present some results that suggest that financial behavior and accumulation trajectories do contribute to getting rich.

Another way to explore the role that asset ownership plays in getting rich is to ask whether the rich are more likely to have received part of their wealth from their parents and whether they are more likely to have been entrepreneurs. Both questions have arisen in other parts of this book, but both are worth asking again in this context. In particular, it is interesting to note that although only 5 percent of the total sample ever received a trust account – an indicator that the respondents did not accumulate all of their wealth independently – 20 percent of the millionaires in the NLS-Y sample had trust accounts. Similarly, 14 percent of those in the next segment of the distribution, and 10 percent of those in the third segment pictured in Table 8.6 had trust accounts. This linear trend suggests that there is a distinct, positive relationship between receiving a trust and accumulating large amounts of wealth. Only 3 percent of those with negative net worth had trust accounts. It is not surprising that the percentage of trust owners is much smaller for this group than for the wealthy groups, but it might be a bit surprising that any of the respondents with negative wealth had received a trust account. The table does not show that the value of the trust accounts received by those with negative net worth was considerably lower than the value of the account received by the wealthier respondents. The table also does not show that those who received a trust and have negative net worth tended to be young and to have student loans, business loans, and other loans for investments that account for their negative wealth. Those who *did not* receive a trust and had negative wealth tended to have more consumption debt.

Equally important, the wealthy *and those with negative wealth* are much more likely to own business assets, including investments in their own entrepreneurial endeavors. Chapter 7 explored the role of entrepreneurship in wealth accumulation in more detail, but this table provides additional support for the finding that entrepreneurs tend to accumulate more wealth than others. The business asset measure used in Table 8.6, however, also includes investments in other businesses. It is important to note that the very rich (those with more than $1 million in net worth) are much more likely than the typical respondent to own business assets. Indeed, ownership rates among millionaires were nearly three times as high as in the full sample. Ownership of business assets was nearly as high for those with wealth greater than $500,000 but less than $1 million. What is most interesting is that ownership rates for those with negative net worth were comparable to rates for the very wealthy. This reflects the fact that many of those with negative net worth have debt that they are using to fund business ventures. Clearly these individuals are on a different trajectory than those who are funding consumption with debt that exceeds their savings. The multivariate analyses below explore the degree to which these patterns withstand controlling for the multitude of other behaviors and processes that also shape wealth ownership.

CONTEXT

The context within which persons save – or do not save – also shapes their wealth in ways that cannot always be controlled. Economic conditions, for example, make it more or less easy to accumulate any assets and determine which assets will be more lucrative. A great example of the importance of economic conditions is the degree to which stock ownership paid off during most of the 1990s. There is considerable evidence of a relationship between stock market fluctuations and the concentration of wealth. When the market booms, stock owners get richer and move up in the distribution (Keister 1997; Winnick 1989). Because white, married, college-educated people are more likely than nonwhite, unmarried people who have not graduated from college to own stock, they do well when the stock market booms.

When the stock market booms, the distribution of wealth also tends to become more unequal (Smith 1987; Wolff 1987, 1992). Smith (1987) showed that between 1972 and 1976, the share of wealth held by the top .5 percent of wealth owners dropped from 22 to 14 percent, and the share of the top 1 percent dropped from 28 to 19 percent. He attributed this to a decrease in the value of stocks owned by these top wealth holders. He also demonstrated that the total stock owned by the top 1 percent of wealth holders fell from $491 million in 1972 to $297 in 1976, not because they divested but because share prices declined sharply during that period. Other studies have showed similar patterns using both empirical and simulated data (Keister 1997). Similar, but less dramatic, patterns can be identified for booms and busts in housing and real estate markets.

A related element of context is the generation in which a person is born. Those who spent the 1990s working and at relatively high levels of lifetime earnings were more able to take advantage of stock market booms in building their portfolios. There is also evidence that members of some generations save and accumulate assets in unique ways. Sociologists argue that traits of a cohort can imprint members of the generation in ways that affect members over the entire life (Elder 1995; Morgan 1998). The Great Depression, for example, shaped attitudes, behaviors, and many other later-life outcomes of the people who lived through it. The people who grew up during the Depression tend to be conservative in terms of both their social and work behaviors and their investment behavior

Table 8.7. *Hometown of the Forbes 400 (2003)*

	Number of Forbes 400 Members	Combined Net Worth of Forbes 400 Members	State GDP
Most Forbes Members			
California	93	167	1,359
New York	49	101	826
Texas	36	80	764
Washington	11	93	222
Forbes' wealth > GDP			
Arkansas	7	85	68

Note: Net worth and gross domestic product (GDP) are in billions of 2003 dollars.
Source: Forbes magazine.

(Keister and Deeb-Sossa 2000; Sabelhaus and Manchester 1995). In contrast, the children of the Depression generation – the baby boomers – tend to be socially liberal and to have accumulated relatively more wealth than their parents. Baby boomers have tended to postpone marriage and fertility, and female baby boomers have been more likely than their mothers to complete college and to work even after having children. Baby boomers have had relatively high wages and have lived through fairly favorable economic conditions. As a result, baby boomers have accumulated more wealth relative to their parents. I do not explicitly control for generation of economic conditions in the multivariate models I have shown because I have a unique sample (the NLS-Y sample is age restricted). However, the findings of previous research suggest that the inclusion of context in my conceptual model does reflect the realities of wealth accumulation.

A more concrete element of context that I can test directly is geography. Geography could include indicators of region of the country, state, city, urban or rural residence, and even neighborhood. At each level of geographic aggregation, it is possible that elements of the surroundings affect the way people accumulate assets. In this spirit, *Forbes* magazine regularly tracks the home state of the wealthiest, and in recent years, most of the Forbes 400 called California and New York home. As Table 8.7 shows, 93 Forbes members lived in California, and 49 lived in New York in 2003. This table identifies the four

states with most Forbes members in 2003 and notes the combined
net worth of Forbes 400 members in that state along with the state's
gross domestic product (GDP). Texas had 36 Forbes members, and
Washington (home to Microsoft) had 11. I also included Arkansas
(home of Wal Mart and the Walton fortune heirs) in the table because, in 2003, it was the only state in which the combined wealth of
the Forbes 400 members exceeded the state's GDP. I did not include
states at the lower end of the spectrum in the table – that is, those
with no members of the Forbes 400. Yet in 2003, 10 states tied for last
place: Alaska, Delaware, Iowa, Kentucky, Maine, Mississippi, New
Mexico, North Dakota, Vermont, and West Virginia.

Although it is interesting to look at the areas the rich call home,
there is no effect of state of residence or even geographic region of
residence when these are included in multivariate models using the
NLS-Y. In contrast, residence in an urban area does tend to affect
wealth. In particular, those living in large urban areas, where housing
in particular is expensive, do accumulate assets differently than those
living in areas where housing is more accessible. For these reasons,
I do control for urban residence in all of the multivariate models I
present.

Multivariate Results: Marriage and Wealth

Multivariate analyses provide additional support for the conceptual
model and the empirical relationships that I have discussed throughout this chapter. Table 8.8 includes partial models of adult assets
between 1985 and 2000, highlighting the effects of education, adult
resources, age, and adult family traits. I include two separate equations in the table to demonstrate the independent effect of education
and then to show how the addition of the other adult traits affects the
education results. Once again, these are only partial models, and the
complete model is included in the Appendix. The first model demonstrates that the effect of education is quite strong and increases with
the level of educational attainment. Although these models cannot
directly test the mechanisms that link education with adult wealth,
they provide support for the argument that formal education provides

Table 8.8. *Adult Family Background and Asset Accumulation, (1985–2000)*

	Education Only	Add Adult Traits
Respondent's education		
High school	17.85***	2.56
	(4.86)	(5.36)
Some college	34.11***	10.53*
	(5.72)	(6.26)
College degree	57.58***	28.46***
	(6.64)	(7.20)
Advanced degree	74.57***	40.51***
	(7.41)	(8.00)
Adult resources		
Entrepreneurial income	–	56.22***
		(7.65)
Family income	–	0.00***
		(0.00)
Age	–	8.18***
		(0.37)
Adult family		
Married	–	27.46***
		(3.96)
Separated	–	−15.98*
		(9.87)
Divorced	–	−16.48***
		(5.72)
Widowed	–	55.27**
		(25.26)
Number of children	–	3.46**
		(1.75)

Note: These are PARTIAL MODELS; other test variables and control variables are included but not displayed.
See Appendix for full models. Cells are coefficient estimates with standard errors in parentheses. * $p < .10$; ** $p < .05$; *** $p < .01$.
Source: National Longitudinal Survey of Youth, 1979 Cohort.

the skills, resources, and social connections that facilitate wealth accumulation. The second model introduces the other effects and shows that the strength of the education variables is reduced considerably. Cox tests confirm that the coefficients for education are lower in the second model. I have estimated other models, not included in this book, that in much greater detail experiment with the causal order of the independent variables. These models suggest that for most NLS-Y respondents, family background shapes educational attainment. Educational attainment, then, affects adult work, income, and family patterns that translate into adult wealth accumulation patterns.

Income is a critical variable included in the second model in Table 8.8. Total family income (measured in the previous year to approximate true chronological order) clearly has a strong, positive relationship with wealth. Similarly, entrepreneurial income has a separate, and equally strong, positive association with adult net worth. I experimented with various different ways of measuring income, and there was no real difference in the effect of the different variables. Measuring income as lifetime earnings, for example, is another common way to quantify income. That is, it is possible that the total earnings over the adult working years is what affects adult wealth. Substituting lifetime earnings for total, lagged household income has the same effect on adult assets. Similarly, measure income as respondent's income and including a separate indicator of spouse's income does not affect the results. In other models, I have also controlled for work behavior in various ways. I find that including measures such as time spent in the labor market and quality of employer (e.g., availability of health plans and pension plans) increase wealth. I also find that measures such as number of weeks unemployed, total number of jobs held during the career, and number of job changes decrease total wealth. These effects tend to be mediated to some degree by education, but they continue to affect wealth even when education is controlled.

Next to income, marital status is among the strongest predictors of adult wealth. Married couples have an undisputed advantage in asset accumulation over unmarried people, and the results included in Table 8.8 document the magnitude of this advantage. The omitted marital status is never married people, and the model shows that married couples have significantly more wealth than their never married counterparts. Married people tend to have lower expenses than two people living independently, they tend to join income resources, and they tend to save as a team. Moreover, married people may be more likely to have incentives to save that include potential college expenses for children. Of course, the models in Table 8.8 also control for the number of children a couple has. The models do not control for the prospect of additional children, an incentive that both those with and without children might have. The model also shows that separated and divorced respondents did relatively worse than those who were never married suggesting that these people suffered from the process of splitting joint assets at the end of a marriage. The one group that had accumulated even more wealth than married couples were widows. In fact, the magnitude of the effect for being widowed is more than twice that for being married. Yet because there are relatively few widows in the sample, the widowed indicator is not quite as statistically significant as the married indicator. As the NLS-Y sample continues to age, it will be important to observe how the effect of widowhood on wealth changes.

One question that arises from including all unmarried people together is: How do these effects vary with gender? That is, do women and men experience separation, divorce, and widowhood differently? Similarly, is there a difference between never-married women and their male counterparts? Indeed, there are an increasing number of female-headed households in the United States, and some have argued that this trend is leading to a feminization of poverty (McLanahan and Kelly 1999). Researchers argue that single females are likely to be financially worse-off than their male counterparts. Since the late 1970s, researchers have explored the possibility that an increasingly large percentage of the economically disadvantaged are women (Bianchi 1999; McLanahan and Kelly 1999). Although it has been difficult to determine the extent of the problem, there is convincing evidence that the relative risks of poverty for women increased in the 1970s but decreased starting in the early 1980s due at least in part to a decline in the gender wage gap (Bianchi 1999). Perhaps the most important lesson this research has taught is that there are gender-specific patterns of economic well-being that cannot be ignored. Extending these ideas to the study of wealth implies that there may also be important differences in wealth accumulation by gender and marital status. Previous research on wealth ownership has certainly taken these factors into account, but researchers

Table 8.9. *Gender, Marriage, and Asset Accumulation, (1985–2000)*

	Gender and Marriage	
	Separate	Interacted
Male	8.37	–
	(3.18)	
Marital status		
Married	28.50***	–
	(4.80)	
Female never married	–	−29.05***
		(7.85)
Female separated	–	−23.32**
		(0.03)
Female divorced	–	−29.02***
		(6.44)
Female widowed	–	49.63**
		(25.07)
Male never married	–	−24.84***
		6.89
Male separated	–	−24.03*
		(13.42)
Male divorced	–	−22.09***
		(7.37)
Male widowed	–	6.04
		42.79

Note: These are PARTIAL MODELS; other test variables and control variables are included but not displayed. Model also includes all control variables included in previous model. Cells are coefficient estimates with standard errors in parentheses. * $p < .10$; ** $p < .05$; *** $p < .01$.

Source: National Longitudinal Survey of Youth, 1979 Cohort.

seldom explore the extent to which the interaction between the two matters. Far from being a trivial point, this oversight implies that research on wealth has not explored the effect that the rise in female-headed households may have on the accumulation and distribution of wealth.

Table 8.9 investigates the role that gender and marital status play in shaping wealth accumulation by including two separate multivariate models. The first model includes separate indicators of gender (male) and marital status (married couples compared to all other couples). Again, these are only partial models, and they control for all other variables discussed throughout this book. The first model shows that marital status has a strong positive relationship with wealth, while there is no direct effect of gender. The second model includes separate indicators of marital status for all unmarried individuals by gender. The omitted category in the second model is that of married couples. This model shows that both never-married men and women fare significantly worse on asset accumulation than married couples. Women appear to do slightly worse than men, but the difference is not statistically significant. Similarly, both separated men and women have fewer assets than married couples, but the separation penalty is equal for men and women.

There is a slightly greater disadvantage of divorce for women, supporting arguments that women fare worse after a divorce than men. However, both divorced men and divorced women do much worse than married couples, and the gender difference is minimal. Exploratory research shows that among the divorced couples in the NLS-Y sample, the women were more likely than the men to be homeowners, particularly in families with children. This suggests that the women were keeping the home after a divorce and adding to their total assets. Widowed females also appear to do better than widowed males, but again, samples sizes for widowed males in the NLS-Y are still much too small to draw definitive conclusions from this finding.

Multivariate Results: Children and Wealth

Table 8.8 shows that wealth increases with the number of children in a family. Consistent with the descriptive statistics covered earlier, larger families have more assets, controlling for all other factors discussed throughout this book. Taken together, the multivariate results and the descriptive results show that parents have more wealth, and this is likely because they tend to be homeowners and to own financial assets. The descriptive statistics also suggested that the number of children in a family matters. That is, there appeared to be an increase in wealth for those with up to three children and a decline in wealth for those with additional children. Table 8.10 repeats

Table 8.10. *Children and Asset Accumulation, (1985–2000)*

	Children One Measure	By Group
Number of children	3.46**	–
	(1.75)	
1	–	10.08
		(7.54)
2	–	21.27***
		(7.58)
3	–	23.08**
		(9.64)
4 or more	–	3.8
		(13.08)

Note: These are PARTIAL MODELS; other test variables and control variables are included but not displayed. Model also includes all control variables included in previous model. Cells are coefficient estimates with standard errors in parentheses. * $p < .10$; ** $p < .05$; *** $p < .01$.
Source: National Longitudinal Survey of Youth, 1979 Cohort.

the model included in Table 8.8 but includes separate indicators for the number of children in the family. The multivariate results corroborate the argument that those with two or three children have relatively more assets, all other factors controlled. This model suggests, however, that once other factors are controlled, the apparent penalty for having four or more children is no longer significant. Similarly, the multivariate results suggest that there is no advantage to having one child but that the increased savings appears only after the family has two children. It would be tempting to attribute this effect to age, but again, this model controls for all other factors, including age.

MULTIVARIATE RESULTS:
FINANCIAL BEHAVIOR AND WEALTH

I also argued that financial behavior and the trajectory or the path along which people accumulate wealth shapes the assets they own. Understanding of financial decision making comes from formal channels, such as formal education, and informal channels, including

Table 8.11. *Financial Behavior, Accumulation*
Trajectory, and Asset Accumulation (1985–2000)

Percent stocks and bonds	414.94***
	(39.43)
Percent housing assets	−38.46***
	(8.05)
Early transition to financial wealth	119.42***
	(71.57)
Traditional accumulation path	−130.06***
	(13.33)

Note: These are PARTIAL MODELS; other test variables and control variables are included but not displayed. Model also includes all control variables included in previous model. Cells are coefficient estimates with standard errors in parentheses. * $p < .10$; ** $p < .05$; *** $p < .01$.

parents' behavior and the lessons parents teach. Those with more education tend to make financial decisions that yield higher wealth; likewise, those who learn about financial behavior from their parents are likely to make better financial decisions, to save earlier, and to accumulate wealth faster. In Table 8.11, I replicate the full regression model and introduce four indicators to explore the effect of financial behavior and accumulation trajectory on assets. In the Appendix I explain in more detail that the first two variables capture the effect of financial behavior. The first variable is the percentage of the portfolio that is accounted for by stocks and bonds, high-risk assets that tend to grow more rapidly. The second variable is the percentage of the portfolio accounted for by housing. Having a higher percentage of the portfolio invested in stocks and bonds yields more wealth, and having a higher percentage of the portfolio invested in housing decreases wealth, all other factors controlled. Similarly, those who made an early transition to financial wealth (invested in stocks and bonds early and before other assets) increased the value of their wealth considerably. In contrast, those who followed a more traditional path in their savings accumulated markedly less than other investors. I included respondents in the traditional accumulation group if they purchased a home during adulthood, did not own more than $1,000 in stocks and bonds before owning a house, and continued to own a home for at least five years. The omitted category is that of all other respondents. The Appendix describes the various ways in which I experimented with measuring trajectories and explains that the basic finding is robust across many different definitions of the independent variables.

CONCLUSION

This chapter explored the remainder of the elements of the conceptual model that has guided this book. I showed that married couples have considerably more wealth than others even when other factors are controlled. In contrast, those who are divorced or separated have considerably less wealth than those who have never married. Widows, particularly widowed females, appear to have a wealth advantage, but this finding should be interpreted with some caution given the young age of the NLS-Y sample. I also showed that there are only limited gender differences in wealth ownership for unmarried respondents; rather, the difference across those who are not currently married appears to be in whether they were ever married in the past. Families with children had more wealth net of other factors including marital status and age, probably because they have additional reasons to save. Finally, I showed that there are important differences in wealth accumulation given investment behavior and the trajectory along which saving occurs. Those who take risks and invest in high return assets are rewarded, while those who save more conservatively enjoy lower returns. These patterns corroborate findings in previous research, and demonstrate the workings of the final segments of my conceptual model.

CHAPTER NINE

CONCLUSION: BORN TO BE RICH

This book began by asking what factors account for wealth accumulation and mobility. That is, why do some people get rich while others never seem to get ahead. Wealth is the things people own, including their homes, savings, investments, other real estate, businesses, and vehicles. Recent shifts in economic conditions propelled some people to great wealth and ignited interest in how this process unfolds. Subsequent economic downturns highlighted the fact that wealth can be – and often is – fleeting. Researchers have been more interested in wealth in recent years, perhaps than at any other point in history. We now have many excellent sources of information about household asset and debt ownership, and this has allowed us to specify very precisely the nature of wealth distribution. That is, we know a great deal about how wealth ownership is allocated across people: what percentage of the total pie is owned by what percentage of the population. The bottom line is that a very small percentage of Americans owns the vast majority of wealth. Yet even with this increased interest in wealth and our improving ability to understand wealth, we know very little about the process by which people accumulate assets. What is it about their backgrounds and the paths they follow through their lives that makes some people accumulate lots of assets while others never seem to save much of anything? Is it simply that those who start off with more end with more? Or are there opportunities for even those at the bottom to move up? If so, what factors make it more possible to get rich over time?

Questions about wealth accumulation and mobility are interesting because there seems to be no end to our fascination with the very wealthy. However, these questions are also central to understanding how people are sorted and why. Having at least some savings is very important to well-being. Assets such as the home provide current use as well as an investment that can be drawn on later in life. Other savings can be used in the event of a financial or medical emergency or in the event of the unemployment of a primary breadwinner. There are, of course, additional advantages of having wealth that exceeds the minimum needed to prevent financial disaster. Wealth can produce political or social influence, it can be used to purchase luxuries and a safe living environment, it can be used to buy leisure, it can be used to improve educational and occupational advantages, and it can be used to create more wealth. Unlike income, wealth can also be directly transferred to future generations, allowing the advantages it entails to be passed along as well. I showed in the first chapter that the total wealth owned by households has increased considerably in recent decades, and I also showed that the average wealth owned by each household has also risen. Yet even while wealth has increased, nearly 20 percent of the population continues to have no savings or to have debt that exceeds their savings. So while understanding wealth accumulation and mobility does shed light on the very rich, it also tells us a great deal about the rest of the population. In exploring questions about wealth accumulation, then, this book also asks about the degree to which opportunities are equal or at least available at various parts of the financial spectrum.

This book is unique in several ways. Perhaps most important, this book is unique in that it is focused on wealth. There is no lack of interest in the availability of opportunities or in questions about who gets ahead and why. A quick look at both popular titles and scholarly publications on inequality and stratification suggest that attention to questions of mobility and well-being is not lacking. Yet most of this attention is still given to income. Even when the word wealth is used, it is often used to refer to financial streams that I refer to as income. Wages and salaries from work, interest from savings, dividends from investments, and government transfer payments such as social security payments are all forms of income. It is certainly important to understand what factors affect how much income a person or a household has, but understanding how much wealth they have is also important. Wealth is the reserve of financial resources owned at a point in time. Attention to income has been more common largely because data on income are more easily available. It is only relatively recent that data on wealth are available, and both academics and popular writers have just begun to explore the role that wealth plays in people's well-being. This book is unique in that it pushes our understanding of wealth a few steps by exploring the processes by which people accumulate their assets and by which some people get rich.

This book is unique because it explores how a person's wealth changes over time. Because I ask about accumulation, I was forced to ask how behaviors and processes that affect wealth change over time. Because I ask about wealth ownership and mobility, I was forced to address how childhood behaviors and processes interact with adult behaviors and processes to ultimately create adult wealth. It is sensible to think that the process of wealth accumulation must take processes at various stages of the life course into account, but doing so can become complicated. Just enumerating the factors that must be accounted for at each stage of the life course is complex. Understanding how they interact with each other adds another level of complexity, and then modeling these processes empirically creates its own challenges. One of the primary goals of this book was to identify the relevant factors and to make a case for the manner in which they are related to each other. This was the focus of Part I of the book. A second goal of this book was to explore these processes empirically. That was the purpose of Part II. While it would take several volumes to investigate all of the factors that affect wealth accumulation, my goal was to identify and investigate the major causes. In some cases, the analyses I presented raised additional questions, and as a result, this book also raised questions that will hopefully be taken up in future research.

This book is also unique because it began with a multi-dimensional conceptual model that incorporates numerous factors from throughout the life course and presents a cohesive model of how these affect wealth ownership. It is appealing to explain wealth accumulation exclusively as a result of initial advantage and market fluctuations: those

who start out with more end up with more, and those who have
wealth get richer during good economic times. Yet, there I argued
that the process of wealth accumulation is likely more complex than
that. Family background matters in the sense that experiences and
events from childhood shape the paths people take during their lives.
More specifically, I proposed that traits such as parents' attainment,
family size, and family culture and religion shape the trajectory on
which people enter adulthood and affect where they end up. I argued
that much of the effect of family background operates through its
effect on education and educational attainment. I argued that these
processes then interact with adult behaviors and processes to shape
wealth ownership. Specifically, I proposed that educational attainment shapes work experiences, financial behavior, and adult family
behavior in ways that will influence the degree to which a person is
upwardly mobile. I proposed that financial well-being during childhood does have an effect on adult wealth – both directly and through
its effect on education – but that these other processes operate even
at comparable levels of childhood finances.

Finally, this book is unique because it explored these processes
by drawing on multiple data sets, including the National Longitudinal Survey of Youth, 1979 cohort (NLS-Y). For instance, I drew on
data from the Survey of Consumer Finances (SCF), largely regarded
as the most accurate cross-sectional (at one point in time) source
of information about household wealth. Using the SCF allowed me
to explore patterns of wealth ownership in recent years in order to
understand who is rich now. I also used data from the Panel Study
of Income Dynamics (PSED), a data set that contains information
about a large sample of people who are beginning to start their own
businesses. Using the PSED allowed me to explore the degree to
which business owners begin rich as opposed to getting rich because
of their entrepreneurial activities. I drew most heavily on the NLS-Y,
however, because it contains information on individual and family
traits at each point that I emphasize in the conceptual model. The
NLS-Y surveyed nearly 13,000 individuals in 1979 and has followed
them closely nearly every year since that time. The data set contains
very detailed information about the family background, educational
attainment, work experiences, and other life events for the large

majority of the sample through 2000. The NLS-Y also contains detailed information about the wealth ownership and accumulation
patterns of this sample, making it possible to develop empirical models that incorporate multiple interacting process that affect wealth
accumulation. Finally, I used other, supplementary data sets where
necessary to explore as many aspects of wealth mobility as possible.

Wealth Mobility: Is there Anything to Explain?

The first question that arises in a study of mobility is: Is there anything to explain? That is, if we are going to understand who is mobile,
we need to know that there are enough people who change positions
over time to explain what accounts for the change. In Chapter Two,
I drew on previous estimates, public and historical records, and my
own analyses of updated data to provide new estimates of the degree
to which Americans experience wealth mobility. I showed that there
is, indeed, a great deal of persistence in wealth ownership both across
generations (i.e., from parents to children) and within generations
(i.e., over a person's own life). Yet I also showed that a considerable
amount of wealth mobility does occur. I drew on historical records
to show that, to the extent to which it is possible to know, there was
very little upward mobility in the early phases of American history.
Estimates from more modern history suggest that while mobility is
certainly limited, it has increased since the 1800s and early 1900s.
Compared to education and income, there appears to be greater persistence in wealth ownership over time. Yet, mobility tables (i.e.,
tables showing the percentage of people in particular segments who
remain in those segments or move to other segments) suggest that
there is still a considerable amount of upward wealth mobility. This
does not suggest that opportunities are equal, but it does mean that
more people, than we would expect by chance, experience upward
wealth mobility over their lives.

After showing that there is at least enough wealth mobility to
explain, I began the process of exploring who does get rich. In
Chapter Three, I provided an overview of who the wealthy are, where
they came from, and how wealthy they are. I used Forbes lists to

identify specific wealthy individuals and then broadened the portrait by using survey data to understand the traits shared by those in the top of the wealth distribution. I found that the wealthy are unique in some important and insightful ways. They have different patterns of saving and investment than those who are not rich. They are also a very well-educated group, and I argued that it is likely that today's rich are more educated than the rich of previous generations. This is important and surprising to the extent to which education allows people to move up in the wealth distribution either between childhood and adulthood or during their adult lives. Historically, good breeding and family connections were likely more important than personal attainment in determining mobility. Yet the evidence suggests that personal traits, particularly education, are now at least a very important part of the picture. The basic portrait of the wealthy that Chapter Three included did not consider other factors that might affect wealth mobility, nor did it attempt to understand whether education facilitates mobility or wealth increases educational attainment. That task, and related tasks, were the subject of the remainder of the book.

The Rich – and Many Others – Get Richer

The second part of this book started with the understanding that there is enough wealth mobility to explain who experiences mobility, and then began to explain who is more fortunate than others. To do this, I developed and explored the meaning of a series of descriptive statistics and multivariate analyses of wealth accumulation and changes in wealth accumulation over time (both from childhood to adulthood and during adulthood). Chapter Five showed that yes, the rich do get richer. Those who inherit wealth, accumulate more wealth as adults than those who do not inherit or who inherit very little. This chapter also showed that parents' attainment – education attainment, occupational well-being, and other financial resources – allow their children to accumulate more wealth than their less fortunate counterparts, all other factors controlled. Those with successful parents also experienced greater changes in their wealth over time, all other factors controlled.

Chapter Five also isolated and explored how other elements of family background shape adult wealth. I showed that the size and structure of the family of origin shaped wealth accumulation and mobility even when all other factors were held constant. Those who came from larger families accumulated less wealth as adults. Consistent with the conceptual model I proposed, the findings suggested that siblings reduced adult wealth by decreasing the material and non-material resources available during childhood. I also found that the persistent racial divide in wealth ownership may be at least partially due to family processes during childhood. These findings do not imply that the relationship between family background and adult wealth is anything but complex, but they do suggest that family background shapes adult wealth in ways that should not be ignored.

Chapter Six explored the role of family background in more detail by addressing the role that family culture, particularly religious upbringing, plays in adult wealth accumulation. I argued that religion is an important determinant of wealth ownership, and I showed patterns in the relationship between religion and wealth. I showed that childhood religion can influence adult wealth both indirectly and directly. I proposed that religion affects adult wealth indirectly by shaping fertility and marriage, education, work patterns, and other behaviors that indirectly affect wealth ownership.

I also showed that religion has a direct effect on wealth, even when all other factors are held constant. I argued that this effect remains because religion is a key component of family culture, and it shapes the goals that people attempt to achieve during their lives and the ways they go about trying to achieve those goals. As a result, religion contributes to the strategies that people use to make important decisions, including decisions about how much to save, how to save that money, how much debt to accumulate, and how to spend their reserves. In addition, it is likely that attending religious services also shapes the nature of social contacts during childhood and into adulthood, and these contacts contribute to the opportunities to save and invest and also shape the strategies that people use in making decisions about wealth. The strong findings in this chapter suggest that religious upbringing does matter, but they do not propose that conversion to religions that are associated with higher wealth is a reasonable response. Rather these findings suggest that there is something very important about the processes that occur in families that shapes adult wealth. Religion is merely part of this story.

While family background is certainly an important part of the wealth accumulation and mobility story, individual behaviors and processes definitely factor in as well. In the final two chapters, I highlighted the importance of work patterns and family life in order to explore the degree to which adult processes matter. In Chapter Seven, I showed that work and occupations do influence adult wealth accumulation. Most interesting, I found that self-employment is related to much higher levels of wealth ownership. Because this relationship raises questions about whether entrepreneurship is a path to becoming rich or the rich are simply more able to start their own businesses, I took a somewhat different approach to analysis. That is, I first use the NLS-Y to show that entrepreneurship increases wealth, even when other influences on wealth accumulation and mobility are held constant. I then drew on data on people who are in the process of starting their own businesses to explore whether wealth ownership increases the chances that they will become entrepreneurs. I found that when other factors are controlled, wealth ownership did not affect the transition to self employment. This simple finding is really quite important because it suggests that entrepreneurship may be a viable route for those who begin with little wealth to get rich.

At the other end of the spectrum, I explored how those who work in nonstandard jobs such as temporary jobs, accumulate assets. The analyses in Chapter seven showed that temporary workers accumulate less wealth than those who had not spent time in temporary positions, even when other factors including marital status, income, time in position were controlled. The findings also suggested that the more time people spend in temporary jobs, the worse they do. The low benefits, such as pension and healthcare benefits, that temporary workers receive are likely to blame for this pattern, a pattern that is consistent with the growing literature on the detriments of nonstandard work of various sorts.

Adult behaviors and processes are also likely to shape wealth ac-cumulation and mobility. These factors have received a great deal of attention from researchers because they are clearly connected to wealth ownership, but also because they are relatively easy to study. For instance, data on the relationship between marital status or family size and wealth are much more accessible than data on the relation-ship between childhood religion and wealth. While the relationship between adult family traits and wealth accumulation have been stud-ied before, the relationships have not been studied exhaustively and are more nuanced than previous research would suggest. I found, for example, that married couples do have more wealth than their unmarried counterparts. However, I also showed that there is lit-tle difference in wealth accumulation across the single households when gender is taken into account. Both males and females who are divorced and separated accumulated fewer assets than married cou-ples. Widowed women, in contrast, accumulated more assets than married couples, while widowed men were not statistically different from married couples. The finding regarding widowhood should be interpreted carefully, however, because the NLS-Y data on which it is based is age restricted, and the finding may change as the respondents age.

This chapter also showed that family size increases wealth, partic-ularly for those with two or three children, perhaps because children encourage saving. Finally, this chapter identified patterns in sav-ing behavior and wealth accumulation trajectories during adulthood, which shape wealth accumulation. Namely, those who start saving early and save in more high-risk, nontraditional ways accumulate assets relatively quickly and tend to be upwardly mobile. Together, these findings suggest that adult behaviors and processes – some of which can be taught and changed – are also critical to the process of wealth accumulation and mobility.

CAVEATS, QUALIFICATIONS, AND EXTENSIONS

This book is not perfect. The conceptual model is comprehen-sive, and the analyses in the book suggest that the model is highly

consistent with empirical reality. However, there may be flaws with
the model and ways in which the analyses could be improved. There
may be other paths that are not included, and there may be factors
that are important determinants of wealth mobility that I neglected
entirely. Moreover, the model may be even more complex than I suggest. Some of the paths are certainly more important than others, I
have not made the relative importance of the factors a central theme
in my discussions.

Empirically, I did not test every possible path, and I did not explore many of the specific factors that are included in the model (e.g.,
the effect of other family background traits or alternative work arrangements). My objective was to test the basic model and to demonstrate how it works. I also focused on testing and discussing the factors
that were particularly relevant. In doing so, I certainly neglected important influences or ignored them entirely. I also did not address the
issue of downward mobility – What accounts for those who move
in the other direction? Not dealing directly with these issues was
not oversight but rather a function of limited space, and of course,
limited time. On the issue of downward mobility, the answer is essentially a mirror of the answer I provide for upward mobility. Yet,
it would be interesting to explore how the two differ. Of course,
as I have pointed out throughout the book, future research ought
to be able to pick up where this book ends and examine exten-
sions of these ideas, test alternative specifications, and explore the
links and relationships that I unfortunately was not able to address
here.

Another important caveat is about data. I used multiple data sets
to test these ideas, and my aim was to be broad in drawing on data
while remaining focused on answering the central question. I drew
largely on data from the NLS-Y 1979 cohort because of its longitudinal coverage and comprehensive interview schedule. However, this
sample is age-restricted. That is, it is a single cohort who have not
reached retirement yet. I did use the NLS mature men sample to estimate mobility patterns, and I found that the sample exhibited very
similar mobility patterns. Yet that does not mean that patterns in the
NLS-Y will not change as the sample ages. In fact, they are likely

to change in important ways, and it will only be with additional studies of the sample that the relevance of the differences will be clear. I might also have drawn on other longitudinal data sets such as the Panel Study of Income Dynamics, but I did not because the sample size and demographics of the NLS-Y sample are comparable, and I find the wealth information in the NLS-Y to be superior in both breadth of coverage over time and within single households. Of course, additional research that compares the two data sets would indicate whether there are discrepancies between the two that need to be addressed.

A related issue is history: this study occurs during an unusual period in U.S. history. Part of my argument was that there are different forces affecting how people are sorted economically and socially now than there were in previous points in history. Moreover, I addressed – albeit very briefly – the issue of context and economic conditions. Yet I do pretend to have done a comprehensive job exploring the way this time period differs from other periods. Differences in economic performance, political differences, and social differences that cohorts experience will all shape the way they accumulated wealth and will, therefore, affect wealth mobility patterns. The time period I studied also saw the proliferation of wealth based on services, investment, knowledge, information, software, and related endeavors. During previous historical periods, land ownership, banking, and industry were dominant. An important implication of not dealing more directly with time period is, as Chaim Waxman pointed out, that the former set of industries (services, finance, investment, etc.) tend to have more Jews working in them than the latter. If I had done this study using data from 50 years earlier, my religion findings might have been very different. Similarly, family size has different implications today than it did when agriculture demanded family labor. Again, if I had done this study in previous decades I would have found some very different patterns. While these caveats are certainly true, they do not negate the findings. In fact, part of my argument is that these patterns reflect today's reality and the fact that today's reality is different from what we suspect historical reality to have been is quite interesting.

Final Comments

While this book is not perfect, it does make a contribution to our understanding of the processes by which people are sorted socially and economically. The findings imply that mobility is possible and that there are behaviors that people can use to affect how much mobility they experience. I find that education is central to the process of wealth accumulation. I also find that it is not just the rich who become entrepreneurs, yet entrepreneurs really do accumulate more wealth on average than those who are not self employed. While these findings do not exhaust the means by which getting rich is possible, they do suggest that it is possible to get rich despite a difficult starting point.

My findings also provide support for very specific arguments about such influences as sibship size and religion, work behavior, and the timing of family events. The negative relationship between sibship size and adult education is among the most persistent findings in research on education (Blake 1989; Downey 1995b), but debate regarding the conditions under which the relationship holds and the reason for the effect has continued (Downey et al. 1999; Guo and VanWey 1999). My results extend the discussion of resource dilution beyond the study of education and demonstrate that additional siblings do, indeed, reduce the financial resources that parents transfer directly to their children in the form of inheritance. Similarly, the findings regarding religion extend the growing and increasingly important literature on the implications of religion by showing that religion may shape wealth accumulation and mobility. Perhaps most important, these findings also underscore the importance of family processes in the accumulation of wealth.

Perhaps most important, my findings have implications beyond the somewhat facetious notion of getting rich. As the twenty-first century begins, wealth inequality is at a level that really is unacceptable and likely unsustainable. Understanding how people accumulate wealth is the first step toward understanding what behaviors and processes at the level of individuals and families can be affected to change saving and thus wealth ownership. Of course, eliminating wealth inequality is not easy. Persistent inequality in wealth ownership is deeply embedded in inequality in earnings, education, and other behaviors and processes that indirectly affect wealth ownership. Not until these disparities are eliminated will current differences in asset ownership be reduced to tolerable levels.

Research Design and
Measurement Issues

Data Details: Supplementary Data

I draw on numerous data sources to provide estimates of wealth ownership and mobility. Table A.1 highlights the strengths and limitations of these sources.

BALANCE SHEETS FOR THE U.S. ECONOMY, 1994–2003

The *Balance Sheets for the U.S. Economy* (the flow of funds) is a time series of flows and levels (stocks) of aggregate wealth holdings for various sectors of the economy. The Board of Governors of the Federal Reserve System has prepared and published annual flow of funds estimates since 1945 and additional quarterly estimates since 1952. These accounts provide a broad estimate of investment activity by measuring the value of real assets and financial assets held and transferred throughout the U.S. economy and by simultaneously tracking the sources of funds used to acquire these assets. The purpose of the flow of funds is to produce estimates of total sources of funds moving among economic sectors, including the household sector and 26 other sectors, such as state and local governments and nonfinancial corporations. These accounts also track each sector's use of the funds by estimating the movement of assets and liabilities among financial instruments.

Flow of funds data are taken from various private and public reports and publications and are constructed on the basis of the principle that total sources of funds must equal total uses of funds. That is, any funds that leave one sector must enter another sector, and any funds

Table A.1. *Wealth Ownership Data: Strengths and Limitations*

Data Type	Examples	Strengths	Limitations
Aggregate data	Balance Sheets of the U.S. Economy (flow of funds)	• Accurate information on all households • Consistent with other government estimates	• No information at the household level • No information on changes over time in particular households
Cross sections	Surveys of Consumer Finances	• Accurate estimates of wealth distribution • Includes high-wealth households • Detailed wealth information	• Limited family background data • Limited life transition data • Very limited information on changes in wealth over time
	Forbes data	• Glimpse of the very wealthy • Indicator of amount of wealth held by the top of the distribution • Captures wealth not included in surveys	• No information about rest of the distribution • Not longitudinal
Longitudinal surveys	National Longitudinal Surveys	• Observations of transitions over time • Ability to model delayed impact of key variables • Ability to study intergenerational effects	• Restricted sample (e.g. white, young men) • Samples size reduces over time because of attrition • Cohort effects

Note: This is collaborative research with Phillip Kim and Howard Aldrich.

that leave one financial instrument must enter another financial instrument. As a result, flow of funds estimates are highly internally consistent. Flow of funds estimates of national saving are also reconciled with national income and product accounts data produced by the Bureau of Economic Analysis of the Department of Commerce to ensure that flow of funds estimates are also consistent with external sources of income and saving data (Federal Reserve System 2003).

DOW JONES INDUSTRIAL AVERAGE, 1994–2003

The Dow Jones Industrial Average (DJIA) is calculated and maintained by the editors of the *Wall Street Journal*. The DJIA is a stock index that serves as a measure of the performance of the entire U.S. economy because it includes a diverse set of industries ranging from financial services to technology, retail, and consumer goods.

FORBES, 1982–2003

Forbes magazine's annual lists of the 400 wealthiest Americans have been compiled annually since 1982 and provide background details for more than 1,000 wealthy individuals. The compilers of these lists estimate the size of fortunes and compensation from secondary sources. They augment this with information about the source of the person's wealth and demographic descriptions. Because business press rosters such as the Forbes 400 highlight only the very wealthiest individuals, there is a relatively large gap between the bottom of the Forbes lists and the top of most surveys. To avoid the problems associated with sampling on the dependent variable, I use the Forbes 400 for anecdotal evidence only.

NATIONAL LONGITUDINAL SURVEY OF MATURE MEN, 1966–1981

I also draw on data from the National Longitudinal Survey of Mature Men. An earlier companion survey to the NLS-Y79, this survey included information on wealth holdings in 1966, 1971, 1976, and 1981. The original sample in this survey represented the U.S. population of men aged 45–59 years in 1966. The men were reinterviewed regularly and reported detailed information about their wealth. While this is an unusual sample, it has some benefits for estimating wealth mobility. In particular, there is evidence that households in this age range own the bulk of assets in the United States. Used as a supplement to the NLS-Y, this data set allows me to gauge the reliability of both data sets and to explore wealth mobility patterns in another subgroup of Americans.

The Survey of Consumer Finances (SCF) is a panel survey sponsored by the Federal Reserve Board and collected by the Survey Research Center. I include estimates from several years of the SCF, including 1962, 1983, 1989, 1992, 1995, 1998, and 2001. The 1962 survey, the Survey of the Financial Characteristics of Consumers (SFCC), was the first thorough survey of family wealth in the United States. It was conducted between the 1960s and the 1980s, but it did not include detailed wealth information. Starting in 1983, however, the Federal Reserve Board began to conduct a detailed survey of U.S. household wealth every three years. Each survey includes a cross section of American households that is supplemented with a sample of high-income households. The high-income households are drawn from the Internal Revenue Service's Statistics of Income data file and are included to overrepresent rich families in an effort to include some very wealthy households (Kennickell and Starr-McCluer 1994; Kennickell, Starr-McCluer, and Sunden 1997; Wolff 1995a, 1995b).

THE WEALTHY 100

Michael Klepper and Robert Gunther (1996) used various sources of information to compile a list of the one hundred wealthiest Americans of all times. They supplement their list with basic information about the origin of the wealthy individuals' fortunes. Table A.2 includes the full list of 100 individuals.

DATA DETAILS: THE NATIONAL LONGITUDINAL SURVEY OF YOUTH (NLS-Y79)

My analyses of wealth mobility come primarily from the National Longitudinal Survey of Youth, 1979 cohort (NLS-Y79). The NLS-Y is a nationally-representative longitudinal survey that was administered to the same individuals 19 times between 1979 and 2000. The NLS-Y includes detailed information about a large sample of young adults and is well-suited for assessing the effect of traits of the

Table A.2. *The 100 Wealthiest Americans Ever*

	Wealth Source	Category from Table 2.1
1. John D. Rockefeller	Oil	Oil
2. Cornelius Vanderbilt	Shipping	Transportation, long distance
3. John Jacob Astor	Fur/land	Natural resources
4. Stephen Girard	Banking	Banking/finance
5. Andrew Carnegie	Steel	Industry, heavy
6. Alexander Turney Stewart	Retail	Retail
7. Frederick Weyerhaeuser	Lumber	Natural resources
8. Jay Gould	Finance	Banking/finance
9. Stephen Van Rensselaer	Inheritance	Inheritance
10. Marshall Field	Retail/land	Retail
11. Henry Ford	Automobiles	Industry, heavy
12. Andrew W. Mellon	Banking	Banking/finance
13. Richard B. Mellon	Banking	Banking/finance
14. Sam Moore Walton	Retail	Retail
15. James G. Fair	Mining	Natural resources
16. William Weightman	Chemicals	Industry, light
17. Moses Taylor	Banking	Banking/finance
18. Russell Sage	Finance	Banking/finance
19. John I. Blair	Railroads	Transportation, long distance
20. Cyrus H. K. Curtis	Publishing	Publishing/communications
21. Edward Henry Harriman	Railroads	Transportation, long distance
22. Henry Huddleston Rogers	Oil	Oil
23. John Pierpont Morgan	Finance	Banking/finance
24. Col. Oliver Payne	Oil/finance	Oil
25. Henry C. Frick	Steel	Industry, heavy
26. Collis Potter Huntington	Railroads	Transportation, long distance
27. Peter A. Widener	City transit	Transportation, local
28. James Cair Flood	Mining	Natural resources
29. Nicholas Longworth	Land	Natural resources
30. Philip Danforth Armour	Meatpacking	Agriculture/food/beverage
31. Bill Gates	Software	Technology
32. Mark Hopkins	Railroads	Transportation, long distance
33. Edward Clark	Sewing machines	Industry, light
34. Leland Stanford	Railroads	Transportation, long distance
35. William Rockefeller	Oil	Oil
36. Hetty Green	Finance	Banking/finance
37. James Jerome Hill	Railroads	Transportation, long distance
38. Elias Hasket Derby	Merchant/shipping	Transportation, long distance
39. Warren Buffett	Finance	Banking/finance
40. Claus Spreckels	Sugar	Agriculture/food/beverage
41. George Peabody	Finance	Banking/finance
42. Charles Crocker	Railroads	Transportation, long distance

(*continued*)

Table A.2 (*continued*)

	Wealth Source	Category from Table 2.1
43. William Andrews Clark	Mining	Natural resources
44. George Eastman	Photography	Industry, light
45. Charles L. Tiffany	Jewelry	Retail
46. Thomas Fortune Ryan	City transit	Transportation, local
47. Edward Stephen Harkness	Inheritance	Inheritance
48. Henry M. Flagler	Oil/resorts	Oil
49. James Buchanan Duke	Tobacco	Agriculture/food/beverage
50. Israel Thorndike	Merchant/shipping	Transportation, long distance
51. William S. O'Brien	Mining	Natural resources
52. Isaac Merritt Singer	Sewing machines	Industry, light
53. George Hearst	Mining	Natural resources
54. John Hancock	Merchant/shipping	Transportation, long distance
55. John W. Garrett	Railroads	Transportation, long distance
56. John W. Mackay	Mining	Natural resources
57. Julius Rosenwald	Catalog retail	Retail
58. George F. Baker	Banking	Banking/finance
59. George Washington	Land	Natural resources
60. Anthony N. Brady	Transit/utilities	Transportation, local
61. Adolphus Busch	Beer	Agriculture/food/beverage
62. John T. Dorrance	Canned goods	Agriculture/food/beverage
63. George M. Pullman	Railroad cars	Industry, heavy
64. Robert Wood Johnson, Jr.	Medical supplies	Industry, light
65. John Francis Dodge	Automobiles	Industry, heavy
66. Horace Elgin Dodge	Automobiles	Industry, heavy
67. J. Paul Getty	Oil	Oil
68. William H. Aspinwall	Shipping	Transportation, long distance
69. Johns Hopkins	Merchant/railroads	Transportation, long distance
70. John Werner Kluge	Communications	Publishing
71. Samuel Colt	Guns	Industry, light
72. James Stillman	Banking	Banking/finance
73. William Collins Whitney	Transit	Transportation, local
74. William Thaw	Canals/railroads	Transportation, long distance
75. Paul Allen	Software	Technology
76. Cyrus H. McCormick	Farm equipment	Industry, heavy
77. Arthur Vining Davis	Aluminum	Industry, heavy
78. Thomas Handasyd Perkins	Merchant/shipping	Transportation, long distance
79. Joseph Pulitzer	Publishing	Publishing/communications
80. Daniel Willis James	Merchant	Retail
81. Howard Hughes	Oil/aviation	Oil
82. Frank W. Woolworth	Retail	Retail
83. John McDonogh	Land	Natural resources
84. Samuel Slater	Textiles	Industry, light

	Wealth Source	Category from Table 2.1
85. August Belmont	Finance	Banking/finance
86. Benjamin Franklin	Land/printing	Natural resources
87. Sumner Murray Redstone	Communications	Publishing/communications
88. Capt. Robert Dollar	Shipping	Transportation, long distance
89. Richard Warren Sears	Catalog retail	Retail
90. H. L. Hunt	Oil	Oil
91. Jay Van Andel	Direct merchandising	Retail
92. Richard Marvin DeVos	Direct merchandising	Retail
93. Henry Phipps	Steel	Industry, heavy
94. Lawrence J. Ellison	Software	Technology
95. Ronald Owen Perelman	Finance	Banking/finance
96. Peter Chardon Brooks	Merchant/shipping	Transportation, long distance
97. Charles W. Post	Cereals	Agriculture/food/beverage
98. Samuel I. Newhouse	Publishing	Publishing/communications
99. William Wrigley, Jr.	Chewing gum	Agriculture/food/beverage
100. David Packard	Computers	Technology

Note: This information was used to construct Table 2.3.
Source: Klepper and Gunther 1996.

family of origin on later life outcomes (McLanahan and Sandefur 1994; Sandefur and Wells 1999; Wu 1996). The survey first interviewed 12,686 individuals who were born between 1957 and 1964 and who were aged 14 through 22 in 1979. Respondents were between the ages of 35 and 43 in 2000. The original sample included three subsamples: a nationally representative sample of 6,111 young adults; a supplemental sample of 5,295 poor white, black, and Hispanic respondents; and 1,280 men and women in the military. Although funding cutbacks forced the elimination of most of the poor and military oversamples, nearly 10,000 respondents were regularly interviewed through 2000. Missing values on wealth variables force my sample size to be lower in the analyses I report here.

An extensive battery of wealth questions was added to the NLS-Y in 1985 when the respondents were between the ages of 20 and 28. I used data from 1985 through 2000 to model wealth accumulation and mobility. I also drew on the 1979 survey and other years between 1979 and 1985 to create family background and other measures. The

NLS-Y wealth modules first ask respondents if they own a series of assets and debts. For those who are owners, the survey then asks for the current market value. Wealth questions were not asked in 1991 for budgetary reasons. Starting in 1994, the NLS-Y was administered every other year rather than every year to reduce costs and respondent burden. As a result, there are no data for 1991, 1995, and 1997 (Zagorsky 1997). The NLS-Y is one of the few data sets that contains detailed, longitudinal wealth data for a large sample. Because the survey has been conducted frequently and has maintained high participation rates, it contains extensive information on the dynamics of wealth ownership (Zagorsky 1999).

The combination of its information on family processes in childhood, transitions to adulthood, and detailed wealth data make the NLS-Y appropriate for exploring the relationship between family background and adult wealth. Of course there are other sources of survey data that I might have used. The Survey of Consumer Finances, described above, oversamples high-income households and thus provides better coverage than the NLS-Y of top-wealth holders. The SCF also more accurately capture the distribution of wealth (Kennickell and Starr-McCluer 1994; Kennickell, Starr-McCluer, and Sunden 1997; Wolff 1995). Because the NLS-Y does not oversample high income households, there is some evidence that it slightly underestimates the value of wealth (Juster and Kuester 1991; Juster, Smith, and Stafford 1999). However, the underestimates are slight and the cross-sectional estimates of the distribution of wealth are largely consistent with the SCF. Moreover, the oversample is less important here than it would be in analyses of wealth distribution. Studying the relationship between processes at different stages of the life course requires longitudinal coverage and information on wealth holdings, both of which the NLS offers and the SCF does not. The Panel Study of Income Dynamics (PSID) and the Survey of Income and Program Participation (SIPP) are two other longitudinal data source that have been used to study changes in wealth over time. I opted to use the NLS-Y rather than either the PSID or SIPP because the NLS includes more detailed information about adult wealth. A description of the NLS-Y79 is contained in the NLS-Y79 User's Guide (1999),

Table A.3. *Wealth Estimates from Various Surveys (Thousands of 2000 Dollars)*

	Net Worth	
	Median	Mean
National Longitudinal Survey (NLS-Y79)		
1996	46.3	179.8
2000	66.2	198.5
Survey of Consumer Finances		
1995	50.2	228.8
1998	63.6	283.2
2001	65.7	325.2
Panel Study of Income Dynamics		
1984	50.4	158.8
1989	51.1	173.6
1994	54.6	170.4
Survey of Income and Program Participation		
1984	54.1	130.5
1988	52.1	133.9
1993	44.7	118.9

Notes: NLS-Y79 and Survey of Consumer Finances estimates are author's estimates. Panel Study of Income Dynamics Estimates are from Hurst, Luoh, and Stafford (1998). Survey of Income and Program Participation Estimates are from Wolff (2001).

available from the Center for Human Resource Research, the Ohio State University, Columbus, OH 43210.

Wealth and demographic data in the NLS-Y is comparable to that available in the Survey of Consumer Finances (SCF), the Panel Study of Income Dynamics (PSID), and the Survey of Income and Program Participation (SIPP). Table A.3 compares wealth estimates from all four surveys. Median wealth from the NLS is lower in initial years than it is in the other data sets, primarily because of the age of the NLS sample. By the later years included in the table, median wealth in the NLS exceeds estimates from the PSID and SIPP and is more comparable to the SCF estimates. Mean wealth in the NLS is lower than mean wealth in the SCF because the SCF includes high-income households. Table A.4 demonstrates that on key demographic dimensions, the samples in the NLS-Y and SCF are comparable. One difference is that the NLS sample is somewhat

Table A.4. *Demographic Comparison of NLS-Y and SCF Data by Total Net Worth*

	Millionaires		$500K–$999K		$300–$499K		$0–$299K		Negative		All	
	NLS	SCF	NLS	SCF	NLS	SCF	NLS	SCF	NLS	SCF	NLS	SCF
Age	40.0	57.9	39.8	57.2	39.6	54.7	39.3	47.7	39.2	37.9	39.5	49.0
Education	15.9	15.6	15.0	14.7	14.8	13.9	13.1	12.6	12.7	12.0	13.3	13.1
Children	1.6	1.7	1.8	1.9	1.8	1.8	1.8	1.9	1.9	1.8	1.8	1.9

Note: Age and education are in years. "Children" is number of people aged 18 or less and living in the home. Millionaires are those with net worth greater than or equal to $1 million. Estimates in this table are consistent with estimates in Table 3.5.
Source: The 2000 National Longitudinal Survey of Youth, 1979 Cohort (NLS), and the 2001 Survey of Consumer Finances.

younger because of the design of that survey. This suggests that as the NLS sample ages, the mean and median wealth values for the surveys will converge.

NLS-Y79 VARIABLES

WEALTH MEASURES

I used four dependent variables (wealth measures) in my descriptive statistics and regression analyses of the NLS-Y data: one main outcome measure and three supplementary measures. The primary outcome, adult net assets, allowed me to test the main set of arguments depicted in Figure 1.1. The supplementary measures were the probability of receiving a trust account, the probability of receiving an inheritance, the probability of owning a home, and the probability of owning stocks. I modeled the supplementary measures to explore the mechanisms that underlie the main theoretical model.

Throughout the text of the book, I present pieces of a set of full regression models. I include only partial models in most chapters to conserve space and because full model details are not necessary for most of the discussions. I include full models in the paragraphs that follow.

In my primary regression analyses, I modeled the dollar value of the net assets in the respondent's adult family, and I allowed this value to vary yearly between 1985 and 2000. *Net assets* is the value of total assets less the value of total liabilities. The financial assets included the value of stocks, bonds, and mutual funds; cash accounts such as checking accounts; trust accounts; Individual Retirement Accounts; 401K plans; and Certificates of Deposit. The real assets included the current market value of the primary residence or home; businesses, farms, and investment real estate; cars and other vehicles; and other possessions. The debts included mortgages on the primary residence; debt on businesses, farms and investment real estate; debt on automobiles; and other debt. I used the Consumer Price Index (CPI) to adjust all asset and debt values to 2000 dollars.

For the regression analyses, I standardized net assets by adding a constant to all values. I also experimented with numerous methods of reducing this variable's skew. Net assets is skewed as wealth ownership is concentrated in the hands of a relatively small portion of the population. Logging the variable, double logging it, taking the square root, and otherwise transforming it does not markedly reduce the skew because a large portion of households have zero net assets. Removing those individuals does not, however, change the results in substantive ways. Similarly, using alternative definitions of wealth does not change the results in substantive ways. For example, I experimented with modeling gross assets (i.e., the sum of all assets not reduced by liabilities), total financial assets, total nonfinancial assets, total liabilities, and other measures of household wealth. I found little difference in the results. I explored how removing outliers affects the results and found that given the large sample size, the results are robust to the removal of outliers. Thus, in the analyses I report, I used the un-logged value of net assets and included all people who responded in each year and who reported usable wealth data when wealth questions were asked.

In the additional analyses, I modeled four dichotomous variables.[1] First I modeled the likelihood that the respondent ever received a *trust account* from their parents. Second, I modeled the likelihood that the respondent ever received an *inheritance*. This includes inheritances received both during the 1985–2000 period when the NLS asked specific questions about wealth and inheritances received prior

---

[1]   Models of other assets and debts produced similar results.

to 1985. The dependent variable is a dichotomous indicator that the respondent ever received an inheritance.[2] Third, I modeled the likelihood that the respondent *owned a home*, and fourth, I modeled the likelihood that the respondent *owned stocks*. I report models in which the dependent variable is the dichotomous indicator that the respondent owned a home or stocks. However, the substantive results of models of the value of the home and stocks were not different from those I report.

FAMILY BACKGROUND CHARACTERISTICS

I introduced numerous individual – and family-level – attributes to explore my arguments about the relationship between family background and adult wealth.[3] I controlled for financial resources in the family of origin by including a measure of parents' net *family income* in 1978 (logged). I also included a dummy variable indicating that the respondent had not provided information about family income in 1978 to control for patterns that might be common to those with missing values on this key variable (Sandefur and Wells 1999).

I included several measures of *parents' education*: separate dummy variables indicating whether the respondent's father and mother had completed high school, some college, a bachelor's degree, or an advanced degree. The omitted category for education is respondents who had not completed high school. The detailed education measures provide insight into the level of education that was relevant to children's attainment in this cohort. Taken together, parents' income and education provide an excellent proxy for their wealth, which is not available in this survey. When I also include measures of trusts and inheritances received (described below), I capture both the parents' ability to generate wealth and the actual wealth they acquired. Previous research suggests that these measures account for most of the variance in parental wealth (Keister 2000b). Preliminary exploration

---

[2] Modeling the value of the inheritance received produced similar results.
[3] I do not explain in detail the theoretical rationale for each control but will provide additional information on request.

using imputation, simulation, and synthetic wealth measures for the parents produced identical substantive outcomes. To ease interpretation, I opted to include income and education in most models. In the final model, I do include an estimated wealth measure (described below).

I included two dummy variables to indicate whether the respondent was *black* or *Hispanic*, as opposed to white. I included a dummy variable indicating whether the respondent was *male*.

To measure the effect of family disruption on family resources and children's well-being (Mechanic and Hansell 1989), I included two indicators of the respondent's *family structure at age 14*. The variables indicate whether the respondent lived in a stepparent family or a single-parent family, as opposed to respondents who lived in a two–biological parent family at age 14. While I explored including various other indicators of the structure of the respondent's family of origin, this combination of variables proved to most effectively capture the relationship between family structure and wealth outcomes.

I used the *total number of siblings* the respondent ever had, reported in 2000, to indicate family size in childhood. Decomposing the total number of siblings in various ways (e.g., number older, number younger) did not improve the fit of any of the models. Likewise, controlling for position among siblings and related measures (e.g., oldest, youngest, middle, spacing of siblings, gender of siblings) did not improve the explanatory power of the models.[4]

I also included two dichotomous measures of whether the respondent's *mother and father worked full time* in 1979. These are proxies of the amount of time parents spent with the respondent. Ideally I would also be able to control for parents' nonmaterial resources, such as the frequency with which respondents spent time with their parents, whether the parents knew their children's friends, and the parents' educational aspirations for their children (Downey 1995a, 1995b; Thomson, Hanson, and McLanahan 1994). Unfortunately,

---

[4] I include stepsiblings and half-siblings who lived in the home. Removing non-biological siblings from the analysis and including only siblings who lived in the home for extended periods did not substantively affect the results.

data on parents' nonmaterial resources and time investment in their children are not available in the NLS, nor are there other data sets that contain both parental time measures and adult wealth.

I included a series of dichotomous variables, coded from reports in the 2000 data wave, to indicate *religious affiliation* in childhood. In the regression models I report, I included measures that the person was Jewish, Baptist, or another type of conservative Protestant. The omitted category is that of all other religious affiliations. I based my classification of Protestants largely on categories used by Lehrer (1999) and Lehrer and Chiswick (1993). In some of the descriptive tables, I also distinguish mainline Protestants by denomination. The mainline Protestants include Episcopalians, Lutherans, Methodists, Presbyterians, Unitarians, and related groups. The conservative Protestant group includes Baptists, Seventh-Day Adventists, and other conservative groups. Jehovah's Witness, Christian Science, Muslim, Mormon, and all other religious affiliations are included in category called "other."

Measures for those who were raised Roman Catholic and mainline Protestant were not significantly different from zero. I did not include these measures in the final regression models because people raised as Roman Catholic and mainline Protestant comprise the bulk of the population. I did not include measures for more underrepresented religious groups (e.g., Muslims) or separate indicators for Orthodox Jews and those raised with no religious affiliation, because I did not want to compromise the models with small samples on such measures.

I experimented with a very wide range of classifications of the denominations, including categorizing those who are evangelical as conservative regardless of the standard classification and including relatively small sects and relatively distinct sects of conservative Protestants in their own categories and in various combinations of categories. Across a multitude of specifications, the results did not change in a substantive way. The models were extremely robust to changes in the way I grouped religions. Including separate indicators for various groups that might seem unique did not change the results. For example, including separate indicators for Mormon,

Hindu, Buddhist, Christian Science, and Unitarian did not change the results. Also, results in Chapter Six suggest that Episcopalians are somewhat unique among mainline Protestants, but including separate indicators for Episcopalians did not change the results. The measures I use are from reports in the 2000 survey. I also experimented with using earlier data, from 1980, to report religious affiliation. Using data from the earlier year also did not change the substance of the results. Finally, including measures of adult religious affiliation does not change the substance of the findings because the correlation between childhood and adult religion is relatively high for all religious groups.

EDUCATION AND WORK BEHAVIOR

I included a series of *education* dummy variables indicating whether the respondent had completed high school, some college, a bachelor's degree, or an advanced degree. The omitted category for education is that of respondents who had not completed high school.

To capture the level of nonwealth financial resources available in the respondent's household, I controlled for the respondent's *income* (logged) and the respondent's *spouse's income* (logged) in the current year. I included a variable indicating the amount of income from *entrepreneurial activities* to capture the effect of entrepreneurship on wealth accumulation. I also included a continuous variable indicating the number of *weeks the respondent's spouse worked* in the previous year. In including indicators of the respondent's spouse's contribution to the household economy, I hope to capture the effects of added financial resources that came into the household through either the spouse's work or independent wealth.

ADULT TRAITS: INDIVIDUAL AND FAMILY

I indicated *age* in number of years in the current year. I did not control for the square of age because wealth accumulation does not typically follow the standard curvilinear relationship with age that income follows. Preliminary investigation confirmed that the squared age term was not a significant predictor of asset ownership in these data.

I included dummy variables indicating whether the respondent was *married, separated, divorced,* or *widowed.* The reference category was those who were never married. I experimented with more detailed marital status controls, including for timing of divorce, timing of widowhood, and various combinations of marital status changes. However, my findings were robust, the more detailed marital status controls did not improve the fit of the models, and I had no theoretical reason to control for marital status and status changes other than those I have included in the models reported later. I included a variable indicating the *number of children* born to the respondent.

To capture the effects of assimilation on wealth ownership, I included dichotomous indicators of whether the respondent was *born out of the United States* and whether the respondent's father or mother (separate indicators) was born out of the United States. These measures control for differences in wealth behavior between immigrants (including second-generation immigrants) and native citizens. I included four dummy variables indicating region of residence to capture variations in economic conditions and opportunities. An indicator of *urban* residence captures urban–rural differences in wealth ownership. This variable uses census data to indicate whether the county of residence had a central core city and adjacent, closely settled area with a total combined population of 50,000 or more. I found no unique effect for residence in the multivariate models. A set of three dummy variables *indicates region of residence* in the current year, including residence in north central states, southern states, and western states, versus residence in northeastern states.

INTERGENERATIONAL TRANSFERS

To measure intergenerational transfers of resources, I included a dummy variable in appropriate models indicating whether the persons *received a trust account* from their parents and whether they *ever inherited.* Including a continuous variable indicating the amount inherited by year had the obvious effect of increasing wealth. I did not include it because it did not change the substance of the findings. Including those who did not inherit (i.e., those with a zero value) did not change the results appreciably. I use the amount inherited ever because it more closely matches the concept I argue will affect wealth ownership. While it can be difficult to generate accurate estimates of inheritance, the NLS-Y estimates are consistent with measures of inherited wealth in other studies (McNamee and Miller 1998).

I included a value for the estimated family wealth in 1979. I calculated this variable using other family measures in 1979, including income, family structure, parents' education, other parent traits, and other individual traits. This variable has an expected positive effect on wealth and allows interpretation of the final regression model in terms of change in wealth since childhood. Controlling for wealth in 1985 – in order to explore change since early adulthood – produced comparable results.

FINANCIAL BEHAVIOR AND TRAJECTORIES

Finally, in a separate model presented in Chapter Eight, I included four measures to explore the role that financial behavior and saving trajectory play in this process. The first two variables in that model capture the effect of *financial behavior*. The percentage of the respondent's portfolio that is accounted for by stocks and bonds indicates the extent to which the person has invested in financial assets. Financial assets, particularly stocks and bonds, typically grow more rapidly than less risky investments and usually lead to higher overall growth of assets. In contrast, those who invest higher proportions of their assets in fixed investments, particularly housing, tend to accumulate wealth more slowly. Similarly, different *accumulation trajectories* yield different wealth outcomes. In this model, I include indicators that the respondent made an early transition to financial wealth or followed a traditional accumulation path. I included respondents in the early transition to financial wealth group if they owned non-pension stocks or bonds before age 25, owned at least $1,000 in these assets in the earliest year, and continued to invest in stocks and bonds through the latest survey year. I included respondents in the traditional accumulation group if they purchased a home during adulthood, did not own more than $1,000 in stocks and bonds before owning a house, and continued to own a home for at least five years. The omitted category is that of all other respondents.

I experimented with various methods of creating indicators of financial behavior and accumulation trajectories, including easing the dollar value associated with stocks, including a value for housing investments, and including other types of financial investments with stocks and bonds. The grouping of respondents varied little when I made these change, and the substantive analytic findings did not change appreciably. Moreover, in other research, I have used optimal matching to identify accumulation paths. Optimal matching is a method designed to identify common patterns or trajectories and is based on the notion that we can measure how similar two sequences are by determining how difficult it is to transform one into the other. The measures I include here correlate at more than 0.9 with similar measures derived through optimal matching. I use the simplified measures here for ease of interpretation.

NLS-Y79 RESEARCH METHODS

I used pooled cross-section time series analyses to model wealth ownership. Thus the unit of analysis in all models was the person–year between 1985 and 2000, and both independent and dependent variables could change in each year. I used Estimated Generalized Least Squares (EGLS) regression to model net assets, because the error terms were both heteroskedastic and correlated over time.[5] Because the sample I use is large, the estimates have a normal sampling distribution even if the residuals are skewed (Boos and Hughes-Oliver

---

[5]   The White's Test for heteroskedasticy was significant, and the Ordinary Durbin–Watson Test (D-W) for first-order autocorrelation was significantly different from two. Because the Ordinary D-W was significant, it was not necessary to use the General D-W for higher orders of autocorrelation. Practically, I used the Yule–Walker method, also known as the two-step full transform method or Estimated Generalized Least Squares, in SAS Proc Autoreg to estimate the models (Judge et al. 1985).

Table A.5. *Aggregate Household Wealth and Dow Jones Industrial Average,*
1994–2003: Values for Figure 1.1

	Total Assets	Net Worth	Financial Assets	Total Liabilities	DJIA
1994	37,000.1	32,500.1	24,880.1	5,888	3,756.60
1995	38,000.1	32,800.1	25,000.1	5,900	3,838.48
1996	38,689.5	33,081.7	26,165.7	5,934.7	5,177.45
1997	42,210.4	36,005.2	29,275.5	6,205.4	6,442.49
1998	45,751.8	39,126.1	31,985.7	6,625.6	7,965.04
1999	50,350.6	43,285.5	35,813.3	7,065.0	9,184.27
2000	49,177.2	41,717.2	33,711.0	7,460.1	11,357.51
2001	47,650.5	39,821.3	31,410.4	7,829.2	10,646.15
2002	45,606.2	37,616.5	28,987.1	7,989.7	10,073.40
2003	44,319.4	36,117.5	27,548.2	8,201.9	9,800.00

Note: Wealth values are from the Federal Reserve Board's *Balance Sheets of the U.S. Economy* converted to 2000 dollars using the Consumer Price Index (Federal Reserve System 2001). Values for 1994–2002 are for end of the year; values for 2003 are for the first quarter. DJIA is the Dow Jones Industrial Average at the start of the year.

2000). I used logistic regression to model the likelihood that the respondent received a trust or an inheritance, owned a home, or owned stock.

To examine the elements of the theoretical model I proposed, I estimated a series of nested models of net assets. I first regressed net assets on family background traits, including race and gender. I then added family structure at age 14 and childhood religion in separate models. Next I added educational achievement, an outcome that follows both logically in my theoretical model. In the fourth model, I added adult traits that are likely affected by education. Finally, I added measures of intergenerational transfers. In order to further explore the mechanisms underlying the relationship between siblings and net assets, I repeated the full model for the dichotomous dependent variables.

NLS-Y79 Analysis Details

Tables A.5–A.16 provide details about the tables and figures appearing throughout the text.

Table A.6. *Intergenerational Correlation of Well-being, Income and Wealth not Logged:*
Table 2.6 Details

	Baseline[a]	Single Only[b]	18 Years or Less Only[c]	Single and 18 Years or Less Only[d]
All wealth levels	0.235	0.234	0.220	0.220
	(3,296)	(3,249)	(2,626)	(2,612)
Only those with wealth > 0	0.218	0.216	0.205	0.205
	(2,778)	(2,742)	(2,223)	(2,212)
Race[e]				
White	0.204	0.203	0.194	0.193
	(2,608)	(2,574)	(2,089)	(2,089)
Hispanic	0.214	0.216	0.197	0.197
	(243)	(234)	(198)	(194)
Black	0.133	0.133	0.141	0.141
	(445)	(441)	(339)	(339)
Religion during childhood[e]				
Catholic	0.220	0.212	0.200	0.200
	(1,122)	(1,112)	(873)	(868)
Mainline Protestant	0.222	0.220	0.210	0.210
	(951)	(937)	(770)	(766)
Fundamental Protestant	0.150	0.150	0.165	0.163
	(1,001)	(981)	(798)	(796)
Jewish	0.177	0.175	0.190	0.190
	(25)	(25)	(22)	(22)

Note: Cells are author's calculations of Pearson correlations between 1979 household income and 1998 household net worth (total assets less total liabilities) for the National Longitudinal Survey of Youth, 1979 Cohort. Number in parentheses is sample size.

[a] Baseline model includes main NLS-Y79 sample respondents who were living with their parents and whose parents reported household income in 1979.

[b] Same as baseline model but excludes any individuals who were married prior to 1979.

[c] Same as baseline model but excludes any individuals who were older than 18 in 1979.

[d] Same as baseline model but excludes any individuals who were married prior to 1979 or who were older than 18 years in 1979.

[e] Separate estimates by race and religion are for members of the specified group only and include those at all wealth levels, equivalent to row 1.

NLS-Y79 ALTERNATIVE SPECIFICATIONS

I experimented with including the effect of measures of financial behavior and saving trajectory play in the wealth accumulation process. In particular, in models not reported here, I included measures of the percentage of the respondent's portfolio that is accounted for by

Table A.7. *Intergenerational Correlation of Well-being, Logged Income and Wealth:*
Table 2.6 Details

	Baseline[a]	Single Only[b]	18 and Under Only[c]	Single & 18 and Under Only[d]
All respondents	0.308	0.306	0.300	0.299
	(2,778)	(2,742)	(2,223)	(2,212)
Race[e]				
White	0.241	0.238	0.231	0.231
	(2,608)	(2,574)	(2,089)	(2,089)
Hispanic	0.223	0.221	0.288	0.276
	(243)	(234)	(198)	(194)
Black	0.292	0.290	0.267	0.267
	(445)	(441)	(339)	(339)
Religion during childhood[e]				
Catholic	0.267	0.261	0.282	0.275
	(1,122)	(1,112)	(873)	(868)
Mainline	0.276	0.276	0.263	0.264
Protestant	(951)	(937)	(770)	(766)
Fundamental	0.264	0.268	0.260	0.261
Protestant	(1,001)	(981)	(798)	(796)
Jewish	0.108	0.108	0.208	0.208
	(25)	(25)	(22)	(22)

Note: Cells are author's calculations of Pearson correlations between logged 1979 household income and logged 1998 household net worth (total assets less total liabilities) for the National Longitudinal Survey of Youth, 1979 Cohort. Number in parentheses is sample size. Estimates for "all respondents" include only those with wealth greater than 0 in 1998.
[a] Baseline model includes main NLS-Y79 sample respondents who were living with their parents and whose parents reported household income in 1979.
[b] Same as baseline model but excludes any individuals who were married prior to 1979.
[c] Same as baseline model but excludes any individuals who were older than 18 in 1979.
[d] Same as baseline model but excludes any individuals who were married prior to 1979 or who were older than 18 in 1979.
[e] Separate estimates by race and religion are for members of the specified group only and include those at all wealth levels, equivalent to row 1.

stocks and bonds and that indicates the extent to which the person has invested in financial assets. Financial assets, particularly stocks and bonds, typically grow more rapidly than less risky investments and usually lead to higher overall growth of assets. In contrast, those who invest higher proportions of their assets in fixed investments, particularly housing, tend to accumulate wealth more slowly. Similarly,

Table A.8. *Percentage Owning Particular Assets: Values for Figure 3.1*

	Millionaires	$500K–$999K	$300–$499K	All Others
Cash	0.98	0.98	0.96	0.74
Home	0.93	0.93	0.97	0.64
Stock	0.77	0.65	0.59	0.21
Trust funds	0.21	0.14	0.10	0.03
Business	0.28	0.22	0.14	0.09

Source: National Longitudinal Survey of Youth, 1979 Cohort.

Table A.9. *Percentage of Total Assets Accounted for by Various Assets: Values for Figure 3.2*

	Millionaires	$500K– $999K	$300–$499K	All Others
Stock	0.23	0.10	0.06	0.02
Home	0.24	0.37	0.47	0.43
Cash	0.10	0.07	0.07	0.07
Business	0.18	0.12	0.08	0.03
Trust funds	0.08	0.06	0.02	0.00

Source: National Longitudinal Survey of Youth, 1979 Cohort.

Table A.10. *Education Levels of the Wealthy: Values for Figure 3.3*

	Millionaires	$500K–$999K	$300–$499K	All Others
Advanced degree	0.37	0.20	0.19	0.08
College graduate	0.30	0.33	0.29	0.12
Some college	0.18	0.20	0.25	0.22
High school degree	0.13	0.26	0.27	0.47
No degree	0.01	0.01	0.01	0.11

Source: National Longitudinal Survey of Youth, 1979 Cohort.

Table A.11. *Family Background of the Wealthy, Father's Education: Values for Figure 5.2*

	Millionaires	$500K–$999K	$300–$499K	All Others
Advanced degree	0.25	0.14	0.11	0.06
College graduate	0.29	0.18	0.15	0.08
Some college	0.06	0.13	0.18	0.10
High school degree	0.24	0.36	0.35	0.33
No degree	0.15	0.15	0.18	0.34

Source: National Longitudinal Survey of Youth, 1979 Cohort.

Table A.12. *Family Background of the Wealthy, Mother's Education:*
Values for Figure 5.3

	Millionaires	$500K–$999K	$300–$499K	All Others
Advanced degree	0.06	0.05	0.03	0.02
College graduate	0.29	0.11	0.13	0.06
Some college	0.19	0.20	0.16	0.09
High school degree	0.37	0.49	0.52	0.44
No degree	0.09	0.11	0.15	0.34

Source: National Longitudinal Survey of Youth, 1979 Cohort.

Table A.13. *Family Background of the Wealthy, Siblings and*
Education: Values for Figure 5.4

Number of Siblings	Median Net Worth by Highest Education Level (Thousands of 2000 Dollars)				
	All	High School	Some College	B.A.	Advanced Degree
1	62	44	50	140	152
2	49	26	45	133	141
3	40	25	44	119	130
4	24	15	28	111	127
5	17	13	19	80	113
6	15	13	31	47	73
7+	6	6	13	38	50

Source: National Longitudinal Survey of Youth, 1979 Cohort.

I experimented with including measures of accumulation trajectories because it is likely that these yield different wealth outcomes.

I also experimented with including indicators that the respondent made an early transition to financial wealth or followed a traditional accumulation path. I included respondents in the transition to financial wealth group if they owned nonpension stocks or bonds before age 25, owned at least $1,000 in these assets in the earliest year, and continued to invest in stocks and bonds through the latest survey year. I included respondents in the traditional accumulation group if they purchased a home during adulthood, did not own more than $1,000 in stocks and bonds before owning a house, and continued to own a home for at least five years. In these supplementary models, the

Table A.14. *Family Background of the Wealthy, Race,*
Education, and Wealth: Values for Figure 5.5

	Median Net Worth by Highest Education Level (Thousands of 2000 Dollars)				
	All	High School	Some College	B.A.	Advanced Degree
White	75	56	76	168	165
Black	4	4	9	49	82
Hispanic	15	12	36	160	133

Source: National Longitudinal Survey of Youth, 1979 Cohort.

omitted category was that of all other respondents. I experimented with various methods of creating this indicator, including easing the dollar value associated with stocks, including a value for housing investments, and including other types of financial investments with stocks and bonds. The grouping of respondents varied little when I made these changes, and the substantive analytic findings did not change appreciably.

I also experimented with using optimal matching to identify accumulation paths. In the final model of net assets, I did not include these measures because they had predictable effects on wealth and did not change the substance of my other arguments.

DATA DETAILS: THE PANEL STUDY OF ENTREPRENEURIAL DYNAMICS

Understanding the relationship between wealth and entrepreneurship is central to understanding mobility, and yet it is difficult using most data to determine the nature of this relationship. Entrepreneurship is one of the avenues through which it is possible for those who are not wealthy to experience upward mobility. In order to understand whether entrepreneurs have more wealth, I use the NLS-Y to model net assets as a function of entrepreneurial income. It is possible, however, that wealthy people are more likely to become entrepreneurs. To better explore this second question,

Table A.15. *EGLS Parameter Estimates for Adult Net Assets, 1985–2000:*
Full Regression Models

	Base Model	Add Childhood Family	Add Childhood Religion	Add Education	Add Adult Traits	Add Wealth Measures
Parents' financial resources						
Family income	−0.82*	−1.02*	−1.05*	1.05*	1.00	0.90
(log)	(0.50)	(0.51)	(0.51)	(0.50)	(0.55)	(0.52)
Family income	−9.01	−8.23	−7.40	−7.55	6.45	5.44
not reported	(6.25)	(6.28)	(6.27)	(6.27)	(6.81)	(6.80)
Father's education						
High school	18.33***	17.26***	16.34***	12.42***	11.53**	10.65
	(4.47)	(4.54)	(4.54)	(4.55)	(4.85)	(7.04)
Some college	22.73***	20.43***	19.60***	10.25	8.78	12.13
	(6.68)	(6.73)	(6.73)	(6.77)	(7.18)	(10.35)
College degree	40.56***	37.17***	35.20***	21.18***	17.91**	10.63
	(7.13)	(7.20)	(7.22)	(7.34)	(7.77)	(6.95)
Advanced degree	60.81***	55.54***	48.38***	32.38***	31.92***	12.22
	(8.39)	(8.46)	(8.50)	(8.62)	(9.12)	(8.00)
Mother's education						
High school	14.78***	14.00***	12.96***	6.48**	3.56	4.21
	(4.41)	(4.47)	(4.47)	(4.5)	(4.82)	(7.01)
Some college	29.98***	29.39***	28.07***	16.15**	11.63	10.12
	(6.98)	(7.03)	(7.03)	(7.11)	(7.53)	(10.95)
College degree	57.92***	56.67***	50.09***	33.94***	32.41***	16.58
	(8.34)	(8.40)	(8.43)	(8 53)	(9.03)	(13.22)
Advanced degree	23.99**	24.69**	22.81	4.51	5.20	−12.30
	(12.62)	(12.74)	(12.74)	(12.80)	(13.56)	(19.45)
Black	−50.79***	−44.65***	−41.44***	−38.85***	−26.18***	−25.55***
	(5.56)	(5.73)	(6.00)	(5.99)	(6.75)	(9.80)
Hispanic	−21.88**	−32.36***	−32.71***	−31.88***	−29.14***	−24.98**
	(7.17)	(7.75)	(7.79)	(7.77)	(8.59)	(12.34)
Male	−1.21	−1.64	−1.60	2.04	6.79	7.88
	(3.53)	(3.53)	(3.52)	(3.53)	(4.85)	(5.63)
Family at age 14						
Number of	–	−2.84***	−2.62***	−2.53***	−2.52***	−2.82*
siblings		(0.45)	(0.85)	(0.85)	(0.92)	(1.04)
Stepparent family	–	−17.11***	−16.22***	−12.50**	−6.04	−6.24
		(6.39)	(6.39)	(6.38)	(6.81)	(9.81)
Single-parent	–	−8.18	−8.79	−8.14	1.57	−6.39
family		(5.85)	(5.85)	(5.84)	(6.28)	(9.02)

(*continued*)

Table A.15 *(continued)*

	Base Model	Add Childhood Family	Add Childhood Religion	Add Education	Add Adult Traits	Add Wealth Measures
Father worked full-time	–	9.28** (4.73)	9.13 (4.73)	8.45 (4.72)	8.83 (5.07)	6.15 (7.31)
Mother worked full-time	–	−3.64 (3.65)	−2.16 (3.65)	−2.31 (3.65)	−6.51 (3.88)	−1.98 (5.61)
Family religion in childhood						
Jewish	–	–	138.52*** (17.80)	124.08*** (17.80)	111.86*** (19.31)	189.02*** (29.29)
Other conservative Protestant	–	–	−6.65** (2.88)	−12.09** (5.91)	−10.41* (6.21)	−17.95* (8.94)
Baptist	–	–	−8.79** (4.83)	−12.33** (4.87)	−9.51* (5.42)	−7.84* (3.81)
Respondent's education						
High school	–	–	–	17.85*** (4.86)	2.56 (5.36)	−3.75 (7.92)
Some college	–	–	–	34.11*** (5.72)	10.53* (6.26)	−1.37 (9.24)
College degree	–	–	–	57.58*** (6.64)	28.46*** (7.20)	21.44** (10.82)
Advanced degree	–	–	–	74.57*** (7.41)	40.51*** (8.00)	35.68** (11.89)
Adult resources						
Entrepreneurial income	–	–	–	–	56.22*** (7.65)	61.17*** (10.89)
Temporary work (weeks)	–	–	–	–	−8.01* (3.80)	−7.55* (3.05)
Family income	–	–	–	–	0.00*** (0.00)	0.00*** (0.00)
Age	–	–	–	–	8.18*** (0.37)	8.13*** (0.63)
Adult family						
Married	–	–	–	–	27.46*** (3.96)	31.01*** (5.98)
Separated	–	–	–	–	−15.98* (9.87)	−16.68 (14.51)
Divorced	–	–	–	–	−16.48*** (5.72)	−24.30*** (8.25)
Widowed	–	–	–	–	55.27** (25.26)	65.51* (35.46)
Number of children	–	–	–	–	3.46** (1.75)	4.41* (2.40)

	Base Model	Add Childhood Family	Add Childhood Religion	Add Education	Add Adult Traits	Add Wealth Measures
Intergenerational transfers						
Received a trust fund	–	–	–	–	–	334.76*** (11.66)
Ever inherited	–	–	–	–	–	20.62*** (6.60)
Estimated wealth in 1979	–	–	–	–	–	2.21*** (0.45)
Adjusted R^2	0.01	0.05	0.08	0.10	0.13	0.15

Note: Standard errors in parentheses. Number of respondents included in models is 6,110; those with missing data are deleted. Sample across 12 years is 73,330 (person years). Also controlled, but not displayed, are the following indicators: that respondent was born out of the United States, that either parent was born out of the United States, number of weeks worked by spouse, urban residence, and region of residence. *$p < .10$; **$p < .05$; ***$p < .01$.
Source: National Longitudinal Survey of Youth, 1979 Cohort.

I use a unique data set that looks at the process of becoming an entrepreneur.

In particular, I draw on the National Panel Study of Entrepreneurial Dynamics (PSED), also known as the National Panel Study of U.S. Business Start-ups, to explore whether family net worth affects becoming an entrepreneur. The PSED was collected by the Entrepreneurship Research Consortium (ERC), an association of 25 to 30 universities, foundations, research institutes, and government agencies. The purpose of the ERC is to sponsor studies of new, family, small, or growth business start-ups and other participants, human or organizational, in the entrepreneurial process. Successful research will result in representative samples of panel data reflecting business start-up processes, control groups, and county information. I participated in the development of the wealth questions for this survey (Crosa, Keister, and Aldrich 2001; Kim, Aldrich, and Keister 2004).

The PSED identified a very large sample of nascent entrepreneurs, people in the process of starting a business, and then selected a sample from this group to include in the survey. The PSED team then followed the nascent entrepreneurs during the business start-up process to explore who attempted to start businesses, who actually

Table A.16. *Logistic Regression Parameter Estimates for Wealth, 1985–2000*

	Ever Inherited	Received a Trust Account	Own a Home	Own Stocks
Parents' financial resources				
Family income (log)	0.01***	0.02***	0.00	0.01
	(0.00)	(0.01)	(0.00)	(0.01)
Family income not reported	−0.05	−0.09	−0.04	0.02
	(0.04)	(0.09)	(0.04)	(0.05)
Father's education				
High school	0.20***	0.08	0.01	0.11***
	(0.03)	(0.07)	(0.03)	(0.04)
Some college	0.16***	0.05	0.20***	0.27***
	(0.04)	(0.09)	(0.04)	(0.05)
College degree	0.36***	0.09	0.03	0.37***
	(0.04)	(0.10)	(0.04)	(0.05)
Advanced degree	0.78***	0.32***	0.19***	0.37***
	(0.05)	(0.10)	(0.05)	(0.06)
Mother's education				
High school	0.07**	0.07	0.12***	0.34***
	(0.03)	(0.07)	(0.03)	(0.04)
Some college	0.20***	0.40***	0.17***	0.35***
	(0.04)	(0.09)	(0.04)	(0.05)
College degree	0.39***	0.74***	0.05	0.52***
	(0.05)	(0.10)	(0.05)	(0.06)
Advanced degree	0.04	0.92***	0.21***	0.36***
	(0.07)	(0.13)	(0.08)	(0.08)
Black	−0.69***	−0.51***	−0.98***	−0.26***
	(0.05)	(0.12)	(0.04)	(0.06)
Hispanic	−0.78***	−0.13	−0.46***	−0.38***
	(0.06)	(0.12)	(0.05)	(0.07)
Male	−0.06	0.06	0.01	0.13***
	(0.04)	(0.05)	(0.02)	(0.03)
Family at age 14				
Number of siblings	−0.05***	−0.08***	−0.03***	−0.04***
	(0.01)	(0.01)	(0.01)	(0.01)
Stepparent family	0.21***	0.05	−0.12***	−0.07
	(0.04)	(0.10)	(0.04)	(0.05)
Single-parent family	−0.14***	−0.19***	−0.12***	−0.04
	(0.04)	(0.07)	(0.04)	(0.05)
Father worked full time	0.05	0.10	0.20***	0.22***
	(0.03)	(0.07)	(0.03)	(0.04)
Mother worked full time	−0.01	0.22***	−0.02	−0.03
	(0.02)	(0.05)	(0.02)	(0.03)

	Ever Inherited	Received a Trust Account	Own a Home	Own Stocks
Family religion in childhood				
Jewish	0.53***	0.34**	−0.41***	0.22**
	(0.10)	(0.16)	(0.11)	(0.11)
Conservative Protestant	−0.08***	−0.18**	−0.10***	−0.10**
	(0.03)	(0.07)	(0.03)	(0.04)
Baptist	−0.27***	−0.07	−0.02***	−0.31***
	(0.03)	(0.08)	(0.01)	(0.04)
Respondent's education				
High school	0.68***	0.46***	0.29***	0.16***
	(0.04)	(0.09)	(0.03)	(0.05)
Some college	1.10***	0.58***	0.34***	0.46***
	(0.04)	(0.10)	(0.04)	(0.05)
College degree	1.43***	0.61***	0.40***	1.03***
	(0.04)	(0.10)	(0.04)	(0.05)
Advanced degree	1.44***	0.48***	0.20***	0.98***
	(0.05)	(0.11)	(0.05)	(0.05)
Adult resources				
Entrepreneurial income	0.34***	0.46***	0.33***	0.03
	(0.05)	(0.09)	(0.05)	(0.06)
Temporary work (weeks)	0.04	0.01	−0.07**	0.01
	(0.03)	0.01	(0.03)	(0.01)
Family income	0.01***	0.01***	0.01***	0.01***
	(0.00)	(0.00)	(0.00)	(0.00)
Age	0.01***	0.01	0.15***	0.04***
	(0.00)	(0.01)	(0.00)	(0.00)
Adult family				
Married	−0.03	0.10	1.75***	0.57***
	(0.02)	(0.06)	(0.02)	(0.03)
Separated	−0.55***	−0.16	−0.52***	−0.48***
	(0.07)	(0.16)	(0.06)	(0.09)
Divorced	−0.07**	0.06	−0.14***	−0.13***
	(0.03)	(0.07)	(0.03)	(0.05)
Widowed	0.60***	0.62	0.96***	0.52***
	(0.14)	(0.39)	(0.14)	(0.19)
Number of children	−0.05***	−0.07	0.08***	−0.08***
	(0.01)	(0.05)	(0.01)	(0.01)
N	6,110	6,198	6,008	6,112
−2 log likelihood	61,727***	14,647***	75,017***	41,572***

Note: Standard errors in parentheses. Sample size refers to number of respondents. Models included n × 12 person years. Also controlled, but not displayed, are the following indicators: that respondent was born out of the United States, that either parent was born out of the United States, number of weeks worked by spouse, urban residence, and region of residence. * $p < .10$; ** $p < .05$; *** $p < .01$.

Source: National Longitudinal Survey of Youth, 1979 Cohort.

started them, and which businesses survived long term. The PSED data collection occurred in three stages. Stage one involved selecting a random sample of 670 people trying to start new businesses during 1998 and 1999 (referred to as *nascent entrepreneurs*) and a randomly selected comparison group of typical adults. This sample was selected using random digit dialing from screening interviews with 64,622 respondents. The sample was supplemented with over-samples of women and minorities. Those who qualified as active nascent entrepreneurs were invited to participate in the study. Stage two involved detailed telephone interviews and self-completed questionnaires returned by mail. The nascent entrepreneurs were asked a set of very detailed questions about their backgrounds and the activities involved in starting their new business. The comparison group subsample was also created in two phases. Individuals were invited to participate in a survey of the work and career patterns of Americans. Individuals were then randomly drawn to form the sample and contacted to complete the interview for the comparison group. These respondents answered the same set of basic background questions as the respondents in the nascent entrepreneur subsample. An oversample of minorities and women supplemented the primary comparison group subsample to enhance the quality of data for these respective groups. Because I explore traits of the nascent entrepreneurs during their start-up phase, I reduce selection bias associated with analyzing existing data sets that do not include individuals who have abandoned entrepreneurial pursuits.

The PSED data are unique in their ability to answer questions about the process of becoming an entrepreneur because they include excellent information about a large sample of this relatively rare population. Table A.17 summarizes the strengths and limitations of alternative sources of information on an entrepreneur and highlights the benefits of supplementing analyses of the NLS-Y with analyses of the PSED.

PSED Variables

The empirical work I report using the PSED is collaborative work with Howard Aldrich and Phillip Kim. In these analyses, our

Table A.17. *Entrepreneurship Data: Strengths and Limitations*

Data Type	Examples	Strengths	Limitations
Longitudinal surveys	National Longitudinal Surveys; Panel Study of Income Dynamics	• Observations of transitions into self-employment over time • Ability to model delayed impact of key variables (e.g., financial) • Ability to study intergenerational effects	• Restricted to certain populations (e.g. white, young men) • Samples size reduces over time because of attrition • Cohort effects
Businesses	Characteristics of Business Owners; Dun and Bradstreet	• Large samples • Oversampling of females and minority groups • Industry specific analytical capabilities	• Selection bias toward examining existing businesses
Tax records	Internal Revenue Service Tax Returns	• Assess specific variables related to legal formation of start-up and financial resources	• Lack of key control variables, such as race and education
Survey of Entrepreneurs	Panel Study of Entrepreneurial Dynamics	• Targeted at entrepreneurs • Specific measures of background characteristics	• Comparison group not sampled from primary sample of nascent entrepreneurs

Note: This is collaborative research with Phillip Kim and Howard Aldrich.

dependent variable was a dichotomous indicator that an individual was a nascent entrepreneur. Those who answered yes to one of the following questions were included as nascent entrepreneurs: (1) Are you, along or with others, now trying to start a new business? (2) Are you, along or with others, now starting a new business or new venture for your employer – an effort that is part of your job assignment? Those who answered yes also needed to meet three additional qualifications to be considered nascent entrepreneurs: (1) they were owners or part owners of the new firm; (2) they had been active in trying to start the new firm in the past 12 months; and (3) their effort was still in the start-up phase

Table A.18. *The Effect of Wealth on Becoming an Entrepreneur:*
Full Logistic Models for Table 7.6

Financial Resources		Control Variables	
Household net worth (ln)	0.08	Age (ln)***	−1.80
	(0.09)		(0.08)
Negative net worth	0.30	Male***	0.70
	(0.42)		(0.37)
Household income (ln)	0.02	Black***	0.72
	(0.08)		(0.47)
Human capital		Hispanic	0.45
Education			(0.50)
Vocational/technical	0.04	Other	−0.22
	(0.43)		(0.32)
Some college	0.38*	Foreign born	0.04
	(0.34)		(0.42)
College graduate	0.68**	Either parent foreign born	−0.16
	(0.56)		(0.30)
Advanced degree	0.39	Married	0.30
	(0.46)		(0.25)
Years work experience (ln)	0.39*	South	−0.18
	(0.30)		(0.21)
Years managerial experience (ln)	0.02	Midwest	0.01
	(0.11)		(0.27)
Helped start other businesses	−0.74***	West	0.09
	(0.09)		(0.31)
Currently self-employed	1.54***		
	(1.00)		
Parents self-employed	0.20		
	(0.23)		
Relatives self-employed	0.82*		
	(1.00)		
Friends self-employed	−0.02		
	(0.47)		

Note: This is collaborative research with Phillip Kim and Howard Aldrich. Standard errors are in parentheses. Household income was recoded as a continuous variable from a categorical variable. The first seven categories in the original variable (up to $15,000; $15–19,000; $20–$24,999; $25–$29,999; $30–$39,999; $40–$49,999; $50–$74,999) were recoded to their midpoints. To recode the last category ($75,000 and above), we relied on the median value for these individuals ($100,000). Recoding based on the mean value of $123,750 yielded similar results. $* p < .10; ** p < .05; *** p < .01$

(i.e., they had not been covering expenses for more than three months).

We used two measures of *financial resources*: household net worth and income. Net worth includes the value of total assets (e.g., physical property and investments, including primary residence) net of outstanding debt (e.g., mortgage, home equity and car loans). The wealth questions in the PSED largely replicate those from the Survey of Consumer Finances. Logged income includes all incoming financial flows from work, government benefits, and pension before taxes in the previous year.

In our models of becoming an entrepreneur, we include measures of *education* and *work experience*. Work experience is measured as years of full-time work experience, years of managerial experience, and two dichotomous indicators that the person helped start a business in the past or was currently self-employed. To measure the effect of *family and friends* on the process, we included indicators that the respondent had parents who were business owners, the percentage of relatives who are current business owners, and the percentage of friends and neighbors who are current business owners. Finally, we controlled for age, gender, race, immigrant status, marital status, and geographic region.

PSED RESEARCH METHODS

The dependent variable in the analyses of becoming an entrepreneur was a dichotomous indicator that the person was a nascent entrepreneur. To estimate the models, we used logistic regression weighted to correct for selection bias by age, education, race, and sex (based on the Current Population Surveys conducted by the U.S. Census) and corrected for differences due to differential nonresponse rates. Since these weights were originally calculated on the basis of respective subsamples, we recalculated the weights so that each case accurately reflects the population when both subsamples were combined into one sample. Table A.18 includes the full regression model for Table 7.8.

References

Abbott, Andrew, and Alexandra Hrycak. 1990. "Measuring Resemblance in Sequence Data: An Optimal Matching Analysis of Musicians' Careers." *American Journal of Sociology* 96:144–85.

Adams, Cindy, and Susan Crimp. 1995. *Iron Rose: The Story of Rose Fitzgerald Kennedy and Her Dynasty*. Beverly Hills, CA: Dove Books.

Airsman, Linda A., and Bam Dev Sharda. 1993. "A Comparative Study of the Occupational Attainment Process of White Men and Women in the United States." *Journal of Comparative Family Studies* 24:171–86.

Aizcorbe, Ana M., Arthur B. Kennickell, and Kevin B. Moore. 2001. "Recent Changes in U.S. Family Finances: Evidence from the 1998 and 2001 Survey of Consumer Finances." Federal Reserve Board Working Paper.

Aldrich, Howard. 1999. *Organizations Evolving*. London: SAGE.

Aldrich, Howard, Linda A. Renzulli, and Nancy Langton. 1998. "Passing on Privilege: Resources Provided by Self-Employed Parents to Their Self-Employed Children." Pp. 291–317 in *Research in Stratification and Mobility*, vol. 16, edited by K. Leicht. Greenwich, CT: JAI Press.

Aldrich, Nelson W. Jr. 1988. *Old Money: The Mythology of America's Upper Class*. New York: A. A. Knopf.

Allen, Michael Patrick. 1987. *The Founding Fortunes: A New Anatomy of the Super-Rich Families in America*. New York: E. P. Dutton.

Altonji, Joseph G., and Thomas A. Dunn. 1991. "Relationships Among the Family Incomes and Labor Market Outcomes of Relatives." *Research in Labor Economics* 12:269–310.

Alwin, Duane. 1986. "Religion and Parental Childbearing Orientations: Evidence for a Catholic–Protestant Convergence." *American Journal of Sociology* 92:412–420.

Appelbaum, Eileen. 1992. "Structural Change and the Growth of Part-Time and Temporary Employment." Pp. 1–14 in *New Policies for the Part-Time and Contingent Workforce*, edited by V. L. duRivage. Armonk, NY: Sharpe.

Armor, David J. 2003. *Maximizing Intelligence*. New Brunswick, NJ: Transaction Publishers.

Auchincloss, Louis. 1989. *The Vanderbilt Era: Profiles of a Gilded Age*. New York: Charles Scribner's Sons.

Avery, Robert B., and Michael S. Rendall. 1993. "Estiating the Size and Distribution of Baby Boomers' Prospective Inheritance." American Statistical Association, Proceedings of the Social Statistics Section, pp. 11–19.

Baer, William. 1992. *Race and the Shadow Market in Housing*. Los Angeles: University of Southern California Press.

Baltzell, E. Digby. 1964. *The Protestant Establishment: Aristocracy and Caste in America*. New York: Random House.

Bane, Mary Jo. 1986. "Household Composition and Poverty." Pp. 209–231 in *Fighting Poverty: What Works and What Doesn't*, edited by S. H. Danziger and D. H. Weinberg. Cambridge, MA: Harvard University Press.

Banerjee, Abhijit V., and Andrew F. Newman. 1993. "Occupational Choice and the Process of Development." *Journal of Political Economy* 101:274–98.

Bates, Timothy. 1997. *Race, Self-Employment, and Upward Mobility: An Illusive American Dream*. Baltimore, MD: Johns Hopkins University Press.

Baumol, William J. 1993. *Entrepreneurship, Management, and the Structure of Payoffs*. Cambridge, MA: MIT Press.

Baydar, Nazli. 1988. "Effects of Parental Separation and Reentry into Union on the Emotional Well-Being of Children." *Journal of Marriage and the Family* 50:967–81.

Bednarzik, Robert W. 2000. "The Role of Entrepreneurship in U.S. and European Job Growth." *Monthly Labor Review* July:3–16.

Behrman, J. R., and P. Taubman. 1990. "The Intergenerational Correlation between Children's Adult Earnings and Their Parents' Income." *Review of Income and Wealth* 36:115–27.

Behrman, Jere R., Robert A. Pollak, and Paul Taubman. 1995. *From Parent to Child: Intrahousehold Allocations and Intergenerational Relations in the United States*. Chicago: University of Chicago Press.

Bendix, Reinhard, and Seymour Martin Lipset. 1966. *Class, Status, and Power*. New York: Free Press.

Bhide, Amar. 1992. "Bootstrap Finance: The Art of Start-ups." *Harvard Business Review* Nov./Dec.:109.

Bianchi, Suzanne M. 1999. "Feminization and Juvenilization of Poverty: Trends, Relative Risks, Causes, and Consequences." *Annual Review of Sociology* 25: 307–33.

Biblarz, Timothy J., and Adrian E. Raftery. 1993. "The Effects of Family Disruption on Social Mobility." *American Sociological Review* 58:97–109.

Biblarz, Timothy J., Adrian E. Raftery, and Alexander Bucur. 1997. "Family Structure and Mobility." *Social Forces* 75:1319–41.

Blake, Judith. 1981. "Family Size and the Quality of Children." *Demography* 18:421–42.

Blake, Judith. 1989. *Family Size and Achievement*. Berkeley, CA: University of California Press.

Blanchflower, David G., and Andrew J. Oswald. 1998. "What Makes an Entrepreneur?" *Journal of Labor Economics* 16:26–60.

Blank, Rebecca M. 1998. "Contingent Work in a Changing Labor Market." Pp. 258–94 in *Generating Jobs: How to Increase Demand for Less-Skilled Workers*, edited by R. B. Freeman and P. Gottschalk. New York: Russell Sage Foundation.

Blau, Francine D., and John W. Graham. 1990. "Black-White Differences in Wealth and Asset Composition." *Quarterly Journal of Economics* May: 321–39.

Blau, Peter Michael, and Otis Dudley Duncan. 1967. *The American Occupational Structure*. New York: Wiley.

Blinder, Alan S. 1988. "Comments on Chapters 1 and 2." Pp. 68–76 in *Modeling the Accumulation and Distribution of Wealth*, edited by D. Kessler and A. Masson. Oxford: Clarendon Press.

Boos, D. D., and J. M. Hughes-Oliver. 2000. "How Large Does n Have to Be for Z and t Intervals?" *The American Statistician* 54:121–28.

Bourdieu, Pierre. 1977. *Outline of a Theory of Practice*. Cambridge, U.K.: Cambridge University Press.

Bowles, Samuel, and Herbert Gintis. 2001. "The Inheritance of Economic Status: Education, Class, and Genetics." Pp. 4132–41 in *International Encyclopedia of the Social and Behavioral Sciences*, edited by N. Smelser and P. Baltes. Oxford: Elsevier Press.

Breiger, Ronald L. 1981. "The Social Class Structure of Occupational Mobility." *American Journal of Sociology* 87:578–611.

Breiger, Ronald L., 1990. *Social Mobility and Social Structure*. New York: Cambridge University Press.

Brenner, Reuven, and Nicholas M. Kiefer. 1981. "The Economics of Diaspora: Discrimination and Occupational Structure." *Economic Development and Cultural Change* 29:517–33.

Brimmer, Andrew F. 1988. "Income, Wealth, and Investment Behavior in the Black Community." *American Economic Review* 78:151–55.

Brooks, David. 2000. *Bobos in Paradise: The New Upper Class and How They Got There*. New York: Simon and Schuster.

Broom, Leonard, and William Shay. 2000. "Discontinuities in the Distribution of Great Wealth: Sectoral Forces Old and New." Unpublished.

Burkhauser, Richard B. 1994. "Protecting the Most Vulnerable: A Proposal to Improve Social Security Insurance for Older Women." *The Gerontologist* 34: 148–49.

Callaghan, Polly, and Heidi Hartman. 1991. *Contingent Work: A Chart Book on Part-Time and Temporary Employment*. Washington, DC: Economic Policy Institute.

Campbell, Lori A., and Robert L. Kaufman. 2000. "Racial Differences in Household Wealth: Beyond Black and White." *American Sociological Association*.

Campbell, Richard, and John Henretta. 1980. "Status Claims and Status Attainment: The Determinants of Financial Well-Being." *American Journal of Sociology* 86:618–29.

Canterbery, E. Ray, and E. Joe Nosari. 1985. "The Forbes Four Hundred: The Determinants of Super-wealth." *Southern Economic Journal* 51:1173–83.

Cappelli, Peter. 1999. *The New Deal at Work: Managing the Market-Driven Workforce.* Cambridge, MA: Harvard Business School Press.

Carnevale, Anthony P., Lynn A. Jennings, and James M. Eisenmann. 1998. "Contingent Workers and Employment Law." Pp. 281–305 in *Contingent Work: American Employment Relations in Transition,* edited by K. Barker and K. Christensen. Ithaca, NY: ILR Press.

Caskey, Richard. 1994. *Fringe Banking: Check-cashing Outlets, Pawnshops, and the Poor.* New York: Russell Sage Foundation.

Cassirer, Naomi. Forthcoming. "Work Arrangements Among Women in the United States." In *Nonstandard Work Arrangements in Europe, Japan, and the U.S.,* edited by S. Houseman and M. Osawa.

Champernowne, David G. 1973. *The Distribution of Income between Persons.* Cambridge: Cambridge University Press.

Chandler, Alfred, Jr., and Stephen Salsbury. 1971. *Pierre S. du Pont and the Making of the Modern Corporation.* New York: Harper and Row.

Chang, Mariko. 2002. "I Get By with a Little Help from My Friends." Harvard University Department of Sociology Working Paper.

Cherlin, Andrew J. 1979. "Work Life and Marital Dissolution." In *Divorce and Marital Separation,* edited by G. Levinger and O. C. Moles. New York: Basic Books.

Cherlin, Andrew J. 1981. *Marriage, Divorce, Remarriage.* Cambridge: Harvard University Press.

Cherlin, Andrew J., P. Lindsay Chase-Lansdale, and Christine McRae. 1998. "Effects of Parental Divorce on Mental Health throughout the Life Course." *American Sociological Review* 63:239–49.

Chiswick, Barry R. 1986. "Labor Supply and Investment in Child Quality: A Study of Jewish and Non-Jewish Women." *Review of Economics and Statistics* 68:700–703.

Chiswick, Barry R. 1988. "Differences in Education and Earnings Across Racial and Ethnic Groups: Tastes, Discrimination, and Investments in Child Quality." *Quarterly Journal of Economics* 103:571–97.

Chiswick, Barry R. 1993. "The Skills and Economic Status of American Jewry: Trends over the Last Half-Century." *Journal of Labor Economics* 11:229–42.

Chiteji, Ngina S., and Frank Stafford. 2000. "Asset Ownership Across Generations." Jerome Levy Institute Working Paper.

Chiteji, Ngina S., and Frank P. Stafford. 1999. "Portfolio Choices of Parents and Their Children as Young Adults: Asset Accumulation by African-American Families." *American Economic Review* 89:377–80.

Cohen, Bernard P. 1989. *Developing Sociological Knowledge: Theory and Method.* Chicago: Nelson-Hall.

Colby, Gerard. 1984. *Du Pont Dynasty: Behind the Nylon Curtain.* Secaucus, NJ: Lyle Stuart.

Conley, Dalton. 1999. *Being Black, Living in the Red: Race, Wealth and Social Policy in America.* Berkeley, CA: University of California Press.

Cooksey, Elizabeth C. 1997. "Consequences of Young Mothers' Marital Histories for Children's Cognitive Development." *Journal of Marriage and the Family* 59:245–61.

Cookson, Peter W., and Caroline Hodges Persell. 1985. *Preparing for Power: America's Elite Boarding Schools*. New York: Basic Books.

Corcoran, M. 1995. "Rags to Rags: Poverty and Mobility in the United States." *Annual Review of Sociology* 21:237–67.

Corcoran, M., and Greg Duncan. 1979. "Work History, Labor Force Attachment, and Earnings Differences Between the Races and Sexes." *Sex Roles* 5:343–53.

Cowles, Virginia. 1979. *The Astors: The Story of a Transatlantic Family*. London: Weidenfeld and Nicolson.

Crosa, Beth, Lisa A. Keister, and Howard Aldrich. 2001. "Access to Valuable Resources: Financial, Social, and Human Capital as Determinants of Entrepreneurship." The Ohio State University Department of Sociology Working Paper.

Dahl, Robert A. 1961. *Who Governs? Democracy and Power in an American City*. New Haven, CT: Yale University Press.

Danziger, Sheldon, Peter Gottschalk, and Eugene Smolensky. 1989. "How the Rich Fared, 1973–1987." *American Economic Review* 79:310–14.

Danziger, Sheldon H., and Peter Gottschalk. 1993. "Uneven Tides: Rising Inequality in America." New York: Russell Sage Foundation.

Danziger, Sheldon H., Robert H. Haveman, and Robert D. Plotnick. 1986. "Antipoverty Policy: Effects on the Poor and Nonpoor." Pp. 50–77 in *Fighting Poverty: What Works and What Doesn't*, edited by S. H. Danziger and D. H. Weinberg. Cambridge, MA: Harvard University Press.

Darnell, Alfred, and Darren E. Sherkat. 1997. "The Impact of Protestant Fundamentalism on Educational Attainment." *American Sociological Review* 62:306–15.

Davies, James B., and Peter Kuhn. 1988. "Redistribution, Inheritance, and Inequality: An Analysis of Transitions." Pp. 123–43 in *Modelling the Accumulation and Distribution of Wealth*, edited by D. Kessler and A. Masson. New York: Oxford University Press.

Davies, James B., and Anthony F. Shorrocks. 1999. "The Distribution of Wealth." Pp. 605–675 in *Handbook of Income Distribution, Volume I*, edited by A. B. Atkinson and F. Bourguignon. New York: Elsevier Science.

Davies, Scott, and Neil Guppy. 1997. "Fields of Study, College Selectivity, and Student Inequalities in Higher Education." *Social Forces* 75:1417–38.

DellaPergola, Sergio. 1980. "Patterns of American Jewish Fertility." *Demography* 17:261–73.

Demo, David H., and Alan C. Acock. 1988. "The Impact of Divorce on Children." *Journal of Marriage and the Family* 50:619–48.

Department of Agriculture, U.S. 2001. "The Cost of Raising a Child." Annual Report 0138.00.

Dolan, Kerry A. 1999. "200 Global Billionaires." *Forbes Magazine*.

Domhoff, G. William. 1978. *Who Really Rules? New Haven and Community Power Reexamined*. New Brunswick, NJ: Transaction Books.

Domhoff, G. William. 1983. *Who Rules America Now?* Englewood Cliffs, NJ: Prentice-Hall.

Domhoff, G. William. 2002. *Who Rules America? Power and Politics, Fourth Edition.* New York: McGraw Hill.

Downey, Douglas B. 1995a. "Understanding Academic Achievement among Children in Stephouseholds The Role of Parental Resources, Sex of Stepparent, and Sex of Child." *Social Forces* 73:875–94.

Downey, Douglas B. 1995b. "When Bigger is Not Better: Family Size, Parental Resources, and Children's Educational Performance." *American Sociological Review* 60:746–61.

Downey, Douglas B., Brian Powell, Lala Carr Steelman, and Shana Pribesh. 1999. "Much Ado About Siblings: Change Models, Sibship Size, and Intellectual Development (Comment on Guo and VanWey)." *American Sociological Review* 64:193–98.

Duncan, Greg J., and Soul D. Hoffman. 1985. "Economic Consequences of Marital Instability." Pp. 427–67 in *Horizontal Equity, Uncertainty, and Economic Well-Being,* edited by M. David and T. Smeeding. Chicago: University of Chicago Press.

Duncan, Otis Dudley. 1961. "A Socioeconomic Index for All Occupations." Pp. 109–38 in *Occupations and Social Status,* edited by Albert J. Reiss. New York: Free Press.

Dunn, Thomas, and Douglas Holtz-Eakin. 2000. "Financial Capital, Human Capital, and the Transition to Self-Employment: Evidence from Intergenerational Links." *Journal of Labor Economics* 18:282–305.

Dye, Thomas R. 1995. *Who's Running America? The Clinton Years.* Englewood Cliffs, NJ: Prentice-Hall.

Dynan, Karen E. 1993. "The Rate of Time Preference and Shocks to Wealth: Evidence From Panel Data." Board of Governors of the Federal Reserve System Working Paper No. 134.

Easterlin, Richard A. 1987. *Birth and Fortune,* 2nd ed. Chicago: University of Chicago Press.

Easterlin, Richard A., Christine MacDonald, and Diane J. Macunovich. 1990a. "How Have American Baby Boomers Fared? Earnings and Economic Well-Being of Young Adults, 1964–1987." *Population Economics* 3: 277–90.

Easterlin, Richard A., Christine MacDonald, and Diane J. Macunovich. 1990b. "Retirement Prospects of the Baby Boom Generation: A Different Perspective." *Gerontologist* 30:776–83.

Eggebeen, David J., and Daniel T. Lichter. 1991. "Race, Family Structure, and Changing Poverty Among American Children." *American Sociological Review* 56:801–17.

Elder, Glen H. 1974. *Children of the Great Depression: Social Change in Life Experience.* Chicago: University of Chicago Press.

Elder, Glen H. 1995. "The Life Course Paradigm: Social Change and Individual Development." Pp. 101–40 in *Examining Lives in Context: Perspectives* on the Ecology of Human Development, edited by P. Moen, G. H. Elder, and K. Luscher. Washington, DC: American Psychological Association.

Elder, Glen H., and Jeffrey K. Liker. 1982. "Hard Times in Women's Lives: Historical Influences Across 40 Years." American Journal of Sociology 88: 241–69.

Elliott, Osborn. 1959. Men at the Top. New York: Harper. Ellison, Christopher G., John P. Bartkowsi, and Michelle L. Segal. 1996. "Conservative Protestantism and the Parental Use of Corporal Punishment." Social Forces 74:1003–28.

Evans, David S., and Boyan Jovanovic. 1989. "An Estimated Model of Entrepreneurial Choice Under Liquidity Constraints." Journal of Political Economy 97:808–27.

Fairlie, Robert W., and Bruce D. Meyer. 1996. "Ethnic and Racial Self-Employment Differences and Possible Explanations." Journal of Human Resources 31:757.

Featherman, David L., and Robert M. Hauser. 1978. Opportunity and Change. New York: Academic Press.

Federal Reserve System, Board of Governors. 2001. Balance Sheets For the U.S. Economy. Washington, DC: Federal Reserve Board.

Federal Reserve System, Board of Governors. 2003. Balance Sheets For the U.S. Economy. Washington, DC: Federal Reserve Board.

Fischer, Mary, and Douglas Massey. 2000. "Residential Segregation and Ethnic Enterprise in U.S. Metropolitan Areas." Social Problems 47:410–24.

Freear, J., J. E. Sohl, and William E. Wetzel. 1995. "Who Bankrolls Software Entrepreneurs?" Babson College Entrepreneurship Research Conference. April 9–13, London, U.K.

Friedman, Debra, Michael Hechter, and Satoshi Kanazawa. 1994. "A Theory of the Value of Children." Demography 31:375–401.

Fujiwara-Greve, Takako, and Henrich R. Greve. 2000. "Organizational Ecology and Job Mobility." Social Forces 79:547–85.

Furstenberg, Frank F., Jr. 2003. "Teenage Childbearing as a Public Issue and Private Concern." Annual Review of Sociology 29:23–39.

Gale, William G., and John Karl Scholz. 1994. "Intergenerational Transfers and the Accumulation of Wealth." Journal of Economic Perspectives 8:145–60.

Galenson, Marjorie. 1972. "Do Blacks Save More?" American Economic Review 62:211–16.

Gokhale, Jagadeesh, and Laurence J. Kotlikoff. 2000. "The Baby Boomers' Mega-Inheritance – Myth or Reality?" Economic Commentary. Issue Oct. 1. Federal Reserve Bank of Cleveland.

Gokhale, Jagadeesh, Laurence J. Kotlikoff, James Sefton, and Martin Weale. 2001. "Simulating the Transmission of Wealth Inequality via Bequests." Journal of Public Economics 79:93–128.

Gottschalk, Peter, and Sheldon Danziger. 1984. "Macroeconomic Conditions, Income Transfers and the Trend in Poverty." Pp. 185–215 in The Social Contract Revisited, edited by D. L. Bawden. Washington, DC: Urban Institute Press.

Gove, Walter R. 1994. "Why We Do What We Do: A Biopsychosocial Theory of Human Motivation." *Social Forces* 73:363–94.

Grad, Susan. 1996. *Income of the Population 55 or Older.* Washington, DC: Office of Research, Evaluation, and Statistics, Social Security Administration.

Guo, Guang, and Leah K. VanWey. 1999. "Sibship Size and Intellectual Development: Is the Relationship Causal?" *American Sociological Review* 64:169–87.

Hachen, David S. Jr. 1992. "Industrial Characteristics and Job Mobility Rates." *American Sociological Review* 57:39–55.

Hanson, Thomas L., and Sara S. McLanahan. 1998. "Windows on Divorce: Before and After." *Social Science Research* 27:329–49.

Hao, Lingxin. 1996. "Family Structure, Private Transfers, and the Economic Well-Being of Families with Children." *Social Forces* 75:269–92.

Harbury, Colin D., and David M. W. N. Hitchens. 1979. *Inheritance and Wealth Inequality in Britain.* London: George Allen & Unwin.

Harrison, Richard. T., and Colin M. Mason. 1997. "Entrepreneurial Growth Strategies and Venture Performance in the Software Industry." *Frontiers of Entrepreneurship Research.*

Haveman, Heather A., and Lisa E. Cohen. 1994. "The Ecological Dynamics of Careers: The Impact of Organizational Founding, Dissolution, and Merger on Job Mobility." *American Journal of Sociology* 100:104–52.

Henretta, John. 1984. "Parental Status and Child's Home ownership." *American Sociological Review* 49:131–40.

Henretta, John C.1979. "Race Differences in Middle Class Lifestyle: The Role of Home Ownership." *Social Science Research* 8:63–78.

Henretta, John C., and Richard Campbell. 1978. "Net Worth As an Aspect of Status." *American Journal of Sociology* 83:1204–23.

Herrnstein, Richard J., and Charles Murray. 1994. *The Bell Curve: Intelligence and Class Structure in American Life.* New York: Free Press.

Hill, C. Russell, and Frank P. Stafford. 1978. "Intergenerational Wealth Transfers and the Educational Decisions of Male Youth: An Alternative Interpretation." *Quarterly Journal of Economics* 92:515–20.

Hill, M. S., and G. J. Duncan. 1987. "Parental Family Income and the Socioeconomic Attainment of Children." *Social Science Research* 16:39–73.

Holden, Karen C., and Pamela J. Smock. 1991. "The Economic Costs of Marital Dissolution: Why Do Women Bear a Disproportionate Cost?" *Annual Review of Sociology* 17:51–78.

Holtz-Eakin, D, D. Joulfaian, and H. S. Rosen. 1994. "Sticking It Out: Entrepreneurial Survival and Liquidity Constraints." *Journal of Political Economy* 102:53–75.

Horton, Hayward Derrick, and Melvin E. Thomas. 1998. "Race, Class, and Family Structure: Differences in Housing Values for Black and White Homeowners." *Sociological Inquiry* 68:114–36.

Horton, Haywood Derrick. 1992. "Race and Wealth: A Demographic Analysis of Black Ownership." *Sociological Inquiry* 62:480–9.

Horwitz, Allan V., Helene Raskin White, and Sandra Howell-White. 1996. "The Use of Multiple Outcomes in Stress Research: A Case Study of Gender Differences in Responses to Marital Dissolution." *Journal of Health and Social Behavior* 37:278–91.

Houseknecht, Sharon K., and Graham B. Spanier. 1980. "Marital Disruption and Higher Education among Women in the United States." *Sociological Quarterly* 21:375–89.

Houseman, Susan N. 1997. *Temporary, Part-Time, and Contract Employment in the United States* (Report to the U.S. Department of Labor). Kalamazoo, MI: W. E. Upjohn Institute for Employment Research.

Houseman, Susan N. 2001a. "The Benefits Implication of Recent Trends in Flexible Staffing Arrangements." Pension and Research Council Working Paper No. 2001–19, The Wharton School, University of Pennsylvania.

Houseman, Susan N. 2001b. "Why Employers Use Flexible Staffing Arrangements: Evidence from an Establishment Survey." *Industrial and Labor Relations Review* 55:149–70.

Houseman, Susan N., and Anne E. Polivka. 2000. "The Implications of Flexible Staffing Arrangements for Job Stability." Pp. 427–62 in *On the Job: Is Long-Term Employment a Thing of the Past?*, edited by D. Neumark. New York: Russell Sage Foundation.

Hoyt, Edwin. 1962. *The Vanderbilts and Their Fortunes*. New York: Doubleday.

Hurd, Michael D. 1989. "The Poverty of Widows: Future Prospects." Pp. 201–22 in *The Economics of Aging*, edited by D. A. Wise. Chicago: NBER(University of Chicago Press.

Hurd, Michael D. 1990. "Research on the Elderly: Economic Status, Retirement, and Consumption and Saving." *Journal of Economic Literature* 28:565–637.

Hurst, Erik, Ming Ching Luoh, and Frank P. Stafford. 1998. "Wealth Dynamics of American Families, 1984–1994." *Brookings Papers on Economic Activity* 1:267–337.

Hurst, Erik, and Annamaria Lusardi. Forthcoming. "Liquidity Constraints, Household Wealth and Entrepreneurship." *Journal of Political Economy*.

Hurt, Harry, III. 1981. *Texas Rich: The Hunt Dynasty from the Early Oil Days through the Silver Crash*. New York: W. W. Norton.

Jackman, Mary R., and Robert W. Jackman. 1980. "Racial Inequalities in Home Ownership." *Social Forces* 58:1221–33.

Jianakoplos, Nancy A., and Paul L. Menchik. 1997. "Wealth Mobility." *Review of Economics and Statistics* 79:18–31.

Jianakoplos, Nancy A., Paul L. Menchik, and F. Owen Irvine. 1989. "Using Panel Data to Assess the Bias in Cross-Sectional Inferences of Life-Cycle Changes in the Level and Composition of Household Wealth." Pp. 553–640 in *The Measurement of Saving, Investment, and Wealth*, edited by R. E. Lipsey and H. S. Tice. Chicago: University of Chicago Press.

Juster, Thomas F., and Kathleen A. Kuester. 1991. "Differences in the Measurement of Wealth, Wealth Inequality and Wealth Composition Obtained from Alternative U.S. Wealth Surveys." *Review of Income and Wealth* 37:33–62.

Juster, Thomas F., James P. Smith, and Frank Stafford. 1999. "The Measurement and Structure of Household Wealth." *Labour Economics* 6:253–75.

Kaelble, Hartmut. 1985. *Social Mobility in the 19th and 20th Centuries: Europe and America in Comparative Perspective*. Dover, NH: Berg.

Kalleberg, Arne L. 2000. "Nonstandard Employment Relations: Part-time, Temporary and Contract Work." *Annual Review of Sociology* 26:341–65.

Kalleberg, Arne L., Barbara F. Reskin, and Ken Hudson. 2000. "Bad Jobs in America: Standard and Nonstandard Employment Relations and Job Quality in the United States." *American Sociological Review* 65:256–78.

Kalleberg, Arne L., and Jeremy Reynolds. 2000. "Work Attitudes and Nonstandard Work Arrangements in the United States, Japan and Europe." Pp. 423–76 in *Growth of Non-Standard Work Arrangements*, edited by S. Houseman and M. Osawa. Kalamazoo, MI: W. E. Upjohn Institute for Employment Research.

Kalleberg, Arne, Edith Rasell, Naomi Cassirer, Barbara F. Reskin, Ken Hudson, David Webster, Eileen Appelbaum, and Roberta M. Spalter-Roth. 1997. *Nonstandard Work, Substandard Jobs*. Washington, DC: Economic Policy Institute and Women's Research and Education Institute.

Kalmijn, Matthijs. 1991. "Shifting Boundaries: Trends in Religious and Educational Homogamy." *American Sociological Review* 56:786–800.

Kearl, James R., and Clayne L. Pope. 1986. "Unobserved Family and Individual Contributions to the Distributions of Income and Wealth." *Journal of Labor Economics* 4:S48–79.

Keister, Lisa. 1997. *Who Wins When the Stock Market Booms?* Ithaca, NY: Cornell University Department of Sociology Working Paper.

Keister, Lisa A. 2000a. "Family Structure, Race, and Wealth Ownership: A Longitudinal Exploration of Wealth Accumulation Processes." Paper presented at the Levy Institute Conference on Saving, Intergenerational Transfers, and the Distribution of Wealth. Bard College, Annandale-on-Hudson, NY.

Keister, Lisa A. 2000b. "Race and Wealth Inequality: The Impact of Racial Differences in Asset Ownership on the Distribution of Household Wealth." *Social Science Research* 29:477–502.

Keister, Lisa A. 2000c. *Wealth in America*. New York: Cambridge University Press.

Keister, Lisa. 2003a. "Religion and Wealth: The Role of Religious Affiliation and Participation in Early Adult Asset Accumulation." *Social Forces* 82:173–205.

Keister, Lisa A. 2003b. "Sharing the Wealth: Siblings and Adult Wealth Ownership." *Demography* 40:521–42.

Keister, Lisa A. 2004. "Race, Family Structure, and Wealth: The Effect of Childhood Family on Adult Asset Ownership." *Sociological Perspectives*. 47: 161–87.

Keister, Lisa A., and Natalia Deeb-Sossa. 2000. "Are Baby Boomers Richer Than Their Parents? Intergenerational Patterns of Wealth Ownership in the U.S." *Journal of Marriage and the Family* 62:569–79.

Keister, Lisa A., and Stephanie Moller. 2000. "Wealth Inequality in the United States." *Annual Review of Sociology* 26:63–81.

Keller, Suzanne. 1963. *Beyond the Ruling Class: Strategic Elites in Modern Society*. New York: Random House.

Kennickell, Arthur B. 2000. "An Examination of Changes in the Distribution of Wealth From 1989–1998: Evidence from the Survey of Consumer Finances." Federal Reserve Board Working Paper.

Kennickell, Arthur B. 2003. "A Rolling Tide: Changes in the Distribution of Wealth in the U.S., 1989–2001." Federal Reserve Board Working Paper.

Kennickell, Arthur B., and Myron L. Kwast. 1997. "Who Uses Electronic Banking? Results from the 1995 Survey of Consumer Finances." Unpublished.

Kennickell, Arthur B., and Martha Starr-McCluer. 1994. "Changes in Family Finances from 1989 to 1992: Evidence from the Survey of Consumer Finances." *Federal Reserve Bulletin* October:861–82.

Kennickell, Arthur B., Martha Starr-McCluer, and Annika E. Sunden. 1997. "Family Finances in the U.S.: Recent Evidence from the Survey of Consumer Finances." *Federal Reserve Bulletin* January: 1–24.

Kim, Phillip H., Howard E. Aldrich, and Lisa A. Keister. 2004. "Household Income and Net Worth." Pp 49–61 in *Handbook of Entrepreneurial Dynamics: The Process of Business Creation*, edited by William B. Gartner, Kelly G. Shaver, Nancy M. Carter, and Paul D. Reynolds. Thousand Oaks, CA: Sage.

Kingston, Paul William, and Lionel S. Lewis. 1990. "The High-Status Track: Studies of Elite Schools and Stratification." Albany, NY: SUNY Press.

Kiyosaki, Robert T., and Sharon L. Lechter. 2000. *Rich Dad, Poor Dad: What the Rich Teach Their Kids about Money That the Poor and Middle Class Do Not*. New York: Warner Books.

Klepper, Michael, and Robert Gunther. 1996. *The Wealthy 100: A Ranking of the Richest Americans, Past and Present*. Secaucus, NJ: Citadel Press.

Korporaal, Glenda. 1987. *Afterward to Rupert Murdoch*. Ringwood, Australia: Penguin Books.

Kotlikoff, Laurence J., and Lawrence H. Summers. 1981. "The Role of Intergenerational Transfers in Aggregate Capital Accumulation." *Journal of Political Economy* 89:706–32.

Lampman, Robert J. 1962. *The Share of Top Wealth-Holders in National Wealth, 1922–56*. Princeton, NJ: Princeton University Press.

Lawrence, Emily C. 1991. "Poverty and the Rate of Time Preference: Evidence from Panel Data." *Journal of Political Economy* 99:54–77.

Lee, Dwight R. 1996. "Why Is Flexible Employment Increasing?" *Journal of Labor Research* 17:543–53.

Lehrer, Evelyn L. 1996a. "Religion as a Determinant of Fertility." *Journal of Population Economics* 9:173–96.

Lehrer, Evelyn L. 1996b. "The Role of the Husband's Religion on the Economic and Demographic Behavior of Families." *Journal for the Scientific Study of Religion* 35:145–55.

Lehrer, Evelyn L. 1998. "Religious Intermarriage in the United States: Determinants and Trends." *Social Science Research* 27:245–63.

Lehrer, Evelyn L. 1999. "Religion as a Determinant of Educational Attainment: An Economic Perspective." *Social Science Research* 28:358–79.

Lehrer, Evelyn L., and Carmel U. Chiswick. 1993. "Religion as a Determinant of Marital Stability." *Demography* 30:385–404.

Lenski, Gerhard. 1961. *The Religious Factor: A Sociological Study of Religion's Impact on Politics, Economics, and Family Life*. Garden City, NY: Doubleday.

Lentz, Bernard F., and David N. Laband. 1990. "Entrepreneurial Success and Occupational Inheritance among Proprietors." *Canadian Journal of Economics* 23:563–79.

Lerner, Robert, Althea K. Nagai, and Stanley Rothman. 1996. *American Elites*. New Haven, CT: Yale University Press.

Lipset, Seymour Martin, and Reinhard Bendix. 1959. *Social Mobility in Industrial Society*. Berkeley, CA: University of California Press.

Loew, Rebecca M. 1995. "Determinants of Divorced Older Women's Labor Supply." *Research on Aging* 17:385–411.

Lundberg, Ferdinand. 1939 [1937]. *America's 60 Families*. New York: Halcyon House.

Lundberg, Ferdinand. 1968. *The Rich and the Super-Rich: A Study in the Power of Money Today*. New York: Lyle Stuart.

McAllister, Ward. 1890. *Society as I Have Found It*. New York: Cassell.

McCall, Leslie. 2001. "Sources of Racial Wage Inequality in Metropolitan Labor Markets: Racial, Ethnic, and Gender Differences." *American Socioligical Review* 66:520–41.

McLanahan, Sara S. 1985. "Family Structure and the Reproduction of Poverty." *American Journal of Sociology* 90:873–901.

McLanahan, Sara S., and Erin Kelly. 1999. "The Feminization of Poverty." Pp. 127–46 in *Handbook of the Sociology of Gender*, edited by J. Chafetz. New York: Plenum Press.

McLanahan, Sara S., and Gary D. Sandefur. 1994. *Growing Up with a Single Parent: What Hurts, What Helps*. Cambridge, MA: Harvard University Press.

McNamee, Stephen J., and Robert K. Miller, Jr.. 1998. "Inheritance and Stratification." Pp. 193–213 in *Inheritance and Wealth in America*, edited by Robert K. Miller, Jr. and Stephen J. McNamee. New York: Plenum Press.

Mechanic, David, and Stephen Hansell. 1989. "Divorce, Family Conflict, and Adolescents' Well-Being." *Journal of Health and Social Behavior* 30:105–16.

Menchik, Paul, and Nancy Ammon Jianakoplos. 1997. "Black–White Wealth Inequality: Is Inheritance the Reason?" *Economic Inquiry* 35:428–42.

Menchik, Paul L. 1979. "Intergenerational Transmission of Inequality: An Empirical Study of Wealth Mobility." *Economica* 46:349–62.

Menchik, Paul L. 1980. "Primogeniture, Equal Sharing, and the U.S. Distribution of Wealth." *Quarterly Journal of Economics* 94:299–316.

Menchik, Paul L., and Nancy A. Jiankoplos. 1998. "Economics of Inheritance." Pp. 45–59 in *Inheritance and Wealth in America*, edited by J. Robert K. Miller and S. J. McNamee. New York: Plenum Press.

Mensch, Barbara S., and Dianne Kandel. 1988. "Dropping Out of High School and Drug Involvement." *Sociology of Education* 61:95–113.

Mills, C. Wright. 1956. *The Power Elite*. New York: Oxford University Press.

Mintz, Beth, and Michael Schwartz. 1985. *The Power Structure of American Business*. Chicago: University of Chicago Press.

Mizruchi, Mark S., and Linda Brewster Stearns. 1994a. "A Longitudinal Study of Borrowing by Large American Corporations." *Administrative Science Quarterly* 39:118–140.

Mizruchi, Mark S. 1994b. "Money, Banking, and Financial Markets." Pp. 331–41 in *The Handbook of Economic Sociology*, edited by N. J. Smelser and R. Swedberg. Princeton, NJ: Princeton University Press.

Modigliani, Franco. 1988a. "Measuring the Contribution of Intergenerational Transfers to Total Wealth: Conceptual Issues and Empirical Findings." Pp. 21–52 in *Modelling the Accumulation and Distribution of Wealth*, edited by D. Kessler and A. Masson. New York: Oxford University Press.

Modigliani, Franco. 1988b. "The Role of Intergenerational Transfers and Life Cycle Saving in the Accumulation of Wealth." *Journal of Economic Perspectives* 2:15–40.

Modigliani, Franco, and Richard Brumberg. 1954. "Utility Analysis and the Consumption Function: An Interpretation of Cross-Sectional Data." Pp. 187–206 in *Post-Keynesian Economics*, edited by K. K. Kurihara. New Brunswick, NJ: Rutgers University Press.

Monk-Turner, Elizabeth. 1989. "Effects of High School Delinquency on Educational Attainment and Adult Occupational Status." *Sociological Perspectives* 33:413–18.

Morgan, David L. 1998. "Introduction: The Aging of the Baby Boom." *Generations* 22:5–9.

Mosley, Leonard. 1980. *Blood Relations: The Rise and Fall of the du Ponts of Delaware*. New York: Atheneum.

Mott, Frank L., and S. F. Moore. 1978. "The Causes and Consequences of Marital Breakdown: Dimensions of Change in American Society." Pp. 113–35 in *Women, Work, and Family*, edited by F. Mott and S. H. Sandell. Lexington, MA: Lexington Books.

Mulligan, Casey B.1997. *Parental Priorities and Economic Inequality*. Chicago: University of Chicago Press.

Munster, George. 1985. *Rupert Murdoch: A Paper Prince*. New York: Viking.

Nee, Victor G., and Jimy M. Sanders. 1985. "The Road to Parity: Determinants of the Socioeconomic Achievements of Asian Americans." *Ethnic and Racial Studies* 8:75–93.

Nestel, G., J. Mercier, and Lois Banfill Shaw. 1983. "Economic Consequences of Midlife Change in Marital Status." Pp. 113–35 in *Unplanned Careers: The Working Lives of Middle-Aged Women*, edited by L. B. Shaw. Lexington, MA: Lexington.

Norris, Floyd. 1996. "Flood of Cash to Mutual Funds Helped Fuel '95 Bull Market." *New York Times*, Jan. 1, p. A1.

Oliver, Melvin L., and Thomas M. Shapiro. 1989. "Race and Wealth." *Review of Black Political Economy* 17:5–25.

Oliver, Melvin O., and Thomas M. Shapiro. 1995. *Black Wealth/White Wealth*. New York: Routledge.

Osberg, Lars. 1984. *Economic Inequality in the United States*. New York: M.E. Sharpe.

Parcel, Toby L. 1982. "Wealth Accumulation of Black and White Men: The Case of Housing Equity." *Social Problems* 30:199–211.

Pessen, Edward. 1974. *Riches, Class, and Power*. New York: D.C. Heath and Company.

Peterson, Richard R. 1996. "A Re-Evaluation of the Economic Consequences of Divorce." *American Sociological Review* 61:528–36.

Polsby, Nelson W. 1963. *Community Power and Political Theory*. New Haven, CT: Yale University Press.

Popper, Karl R. 1965. *Conjectures and Refutations: The Growth of Scientific Knowledge*. New York: Harper and Row.

Quadrini, Vincenzo. 1999. "The Importance of Entrepreneurship for Wealth Concentration and Mobility." *Review of Income and Wealth* 45:1–19.

Quillian, Lincoln. 1999. "Migration Patterns and the Growth of High-Poverty Neighborhoods, 1970–1990." *American Journal of Sociology* 105:1–37.

Renzulli, Linda A., Howard Aldrich, and James Moody. 2000. "Family Matters: Gender, Networks, and Entrepreneurial Outcomes." *Social Forces* 79:523–46.

Reynolds, Paul D., and Sammis B. White. 1997. *The Entrepreneurial Process: Economic Growth, Men, Women, and Minorities*. Westport, CT: Quorum Books.

Robinson, Peter B., and Edwin A. Sexton. 1994. "The Effect of Education and Experience of Self-Employment Success." *Journal of Business Venturing* 9:141–56.

Rose, Arnold. 1967. *The Power Structure: Political Process in American Society*. New York: Oxford University Press.

Rosenfeld, Rachel A. 1992. "Job Mobility and Career Processes." *Annual Review of Sociology* 18:39–61.

Ruef, Martin, Howard E. Aldrich, and Nancy M. Carter. 2003. "The Structure of Founding Teams: Homophily, Strong Ties, and Isolation among U.S. Entrepreneurs." *American Sociological Review* 68:195–222.

Ruggles, Richard. 1994. "The Origins of African-American Family Structure." *American Sociological Review* 59:136–51.

Sabelhaus, John, and Joyce Manchester. 1995. "Baby Boomers and Their Parents: How Does Their Economic Well-Being Compare in Middle Age?" *Journal of Human Resources* 30:791–806.

Sandefur, Gary D., and Thomas Wells. 1999. "Does Family Structure Really Influence Educational Attainment?" *Social Science Research* 28: 331–57.

Sander, William. 1995. *The Catholic Family: Marriage, Children, and Human Capital*. Bouider, CO: Westview Press.

Schiller, Bradley R. 1977. "Relative Earnings Mobility in the United States." *American Economic Review* 67:926–41.

Segal, Lewis M., and Daniel G. Sullivan. 1997. "The Growth of Temporary Services Work." *Journal of Economic Perspectives* 11:117–36.

Sewell, William H., and Robert M. Hauser. 1975. *Education, Occupation, and Earnings: Achievement in the Early Career*. New York: Academic Press.

Shane, Scott Andrew. 2003. *A General Theory of Entrepreneurship: The Individual-Opportunity Nexus*. Cheltenham, U.K.: E. Elgar.

Sherkat, Darren E., and Christopher G. Ellison. 1999. "Recent Developments and Current Controversies in the Sociology of Religion." *Annual Review of Sociology* 25:363–94.

Shorrocks, Anthony F. 1976. "Income Mobility and the Markov Process." *The Economic Journal* 86:566–78.

Singer, Burton, and Seymour Spilerman. 1979. "Clustering on the Main Diagonal in Mobility Matrices." *Sociological Methodology* 10:172–208.

Sklare, Marshall. 1971. *America's Jews*. New York: Random House.

Sloane, Leonard. 1995. "Dow Climbs 21.32 Points; Gain for the Year is 33.5%." *New York Times*, Jan. 1, p. B45.

Smith, Christian. 1998. *American Evangelicalism: Embattled and Thriving*. Chicago: University of Chicago Press.

Smith, James D. 1987. "Recent Trends in the Distribution of Wealth in the U.S.: Data, Research Problems, and Prospects." Pp. 72–90 in *International Comparisons of the Distribution of Household Wealth*, edited by E. N. Wolff. New York: Oxford University Press.

Sorokin, Pitirim. 1925. "American Millionaires and Multi-Millionaires." *Social Forces* 4:627–40.

Spilerman, Seymour. 2000. "Wealth and Stratification Processes." *Annual Review of Sociology* 26:497–524.

Stack, Carol. 1974. *All Our Kin: Strategies for Survival in a Black Community*. New York: Harper and Row.

Stafford, Frank P. 1996. "Early Education of Children in Families and Schools." Pp. 219–46 in *Household and Family Economics: Recent Economic Thought*, edited by P. Menchik. Boston: Kluwer Academic.

Steckel, Richard H. 1990. "Poverty and Prosperity: A Longitudinal Study of Wealth Accumulation, 1850–1860." *Review of Economics and Statistics* 72:275–85.

Steckel, Richard H., and Jayanthi Krishman. 1992. "Wealth Mobility in America: A View From the National Longitudinal Survey." National Bureau of Economic Research Working Paper No. 4137.

Steinmetz, George, and Erik Olin Wright. 1989. "The Fall and Rise of the Petty Bourgeoisie: Changing Patterns of Self-Employment in the Postwar United States." *American Journal of Sociology* 94:973–1018.

Stinchcombe, Arthur L. 1965. "Organizations and Social Structure." Pp. 142–93 in *Handbook of Organizations*, edited by J. G. March. Chicago: Rand McNally.

Stinchcombe, Arthur L. 1986. *Stratification and Organization : Selected Papers*. New York: Cambridge University Press.

Stirling, Kate. 1989. "Women Who Remain Divorced: The Long-Term Economic Consequences." *Social Science Quarterly* 70:549–61.

Stovel, Katherine, Michael Savage, and Peter Bearman. 1996. "Ascription into Achievement: Models of Career Systems at Lloyds Bank, 1890–1970." *American Journal of Sociology* 102:358–99.

Stryker, Robin. 1981. "Religio-Ethnic Effects on Attainments in the Early Career." *American Sociological Review* 46:212–31.

Sullivan, Teresa A., Elizabeth Warren, and Jay Lawrence Westbrook. 2000. *The Fragile Middle Class: Americans in Debt.* New Haven, CT: Yale University Press.

Swidler, Ann. 1986. "Culture in Action: Symbols and Strategies." *American Sociological Review* 51:273–86.

Taniguchi, Hiromi. 1999. "The Timing of Childbearing and Women's Wages." *Journal of Marriage and the Family* 61:1008–19.

Tanner, Julian, Scott Davies, and Bill O'Grady. 1999. "Whatever Happened to Yesterday's Rebels? Longitudinal Effects of Youth Delinquency on Education and Employment." *Social Problems* 46:250–74.

Taubman, Paul. 1982. "Measuring the Impact of Environmental Policies on the Level and Distribution of Earnings." Pp. 171–89 in *The Fundamental Connection between Nature and Nurture: A Review of the Evidence,* edited by W. R. Gove and G. R. Carpenter. Lexington, MA: Lexington Books.

Teachman, Jay D. 1987. "Family Background, Educational Resources, and Educational Attainment." *American Sociological Review* 52:548–57.

Terrel, Henry S. 1971. "Wealth Accumulation of Black and White Families: The Empirical Evidence." *Journal of Finance* 26:363–77.

Thomson, Elizabeth, Thomas L. Hanson, and Sara S. McLanahan. 1994. "Family Structure and Child Well-Being: Economic Resources vs. Parental Behaviors." *Social Forces* 73:221–42.

Thornton, Arland. 1985. "Changing Attitudes towards Separation and Divorce: Causes and Consequences." *American Journal of Sociology* 90:856–72.

Tilly, Chris. 1996. *Half a Job: Bad and Good Jobs in a Changing Labor Market.* Philadelphia: Temple University Press.

Tuccille, Jerome. 1989. *Rupert Murdoch.* New York: Donald I. Fine, Inc.

U.S. Census Bureau. 1992. *Economic Census.* Washington, DC: U.S. Government Printing Office.

Useem, Michael. 1979. "The Social Organization of the American Business Elite." *American Sociological Review* 44:553–71.

Useem, Michael. 1980. "Corporations and the Corporate Elite." *Annual Review of Sociology* 6:41–77.

Useem, Michael. 1984. *The Inner Circle.* New York: Oxford University Press.

Vianello, Mino, and Gwen Moore. 2000. *Gendering Elites: Economic and Political Leadership in 27 Advanced Industrialised Societies.* New York: St. Martin's Press.

Warner, W. Lloyd. 1960. *Social Class in America: A Manual of Procedure for the Measurement of Social Status.* New York: Harper.

Warren, John Robert, and Robert Hauser. 1997. "Social Stratification across Three Generations: New Evidence from the Wisconsin Longitudinal Study." *American Sociological Review* 62:561–72.

Watkins, G. P. 1907. *The Growth of Large Fortunes.* New York: A. M. Kelly.

Waxman, Chaim I. 1983. *America's Jews in Transition.* Philadelphia: Temple University Press.

Waxman, Chaim I. 2001. *Jewish Baby Boomers: A Communal Perspective.* Albany, NY: State University of New York Press.

Weicher, John C. 1995. "Changes in the Distribution of Wealth: Increasing Inequality?" *Federal Reserve Bank of St. Louis Review* 77:5–23.

Weicher, John C. 1997. "Wealth and Its Distribution: 1983–1992: Secular Growth, Cyclical Stability." *Federal Reserve Bank of St. Louis Review* 79:3–23.

Weir, David, Robert Willis, and Purvi Sevak. 2000. "The Economic Consequences of a Husband's Death: Evidence from the HRS and AHEAD." Working Paper.

Weitzman, Lenore J. 1985. *The Divorce Revolution: The Unexpected Social and Economic Consequences for Women and Children in America.* New York: Free Press.

Western, Mark, and Erik Olin Wright. 1994. "The Permeability of Class Boundaries to Intergenerational Mobility among Men in the United States, Canada, Norway, and Sweden." *American Sociological Review* 59:606–29.

Westoff, Charles F., and Elise F. Jones. 1979. "The End of 'Catholic' Fertility." *Demography* 16:209–17.

Wilcox, Bradford W. 1998. "Conservative Protestant Childrearing: Authoritarian or Authoritative?" *American Sociological Review* 63:796–809.

Wilhelm, Mark O. 2001. "The Role of Intergenerational Transfers in Spreading Asset Ownership." Pp. 132–61 in *Assets for the Poor: The Benefits of Spreading Asset Ownership*, edited by T. M. Shapiro and E. N. Wolff. New York: Russell Sage Foundation.

Williams, Robin M. 1975. "Race and Ethnic Relations." *Annual Review of Sociology* 1:125–64.

Williamson, Jeffrey G., and Peter H. Lindert. 1980. *American Inequality: A Macroeconomic History.* New York: Academic Press.

Willis, Paul E. 1981. *Learning to Labor: How Working Class Kids Get Working Class Jobs.* New York: Columbia University Press.

Wilson, Derek. 1993. *The Astors 1763–1992: Landscape with Millionaires.* New York: St. Martin's Press.

Wilson, William J. 1987. *The Truly Disadvantaged: The Inner City, the Underclass, and Public Policy.* Chicago: University of Chicago Press.

Winborg, Joakim, and Hans Landstrom. 2000. "Financial Bootstrapping in Small Businesses: Examining Managers' Resource Acquisition Behaviors." *Journal of Business Venturing* 16:235–54.

Winkler, John K. 1935. *The du Pont Dynasty.* New York: Reynal and Hitchcock.

Winnick, Andrew. 1989. *Toward Two Societies: The Changing Distributions of Income and Wealth in the U.S. Since 1960.* New York: Praeger.

Wolff, Edward N. 1987. "Estimates of Household Wealth Inequality in the U.S., 1962–1983." *Review of Income and Wealth* 33:231–56.

Wolff, Edward N. 1992. "Changing Inequality of Wealth." *American Economic Review* 82:552–58.

Wolff, Edward N. 1993. "Trends in Household Wealth in the United States During the 1980s." Unpublished manuscript, New York University.

Wolff, Edward N. 1995a. "The Rich Get Increasingly Richer: Latest Data on Household Wealth During the 1980s." Pp. 33–68 in *Research in Politics and Society*, vol. 5, edited by R. E. Ratcliff, M. L. Oliver, and T. M. Shapiro. Greenwich, CT: JAI Press.

Wolff, Edward N. 1995b. *Top Heavy: A Study of the Increasing Inequality of Wealth in America.* New York: Twentieth Century Fund.

Wolff, Edward N. 1998. "Recent Trends in the Size Distribution of Household Wealth." *Journal of Economic Perspectives* 12:131–50.

Wolff, Edward N. 2001. "Recent Trends in Wealth Ownership, from 1983 to 1998." Pp. 34–73 in *Assets for the Poor: The Benefits of Spreading Asset Ownership*, edited by T. M. Shapiro and E. N. Wolff. New York: Russell Sage Foundation.

Wolff, Edward N. 2002. "Inheritances and Wealth Inequality Trends, 1989–1998." Levy Institute Working Paper.

Wolff, Edward N., and Maria Marley. 1989. "Long Term Trends in U.S. Wealth Inequality: Methodological Issues and Results." Pp. 765–839 in *The Measurement of Saving, Investment, and Wealth*, edited by R. Lipsey and H. S. Tice. Chicago: University of Chicago Press.

Wolfinger, Raymond E. 1974. *The Politics of Progress*. Englewood Cliffs, NJ: Prentice-Hall.

Wong, Raymond. 1992. "Vertical and Nonvertical Effects in Class Mobility: Cross-National Variations." *American Sociological Review* 57:396–410.

Wu, Lawrence L. 1996. "Effects of Family Structure and Income on Risks of Premarital Birth." *American Sociological Review* 61:386–406.

Wuthnow, Robert. 1999. *Growing up Religious: Christians and Jews and Their Journeys of Faith*. Boston: Beacon Press.

Wuthnow, Robert, and Tracy L. Scott. 1997. "Protestants and Economic Behavior." Pp. 260–95 in *New Directions in American Religious History*, edited by H. S. Sout and D. G. Hart. New York: Oxford University Press

Young, R. C., and J. D. Francis. 1991. "Entrepreneurship and Innovation in Small Manufacturing Firms." *Social Science Quarterly* 72:149–63.

Zagorsky, Jay L. 1997. Pp. 135–56 in *NLSY-79 Users' Guide*, vol. 45. Columbus, OH: Center for Human Resource Research, The Ohio State University.

Zagorsky, Jay L. 1999. "Young Baby Boomers' Wealth." *Review of Income and Wealth* 45:135–56.

Zagorsky, Jay L. 2004. "How Do Marriage and Divorce Impact Wealth?" Working Paper.

Zimmerman, D. 1992. "Regression towards Mediocrity in Economic Stature." *American Economic Review* 82:409–29.

Zweigenhaft, Richard L., and G. William Domhoff. 1982. *Jews in the Protestant Establishment*. New York: Praeger.

Zweigenhaft, Richard L., and G. William Domhoff. 1998. *Diversity in the Power Elite: Have Women and Minorities Reached the Top?* New Haven, CT: Yale University Press.

Index